the WARRIOR'S WAY

the WARRIOR'S WAY

england in the viking age

Stephen Pollington

BLANDFORD

First published 1989 by
Blandford Press,
An imprint of Cassell,
Artillery House, Artillery Row, London SW1P 1RT

Distributed in the United States by
Sterling Publishing Co. Inc.
387 Park Avenue South, New York, NY 10016-8810

Distributed in Australia by
Capricorn Link (Australia) Pty Ltd
PO Box 665, Lane Cove, NSW 2066

ISBN 0-7137-2120-0

British Library Cataloguing in Publication Data
Pollington, Stephen
    The Warrior's Way England in the Viking age.
    1. England, 924-1016
    I. Title
942.01'7

Typeset by Litho Link Ltd, Welshpool, Powys, Wales.
Printed and bound in Yugoslavia by Papirographica. ▨

Frontispiece: The Battle of Maldon *was the last, and perhaps
the most important, in a line of Anglo-Saxon vernacular epics.
This illustration shows a page from an eighteenth-century
transcript. The only known manuscript of the poem was
destroyed by fire in 1731. A copy had been made, however, ten
years before; and it is on this manuscript that all later study is
based. The poem recounts the heroic last stand of the elderly
Byrhtnōth, ealdorman of Essex, whose army was destroyed in
991 by an overwhelming Viking force.*

cyning sceal rice healdan
(A king must hold his domain)

GNOMIC VERSE, THE EXETER BOOK

Oct. 19. 1725. Tuesday. Given me by Mr. Graves.
Transcribed by Mr. John Elphinston, late under-Keeper of the Cotton Library, the same that
Num. VII. vide p. XXV. I have printed transcribed beginnings Chartulam, that printed
this Fragmt in the Appendix to John of Glastonbury.

Fragmentum quoddam historicum de Eadrico &c.

Fragmentum capite & calce mutilum, sex
foliis constans, quo Poëtice & Stylo Ced-
moniano celebratur virtus scilicet BEORHT-
NOTHI Ealdormanni & aliorum
Anglo-Saxonum, in prælio cum Danis. Vide
& Smithi Catal. Bibl. Cott. p.67.
& Hickesii Thes. l. II. p. 232.

. . . brocen wurde. het þa hyssa hwæne. hors
forlætan feor afysan ⁊ forð gangan hic
gan to handum ⁊ to hige godu. þ[æt] offan mæg
ærest onfunde þ[æt] se eorl nolde yrhðo ge
þolian he let him þa of handon leofne
fleogan hafoc wið þæs holtes ⁊ to þære
hilde stop. be þa[m] man mihte oncnawan
þ[æt] se cniht nolde wacian æt þa[m] wige þa
he to wæpnu feng eac hi wolde eadric
his ealdre ge læstan frean to ge feohte
ongan þa wæpn beran gar to guþe he
hæfde god ge þanc þa hwile þe he mid han
dum healdan mihte bord ⁊ brad swurd
beot he ge læste þa he æt foran his frean
fechtan sceolde.

Ða þær byrhtnoð ongan beornas trymi
an rad ⁊ rædde rincu[m] tæhte hu
hi sceoldon standan ⁊ þone stede he
aldan ⁊ bæd þ[æt] hyra randan rihte heol
don fæste mid folman ⁊ ne forhtedon
na. þa he hæfde þ[æt] folc fægere ge trymed
he lihte þa mid leodon þær him leofost
wæs þær þær he his heorð werod holdost wiste
þar stod on stæðe stiðlice clypode wicinga
ar

contents

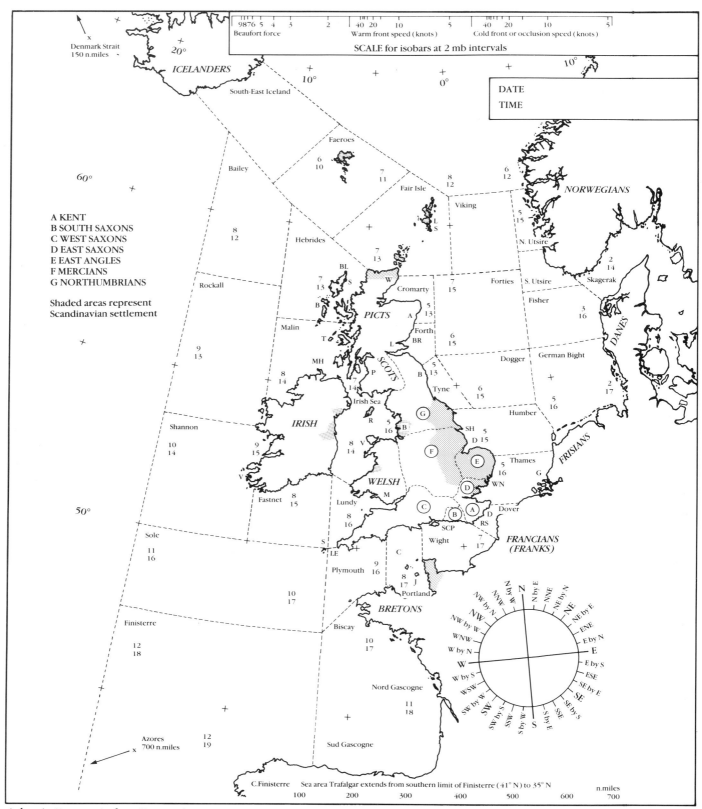

Atlantic Europe in late Saxon times.

chapter 1

england in the viking age

Southern England in summer, AD 991. The fine days and warm nights brought with them great danger; a wind-borne plague from across the sea which struck almost anywhere, at any time, without warning and left men dead or crippled, deprived of a means of living and of the fruits of their labours. This curse upon the land was known to those oppressed as *wicing*.

The summer of AD 991 brought a great host of Vikings coursing westwards out of Scandinavia in long, sleek craft which carried them to the wealthier, more temperate lands on Europe's edge. In small bands, or united into mighty fleets, they drove their keels westwards into the shallows around the British coastline, and heard the look-outs' shouts as the unfortunate fishers and farmers gathered their belonging and raced for the nearest stronghold, or fled by secret woodland ways to prepared hiding-places. Even the towns were not safe against so vast and powerful a force, and this summer witnessed the sacking of Folkestone and Ipswich (among other English centres) and the seizure of a truly enormous quantity of plunder.

The English military forces were too slow, too few in numbers and too widely scattered to get to grips with the raiders before they could cause ruinous damage. By the time the Saxon levies rode up, the towns were plundered, the townsfolk slain or enslaved, the timber buildings set ablaze, and the Viking host was an outline of sails against the seaward horizon. And when the invaders fought the thin, hastily-armed ranks of Englishmen the result was most often a heavy, indeed humiliating, defeat for the natives, ending with the local men deserting to protect their families and livestock rather than continue to face the terrible Danes in open and fruitless warfare.

From the beginning of their adventures, the *wicing* life had attracted the boldest, the strongest, the most enterprising and the hardest men of their times: men determined to force their way in the world in whatever manner seemed most advantageous. It has become an accepted tenet of modern study of Viking life and Viking culture that they were essentially 'decent' warriors who liked nothing better than to feast and hear a complex saga by the fireside after a long journey's exploring. It is worth bearing in mind, however, that in the main they constituted a destructive rather than a constructive force in their effect on the outside world; that they represented (indeed typified) self-serving elements in their contemporary world; and that they became a 'creative' force only when their narrow, purely selfish ambition had been abandoned, at which time they could no longer be said to be Vikings in the true sense of the term.

Just why these nations – Danes, Swedes and Norwegians – suddenly began to search beyond the confines of their known territories, and why they were impelled continuously to look further afield, is far from certain. A frequently-cited motive for the Norwegians is the unification of that country out of the former multitude of small independent earldoms, kingdoms and tribal groups, under the rule of Harald the Fairhaired in the ninth century, which left many aristocratic families with no livelihood, and no skills except in warfare. Yet, while this may be true of ninth-century Norway, it does not explain why the Danes and Swedes acted likewise, nor why any of these peoples began their Viking careers in the late 700s. Interestingly, a Geatish king called Hygelac mounted a kind of 'prototype' Viking raid from his

home in southern Sweden south to the Netherlands in the sixth century, so the phenomenon may be still older than is usually believed. This king's motive was apparently his own pride and the lust of his people for martial glory and treasure won in battle.

Whatever it may have been that set the Scandinavians off on their adventures, there can be little doubt as to what sustained them: it was hunger for gold easily got, whether in trade or in war; greed for prestige and a glorious name, spurring men on to ever more daring exploits; and above all, the ever-present greed for land. Land meant wealth, and the life of a land owner could be comfortable and prestigious. The Vikings' appetite for land was almost insatiable and took them beyond the narrow limits of the Germanic and the European world: eastwards far into Asia; northward to Iceland and the White Sea; southwards to north Africa and the Byzantine Empire; and westwards to Greenland and North America.

It was the Swedes who spread eastwards, first to the offshore islands in the Baltic, such as Gotland and Bornholm. Having established firm links there, they progressed to the southern shores of the Baltic and so up the navigable rivers into 'European' Russia. The Swedish Vikings founded the city of Kiev, from which base they were able to dominate the surrounding Slav tribes. Increasingly, however, they tended to lose their distinctive Scandinavian character, and were slowly Slavicised so that their separate ethnic and cultural identity was only a memory by the twelfth century. Their trading links extended far to the south and east, to the Eastern Roman Empire's capital at Byzantium (Istanbul), and beyond that to the emergent Islamic states in western Asia.

The Danes were hemmed in to the south by the Holy Roman Empire and the German states, and consequently they favoured the western routes into Atlantic Europe from an early date, although there was some Danish expansion along the adjacent Baltic coast into Prussia which was then inhabited by a Slavonic people called the Wends. Danish travellers journeyed to the Low Countries, northern France, the coasts of the Iberian peninsula and through the Straits of Gibraltar into the Mediterranean. They also established routes leading to Britain and Ireland, and

Late Viking sword from Canwich Common, its blade decorated with silver inlay; such weapons were to influence English patterns in sword design. Blades were often imported without hilts and then fitted with whichever blade hilt was fashionable locally.

The Victorian idea of the Viking (right), complete with horned helmet; research and archaeology have dispelled many of the myths concerning Norsemen, but to many people the word 'Viking' still conjures up this image. See the drawing of the horned figure from Birka for a possible origin of the image.

to the Faroes. With the exception of Ireland and the Faroes, these were all well-developed and organised nation-states with urban communities far better established than those of the Danes in their homeland. As a consequence of this they made little impact on the settlement patterns in these countries in the early years of Danish expansion, although they were happy to take over existing estates when the opportunity arose. The Faroes, on the other hand, were sparsely populated and the advent of the Vikings probably did a great deal to open up the islands to long-distance trade, which proved advantageous to the locals and the newcomers alike.

Ireland was different: here a complicated social and governmental system had evolved, but virtually nothing in the nature of urban settlement. The Irish people lived almost exclusively on isolated or self-contained farmsteads, and at this time had only scant trading links with the rest of the world, except southern Scotland and North Wales. Militarily, the Irish were still firmly in the Celtic Iron Age, which had been swept away elsewhere in Europe by the Roman Empire; culturally, they still lived in the late Bronze Age; yet Irish Christianity was a powerful, dynamic force and the Irish church sent its proselytising saints and missionaries over much of Atlantic Europe.

The impact of the Vikings' arrival was influential for the course of later Irish history: Ireland became part of the European Christian community centred on Rome, and soon a long series of bloody civil wars began as the shaky equilibrium of the past was

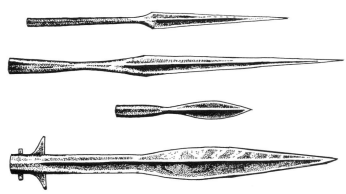

Four English spearheads, the largest of which has metal wings at the base of the socket to prevent the head penetrating into a wound. Tenth and eleventh centuries.

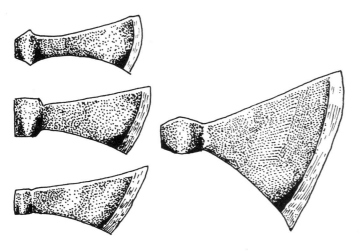

Axeheads found in England, of styles associated with the Vikings. Tenth or eleventh centuries.

Viking raiders at Lindisfarne in 793. It was the plundering of the Holy Island's monastery that really shocked the Church and gave rise to the chronicles' image of a 'wrathful, foreign, purely pagan people'.

replaced by rapid and violent shifts in the balance of power. Danish trading centres were established at suitable coastal sites such as Dublin and Cork, and lordless Danes flocked to these towns to offer themselves as mercenaries in the struggles for control of the island. To their dismay, however, they were not called upon to use their long axes only against lightly-armoured Celtic war-bands: they soon had to face other Scandinavians, Norsemen who had set up their own rival trade centres in the north of the country. These Norwegians had dispersed gradually from western Norway into the Orkneys and Shetland – quite peacefully and with the natives' consent, as far as can be determined – and from these islands had extended their sway over northern Scotland, the Western Isles, Man and, ultimately, parts of Ulster. The Norwegians' voyages also took them northwards and led to the discovery of Iceland, which they settled relatively quickly because the previous inhabitants had been a handful of Irish hermit monks seeking the peace and solitude of that wilderness.

From Iceland, colonies were established on Greenland, and these throve for some time until in the Middle Ages climatic conditions deteriorated and made them uninhabitable, while the lack of newcomers caused desperate social problems among the dwindling native Norse population. Travellers in search of the settlements on Greenland were occasionally driven off course and so discovered new lands further to the west, which they named *Helluland* ('Boulder-land'), *Markland* ('Forest-land'), and *Vínland* ('Meadowland', or possibly 'Vine-land'). A small pioneer settlement was established in Vínland, which is believed to be the first settlement of North America by Europeans, but the distance from the nearest Norse colonies and trade routes was so great, and the quality of life in the New World so miserable, that it was abandoned after a short length of time. Archaeological research within the last thirty years has brought to light houses of a European type and traces of iron-working at sites in Newfoundland – most convincingly at L'Anse aux Meadows – along with some iron artefacts, all of which point to a settlement by an iron-using and distinctly non-native people. This is far from proof that Vínland was situated along the coast of Newfoundland, but it indicates the presence of incomers whose technical achievements and cultural background are consistent with Viking Greenland.

The Vikings traded round and raided the coasts of Britain from the late eighth to the mid-eleventh century. The first true Viking raid of which record survives is that of the monastery on Holy Island

St Mark

St Mark

St Mark

St Matthew

St Luke

St John

The symbols of the Evangelists are recurring motifs in Anglo-Saxon art. They can be seen in many of the illuminated manuscripts and were part of a whole pantheon of symbols representing specific characters or concepts in the Christian tradition.

(Lindisfarne), off the coast of Northumbria, dated 793 AD by English chronicles of the time. A small force of Danes plundered the monastic settlement, drove off some of the monks and killed or enslaved others. The raid had been preceded by 'terrible portents' over Northumbria, possibly a display of the Aurora Borealis, which was taken to be an omen of imminent disaster; and it was not long before church-men were declaring the heavenly spectacle and the raid itself to be signs of divine displeasure and a message that the English should mend their ways. Whether the laymen made good their sins or not, further raiding soon followed. Typically the marauding seamen rushed into some unsuspecting coastal town, sacked it and set sail before the local militia could be summoned, organised and brought to the site of the raid.

These hit-and-run incursions were a nuisance to the kingdoms they affected, and they were an inconvenient drain on English manpower and resources because of the panic and disruption they caused among the farm-workers, but they did not constitute a serious threat to the stability and integrity of the Saxon kingdoms until the year 864. In this year the so-called "Great Army" of Danes decided to remain in Britain all winter rather than sail back north with their plunder, as had been their practice till then. It became obvious that the warriors were no longer content to seize what could be carried away: they had come to stay. They took over the old Anglian kingdoms (Mercia, Northumbria, East Anglia) one by one, killed or forced into exile the royal families and took over large areas of land for themselves. The smaller southern kingdoms were by this time depend-encies of Mercia in their own right, and thus, with its fall soon came within the Danish sphere of influence, although to what degree there was any real inter-ference in these kingdoms' affairs, at any but the

Two English kings (crowned, centre) after a battle; their captive is bound at the wrists and led away by an armed escort.

highest level, is unclear. The kings may have bowed to the Vikings' superior might, but the lives of farmers and peasants went on much as before.

The last English kingdom with its own royal line intact was Wessex, the kingdom of the West Saxons. The royal family traced its origin to the god Wōden, who had supposedly founded the dynasty through one Cerdic who probably ruled over the nucleus of the West Saxon tribes around 470. The Viking attacks looked likely to sweep away this succession of kings which had lasted for four centuries. The old

king, Æthelwulf, had five sons who each took command of given areas south of the Thames; the youngest, however, was in poor health and not thought fit for war – he had, besides, shown intellectual leanings which marked him out for a career in the church. In 870 this sickly youth accompanied his brother to Ashdown, to block the path of an advancing Danish army. While the commander of the English forces, King Ethelred, was still at prayer, the younger king rushed boldly forward with his own men and so unnerved the enemy that they broke and fled! Thus was born the reputation of King Alfred, whom later history was to name 'the Great' – a unique distinction in any age.

Despite this and similar small-scale local victories, Wessex was so hard-pressed by Danish incursions that King Ethelred decided to play for time and buy off the leaders of the raiders, who retired to Mercia with the payment – though not for long. Raids and skirmishes continued and King Ethelred fell in battle: thus it fell to Alfred in turn to assume the responsibilities of ruling the kingdom of Wessex and defending it. His start was not promising: he was beaten time and again by the Vikings, to the extent that their hold on the last remaining English kingdom was so tight that its leading men had to submit to the invaders.

Alfred's 'kingdom' then consisted of an area of Somerset fenland, centred on a makeshift stronghold on the island of Athelney; from this temporary base he planned his strategy for reconquest. For their part, the Danes were keen to be rid of the last threat to their sovereignty over England. With this objective they sent a fleet from South Wales to Devon, to prevent the King from withdrawing west into Cornwall when the campaigning got under way in earnest. However, the fleet was attacked by the men of Devon, with such slaughter that neither force was able to take any further part in military operations. Word was sent from Athelney for the king's allies to assemble at 'Ecgbert's Stone', whence the English set out to meet the Danes at Edgington; there they fell upon the Vikings, and hunted them all the way back to their base at Chippenham, where they later surrendered to Alfred, and their leader, Guthrum, agreed to be baptised, together with the leading men of his army.

England's Danish problems were not over yet, however, for although Alfred's successful campaign had won a measure of security for Wessex, the invaders still held midland and northern England. To bring some degree of stability to this situation, an English-Danish border was agreed, running along the Thames to the river Lea, then up the Lea to its source, thence on to Bedford, along the Ouse to Watling Street. English customs and laws prevailed west and south of this cultural frontier, while beyond it men had to observe Danish practice – hence the name of the Viking area, 'Danelaw'.

Alfred's successors continued his policies, and built upon his success: they attacked the Danes by land and sea and built up their own fleet of warships, said to have been designed by Alfred himself, to end the Viking domination of the seas. Alfred's son, Edward, proved a capable ruler and, in his turn, Edward's eldest son gained control of all England and much of Wales besides. This king, Athelstān, overran the last outpost of the west Welsh – Cornwall – so that he needed not fear attack from the rear by disaffected Celts; and he subdued the Scots – no easy task – so that he became effectively the ruler of all Britain. The Viking warlords looked elsewhere for an easier victim, while the Scandinavians who had already settled in Britain – sons and grandsons of the men who had fought Alfred – breathed a sigh of relief that there would now be more stability in which to enjoy their wealth.

The Vikings' trade centre, the city of Jorvík (York), flourished in the prosperity of its commercial links with the limits of the known world; though populated by as many Scandinavians as Englishmen, it was under the control of the southern King Athelstān, who was keen to promote its unique position as the hub of Viking trade in the North Sea. Not all the Northumbrians were content with this arrangement, however, and they plotted with their Norse kinsmen as well as with the Scots, the free Welsh and the Norwegian Irish, to overthrow the proud English king and end his mastery of the island. In the year 937 they made common cause among themselves, and joined forces in a vast host with which to take on the English. King Athelstān led an army north from his capital at Winchester and engaged the rebels at a spot known as 'Bruna's Stronghold' (Brunanburh), probably somewhere in south Yorkshire, but never reliably identified. A bitter and bloody conflict ensued, in which neither side fled, but stayed and fought it out to the last. The result was a crushing defeat for the king's enemies. Among those who fell in the fighting were five kings, seven Norse jarls (high-ranking noblemen) and a large number of warriors from the royal families of Scotland and Wales. The battle had repercussions all over the Norse world since a great many important men met their death in the fight against Athelstān, and with them died the Norse hope of linking Viking Dublin with Danelaw England in a single political unit.

A generation or more later, Viking attacks on Britain resumed, partly due to a period of turbulence in Norway and partly to the growing power of the Wends in eastern Europe under Norse leadership, which made it less profitable for Viking expeditions to sail east, and so increased the pressure on the west. In England, King Edgar, Athelstān's brother Eadred's son died in 975 at the early age of 32, and different factions of the court and the king's council of advisers (the Witan) supported rival claimants to the throne. The resulting in-fighting and internal turmoil turned English magnates' attention inward to foes at home rather than outward to possible threats from abroad. Edgar's eldest son, Edward was crowned in the year of his father's death while only about sixteen years

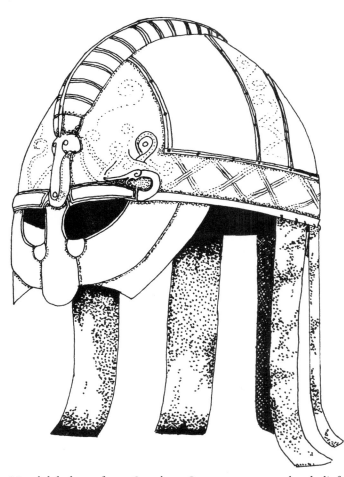

Vendel helmet from Sweden. Contrary to popular belief, Viking helmets did not sprout wings or horns. The half-length face-plate was a practical and effective alternative to the full visor.

cing years, of those men – churchmen and noblemen alike – whose experience and advice were most needed during this time of crisis. Ethelred was not twenty until 988, by which time so much damage had been done to his reputation and standing in the Viking world that he can hardly have been regarded as a threat to Viking designs. Unhappily, at this time the nature of government in England was changing: support and mutual aid between the various shires was gradually giving way to a reluctance to fight if not directly threatened, and prudent leadership was being replaced by bullying and treachery. The Viking raids became more frequent and more audacious. In Denmark, special forts were constructed to house the armies of professional warriors recruited by the Danish king for the assault on England.

The seeds of an ambition which was to occupy them for generations yet to come were being sown among the members of the Skjoldung dynasty: the conquest of Britain and the seizure of the English throne.

the changing vikings

During the centuries of Viking activity, which we may identify as the years 750 to 1050, the nature of the raids of typical Vikings – in so far as such abstract and aggregate creatures may be said to exist – had evolved to such an extent that the latest campaigns, those of Knut Svensson, for example, bore almost no similarity to the early smash-and-grab attacks.

If the early Viking had set out with half a dozen ships full of comrades-in-arms and returned home with more than half of them, and with his sea-chest full of trinkets and silver coins, then he probably counted the campaign a success. At this level, and on this scale, the Vikings were virtually unstoppable because if they were checked in England or met with unusually strong resistance in Northern France, they were free to climb back into their ships and sail for Ireland, Spain, the Baltic, or anywhere else that seemed more promising. But the later settlement of eastern England, Man, Iceland and so on, offered those Vikings who were determined to make their way in the world a new life as land-owning farmers. For those who were younger sons, or sons of unknown fathers, and who could expect little inheritance, such an opportunity must have been irresistible. Instead of gold, land became the main target for Viking acquisitiveness.

Land-ownership did not fulfil all the needs of the

old, but England's luck straight away began to worsen: there was a crop failure and civil unrest. Disaffection among some leading men at Edward's succession led to his treacherous murder in 978 at Corfe Castle, before the very eyes of his younger brother Ethelred, then just ten years old. Although Edward had been singularly unpopular with churchmen during his lifetime, they were not slow to make him into a royal martyr, and the effect this had on the new king may be judged from his later behaviour.

In 980 the Vikings were back in earnest. The accession of the boy-king Ethelred to the throne of one of Europe's most wealthy nations must have been greeted with glee throughout Scandinavia; soon the raiders began sacking coastal towns again, including Thanet, Southampton, Padstow and Portland. The young king was soon deprived, through their advan-

Viking love of glory and adventure, however. It soon came about that men from the Danelaw and Ireland and Iceland took off on their own expeditions, in a second generation of Viking adventuring. One such man was an Icelander whose father and grandfather had come out west from Norway; they came from a strong-minded and successful family. Young Egil, son of Bald Grim, sailed east to Norway where his skilful poetry and ruthless fighting spirit won him much praise, though it also earned him the disapproval of the royal family. Later, he journeyed to England where he fought alongside the English as commander of a small band of Norse mercenaries at the famous battle of Brunanburh, and was reputedly richly rewarded by King Athelstān. He retired to Iceland with great wealth and enjoyed a considerable reputation as a widely-travelled and knowledgeable man, although his war-like ways never softened. There must have been many men of his kind at the beginning of the tenth century, who belonged to the expanded Norse world, and who thought nothing of voyaging from Iceland to Denmark to secure an inheritance or avenge a wronged kinsman.

Political troubles loomed in Denmark, however. It was a matter of some concern to the Danes that they shared a land boundary with the Holy Roman Empire. The Emperors were usually too busy elsewhere to pay much attention to the northern marches, but unfortunate occurrences of Danish raiders laying waste German towns caused the Danes to appear in a very unfavourable light, which led some bishops to suggest that a Holy War should be declared against them, because they were a heathen people. In fact, Christian missionaries were allowed to preach in Denmark and to tend to the spiritual well-being of Christian merchants who stayed at Danish ports; the majority of the Danes continued in their native observances and did not interfere. Fearing the consequences of being attacked by the Germans, King Harald Bluetooth decided to take the bull by the horns and proclaimed that all men should henceforth follow the Christian faith, and should be baptised. He erected a church at Jellinge and had his parents' remains disinterred and reburied with Christian honour beneath the building; he also raised a rune-stone to commemorate his conversion of the nation:

> Harold the King ordered this memorial to be raised in honour of Gorm his father and Thyra his mother; it was that Harald who won all Denmark and Norway and made the Danes Christian.

Harald's somewhat overstated claim that he won 'all Denmark and Norway' is a reference to his intervention in Norwegian politics by supporting a nobleman in his overthrow of the ruling dynasty.

Although the coming of Christianity to the Danes helped secure their border, it alienated them from the other Scandinavians, who were obdurately pagan and sufficiently independent of mind to resist the new faith. In turn, it brought the Danes closer to the English, whom they now had to consider as fellow-Christians instead of potential victims.

The Viking era may be said to end with the death of Harald Hardrāda, a formidable warrior and leader whose career is the very stuff of which Viking sagas were made. He was exiled from his native Norway during his teens, and fled east to the Byzantine court where he became head of the Emperor's personal troop, the Varangian Guard. After many years of successful campaigning in the Mediterranean and Asia Minor, Harald returned to Norway with a large quantity of the Imperial revenues, which he had been sending off into 'safe-keeping' elsewhere. The Norwegian king, Magnus, was involved in a bitter but petty struggle with the king of Denmark over the nominal claim each had to the other's throne. Harald's arrival coincided with the conclusion of a peace treaty, under the terms of which each king should hold the territory he now had, and each should succeed to the other's throne if he died without an heir.

The warlord Harald was not a particularly welcome figure back in the north, but Magnus soon came to an arrangement with him by which they were to rule Norway jointly (this was not exceptional in Northern Europe, and there were many precedents). However, as things turned out, both Magnus and the Danish king died without legitimate sons, and Harald was quick to reinterpret the terms of the treaty to elect himself as Magnus's heir, and give himself a claim on the Danish throne – and a stake in the claim its kings had on the throne of England. Not even the most generous reading of the agreement could render Harald's designs legitimate, but this was too trifling an objection to deter him: he knew that what counted in these matters was military might and the will to use it. In this he was unequalled in Northern Europe, for he had always been a most aggressive and belligerent character and his personal followers were among the finest the Viking nations had ever produced, besides having been given valuable, indeed unrivalled, experience of a variety of types of warfare while in the east. Harald's reputation alone could carry the day in most

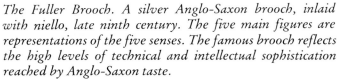

The Fuller Brooch. A silver Anglo-Saxon brooch, inlaid with niello, late ninth century. The five main figures are representations of the five senses. The famous brooch reflects the high levels of technical and intellectual sophistication reached by Anglo-Saxon taste.

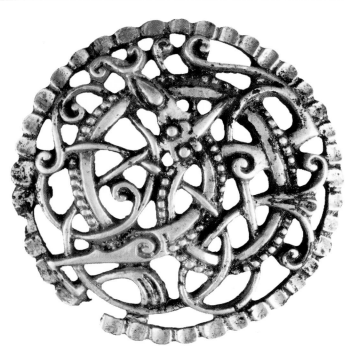

The Pitney Brooch. Anglo-Scandinavian. Second half of eleventh century. An outstanding example of the Urnes style, closer to Scandinavian brooches than others discovered in Britain. Found at Pitney in Somerset. A poorer version, in copper alloy, has been found at Wisbech, Cambridgeshire.

circumstances, and few dared stand against him.

In the event, Harald's campaign to conquer Britain came close to victory, but finally ended in disaster at Stamford Bridge near York, where he went down fighting with his followers while his countrymen fled back to their ships after being defeated at the hands of Harold Godwinesson. It was this bitter fight against Norsemen in the north, however, that made it impossible for Harold to respond quickly or strongly enough to the invasion by William of Normandy on the Sussex coast, and which cost Harold his crown and his life.

Harald Harðraða died with his sword in his hand in 1066, and with him died the Viking ideal that it was possible for a brave man to carve a good name for himself, as well as no small personal fortune, in an inhospitable but exploitable world. Harald was the last of the Vikings in a real sense, yet by no means the least of them.

the viking legacy

Just how much the Vikings contributed to the fabric of Britain in the years of their settlement is not easy to determine, since we obviously cannot know how British history might have progressed if there had been no Viking Age.

Their linguistic contribution is often cited as one of the more evident areas where the Scandinavians made their mark: a good many English words are taken from Norse, or have been influenced by Norse, among the most common being:

anger	drown	seat
axle	egg	skill
bank	kid	skin
birth	law	skull
bull	leg	sky
calf	lift	stack
cast	race	steak
cow (the verb)	rid	take
crawl	root	thrive
cut	scant	want
die	scare	window
droop	scowl	

Perhaps even more surprising is that such a basic English phrase as 'they are' is taken from Norse (*ðeir eru*) and has entirely replaced the native phrase (*hīe*

St Matthew from the famous Lindisfarne Gospels, which were written at the end of the seventh century at the monastery of Lindisfarne. The Viking raid on the Holy Island of Lindisfarne in 793 is often regarded as the start of the Viking Age.

King Edgar offering the New Minister Charter to Christ. Dated 966, the splendidly-illuminated New Minister Charter is at the beginning of the Golden Age of late Anglo-Saxon art (966 – 1066), known as the 'Winchester Style'.

sindon); the reason that this could happen is that the English pronoun *hīe* was too easily confused with the words for he and she (*hē, hēo*), and any alteration which made for greater clarity was an improvement.

Norse speech was introduced first in the Danelaw areas, of course, but words from the region soon escaped into other local dialects, and eventually into 'standard' Old English, the language of Winchester. Early examples are *dreng*, a warrior, *æsc*, a ship, and *ūtlah*, an outlaw.

English and Norse were, at this time, not as different as the modern speech of London is from that of Oslo or Copenhagen, and it was probably possible for Danes to make themselves understood by English-men, and vice versa, by careful selection of vocabulary. Many Norse words were little different from their Saxon equivalents, and would have posed few problems for either nationality; such words include land,

father, mother, man, wife, grass, summer, winter, life, cliff, tree, town and house. Furthermore, a few words abandoned their purely English form in favour of the Norse equivalent, such as 'sister' (Norse *sýstir*, English *sweostor*) and 'egg' (Norse *egg*, English *ey*). This is probably due to confusion between very similar forms, with one or other becoming more popular – there are many examples of Norse words gaining a temporary foothold in the English language and then gradually falling into general disuse, and many Norse words linger on in dialects in the north and east of the country. The most far-reaching effect of the Scandinavian language on English, however, was to weaken the word-endings of English, which at this time were similar to those used in modern German: gradually, since the core of the vocabulary of English and Norse was similar, the distinctive patterns of endings for each language became less important, as people found themselves able to convey ideas without resorting to all the tiresome details which served only to confuse their neighbours.

Danish ideas about the law contributed considerably to maintaining the strong regional identity of the areas they settled until well after their reconquest by the English. Danish legal terms which survive include the word 'law' itself, as well as 'by-law' (Danish *by*, a village or hamlet), 'outlaw' (one who puts himself outside the law, and cannot benefit from its protection), 'husband' (house-dweller), 'fellow' (partner, one who lays out a fee of money), 'husting' (house-meeting) and 'wapentake' (a district, or body of freemen who meet at a common local assembly and brandish their weapons to show their approval of a proposal).

The Danes who settled in England often gave their own names to the places they acquired and these are characterised by elements such as -by (for example, Hemsby, Grimsby) and -toft (Lowestoft, Langtoft). They also often altered existing English names to resemble Norse ones. Many northern English place-names commemorate Viking owners, though hardly any can be identified with historically verifiable persons.

It is perhaps too large a claim to make for these Norse incomers that their particular notions about personal freedom and responsibility moulded later English opinion and led to the present-day view of the proper relationship between the state and the individual. Yet it is fair to say that the Danish freeman enjoyed a degree of freedom within the law greater than that of his English equivalent. This state of affairs was redressed to some extent by the legal amendments of various kings, notably Athelstān and Knut, but there persisted a greater feeling for the rights and privileges of freemen in the East Midlands than elsewhere even as late as the Norman Conquest and beyond.

The passion for individual freedom was the undoing of the Scandinavian empire-builders, for while warriors and petty chiefs were content to follow their leaders on raiding campaigns, they were considerably less inclined to accept any authority imposed by the jarls once they had settled into land-ownership – it was one thing to obey the jarl on the battlefield, but entirely another to have him interfering in the

Alfred's jewel, found at Atheleny. Now in the Ashmolean Museum, Oxford, England.

management of one's household. For this reason, although the Vikings were able to 'muscle in' everywhere, to take over districts and settle them, they were seldom able to establish independent states or consolidate the territories they had won into a political unity. The nearest they came was in Iceland, where they set up a republican system in the previously almost uninhabited land. Although there were no kings or jarls there, the social system imported from Norway soon produced a class of wealthy '*góðar*', priest-chieftains with considerable legal, religious and political authority. The island increasingly leaned towards Norway for support and trade, especially after the conversion to Christianity in the year 1000. Eventually the Icelandic state was reduced to a mere colony of the Norwegian crown.

The fierce independence which sustained the Vikings through hard times in inhospitable places, and which made itself felt wherever they settled, prevented them from taking a wider than purely local view, or abandoning their parochialism in support of the greater good, or of long-term ends. They were capable of achieving great successes, but lacked the co-operation needed to exploit them. Some men, Knut among them, saw the immense possibilities in the resources which needed only to be directed wisely to bring about a lasting Viking empire; some Vikings did manage to realise their ambitions, in part. But social ties were founded on the loyalty of this or that jarl to this or that king, and the death or replacement of a few men could cause the whole edifice to collapse, or the empire to disintegrate, when the personalities which held the state together were removed.

Chapter 2

Byrhtnōth's World

King Athelstān the Victorious was born around the year 895 to Edward, the eldest son and successor of Alfred. The identity of his mother is unknown, but hints in later sources suggest that she was not a suitable mother for a king, indicating either that she was Edward's first wife and of lowly birth, or that she was the king's mistress in his early years. Although Edward had other children by his successive queens, Athelstān was not born while his father was king, and his accession therefore caused raised eyebrows throughout Europe. Athelstān's early years were spent with the formidable Æthelflæd, the 'Lady of the Mercians', his aunt and herself a daughter of Alfred the Great. She was the wife of the Mercian Ealdorman Æthelred.

In all likelihood Edward had intended that Athelstān should succeed his uncle to the post of ealdorman, and had arranged for him to be raised and schooled among Mercians. Edward's designated heir to the throne was his son Ælfweard, but in the event this prince survived his father by only a few days. The Midlanders then chose Athelstān to be, not merely their ealdorman, but king of the entire nation. There was a good deal of resistance to his accession at the time, but faced with the choice of the capable Mercian leader or the late king's younger children, the Witan accepted Athelstān in 925, the year following his father's death. The reaction of the rejected candidates – or those who hoped to gain from the accession of a child-king – was predictable for the period and several attempts were made on his life during the early years of his reign.

By 927, Athelstān had reached formal agreement with the Viking king of York, called Sihtric, who died soon afterwards. The throne of York was seized by his kinsman Óláf, supported by the Dublin Vikings. Athelstān was quick to make his mark on contemporary politics: he marched on York, expelled Óláf, and drove him and his army north into Strathclyde. He summoned all the kings of northern Britain to an assembly at Eamont in Cumberland, and the outcome was that one Guthfrith, a kinsman and supporter of Óláf's, was to be surrendered to him: this first test of his power and resolve allowed him to force his recalcitrant neighbours to obey him. Guthfrith, meanwhile, escaped back to York with the intention of raising a further Anglo-Danish army. He received short shrift from the men of York, however, as they were not keen to try the patience of the English king. Rather than spend the rest of his life a refugee, Guthfrith surrendered to Athelstān, who spared him and transported him back to Dublin.

A further assembly was convened at Hereford with the Welsh kings in order to agree a frontier between England and Wales, and to settle the amount of tribute the Welsh kings should pay him annually. At the meeting was King Hywel Dda (Howell the Good) of Dyfed, who was clearly impressed by the success of the English monarchy in establishing a sense of national identity across various separate districts. Hywel set about introducing a law codex based on the English model.

Elsewhere on the Celtic fringe, Athelstān was at work removing the threat posed to the rear of his kingdom by the continued independence and increasing belligerence of the Cornish. He expelled them from Exeter, fortified it against them, and established the border at the river Tamar. This was not the last of his Celtic problems, however: in 934 there was a resurgence of anti-English feeling

A bronze bucket from Hexham, its rim decorated with pendant triangles of interlace and its handle attached to mounts decorated with human figures, perhaps influenced by Irish styles.

among the Scots, expressing itself in raiding expeditions into English territory. The king was not prepared to tolerate this and he quickly summoned the armies of Wessex and Mercia, as well as the Welsh and the East Anglian Danes, and led them north in a two-pronged movement: one force travelled overland with the king while a fleet sailed along the east coast. The Scots were suitably cowed by this show of military force and avoided battle. Athelstān allowed his army to carry out some minor ravaging, however, as a warning to the northerners. This campaign, if we may so call it, probably represented the first joint effort by the English, Welsh and Anglo-Danes to overcome a common foe. It could only have been effected by a king whose standing with each of these peoples was such that it overrode traditional rivalries between them.

Worse was to come, for the disgruntled Scots courted support for their cause from the more independent elements among the Welsh, and from the Norsemen of Ireland. They must have spoken eloquently and at length of the humiliation which they had all suffered at the hands of the proud English king, for by 937 they had come to a mutual resolve to tackle Athelstān and to overcome him by force of arms. The leader of the alliance is believed to have been Óláf, the ex-king of York. The rebel army met the English King and his army at an unidentified spot called Brunanburh and the fighting continued till nightfall. The exultant English chroniclers were able to record the deaths on that field of five kings and seven jarls; Athelstān's reputation was unassailable, unmatched in his time. Even in distant Iceland men knew of *Aðalsteinn hin sigrsæll, einvaldskonungr yfir Englandi*, 'King Athelstān the Victorious, sole king over England'.

Much as this was the king's victory, it was really a triumph for the English nation and its allies, the friendly Danes and Welsh. After Brunanburh the whole of Britain from Land's End to the Firth of Forth looked to Athelstān as lord, and his authority even extended to Ireland. He began to style himself, not without justification 'Emperor of Britain'. Such was his prestige that his kinswomen were used for strategic marriages: one of his sisters married Hugh, duke of the Franks, others of his female relatives were betrothed to Otto, son of Henry the Fowler of Germany, Konrad of Burgundy and Louis of Aquitaine. Athelstān was also foster-father to the young Hákon, son of King Harald the Fairhaired of Norway.

When not engaged in waging war, subduing foes, dispensing justice, and terrorising his neighbours Athelstān was an avid collector of that most curious, often ghoulish, of medieval currencies: holy relics – chiefly, that is, the bones and personal belongings of saints. Inventories of gifts made to him indicate a more than usual interest in such items, even for a war-like king who believed that one could never have too much good luck. The value of holy relics in the religious culture of the time was the point of physical contact with saints that they offered. The saints could be expected to look favourably on the prayers of those who were tending their mortal remains and ensuring that their miracles or sacrifices were not forgotten. Why Athelstān wanted to surround himself with these bizarre remnants is not clear; it may point to his sometimes strained relations with the church and perhaps served to convince his subjects of his

Christ in majesty from the Trinity Gospels. First quarter of the eleventh century. The Gospels form one of the most lavishly illuminated manuscripts surviving from this period.

fundamental deep concern for Christian tradition. Alternatively, the king may have regarded the holy articles as imbued with a potent spiritual power which he wished to wield for his own ends.

After only fifteen years of rule, aged about forty-four, King Athelstān died. The cause is not recorded, which suggests that it was a natural death, and we are reminded of the poor health of his grandfather Alfred, which, as well as his determination and qualities of leadership, may have been inherited by Athelstān. Fortunately for the nation, he had allowed his half-brother Edmund to share military power during his lifetime, and so Edmund was elected king at the age of eighteen.

Almost immediately there was Viking trouble to contend with. York was declared independent under its own king, Óláf, yet again. After a brief interlude of plundering southwards into England, a truce was patched up by which York was ceded the entire Danelaw in 940. Just two years later Edmund's efforts to regain the territory were crowned with success when the Danelaw was returned to the rule of the English, much to the relief of the inhabitants, who now felt little identity of common interest with the upstart kings of York.

A ninth-century English sword pommel from Fetter Lane, London; the grip features a spread-eagled animal amid vine leaves, executed in niello, a black oxide of silver. The reverse of the pommel incorporates four spiralling serpents set among vine leaves.

King Óláf of York died soon afterwards, to be replaced by another Óláf, son of Sihtric; he was expelled and replaced by one Ragnald, brother of the first Óláf. A very interesting situation developed, as neither Óláf Sihtricsson nor Ragnald was strong enough by himself, nor sure enough of the men of York, to defeat his rival decisively – consequently, both leaders covertly requested the assistance of the king of England in ousting the other. This told Edmund all he needed to know about the strength of either side, and he promptly harried both out of England. In 946, he again marched north, this time to quell an uprising among the men of Strathclyde, which had been instigated by Óláf Sihtricsson; the territory gained was handed over to King Malcolm of Scotland under the terms of a treaty of alliance.

Aged only twenty-five, Edmund met his end in 946 when he was stabbed to death at a feast while single-handedly restraining a warrior whom he had previously outlawed and banished.

Edmund's two sons were both still children, but a succession crisis was avoided by the election of his brother Eadred, who immediately took steps to bring Northumbria and Scotland back under English dominion. The following year he received oaths of allegiance from the leaders of the Northumbrians, led by Archbishop Wulfstān. Wulfstān was a fierce opponent of the Wessex dynasty and a campaigner for Northumbrian independence, and it comes as no surprise to learn that the leaders were soon ignoring their oaths to the king.

In Norway, King Harald the Fairhaired had died, leaving his throne to his son Eirík, who bore the unpromising soubriquet 'Blŏdŏx', 'Bloody-axe'. So stiff was the opposition to this tyrant that he was quickly deposed in favour of Hákon, the foster-son of Athelstān, leaving Eirík little choice but to try to carve out a kingdom for himself elsewhere. Elsewhere proved to be Northumbria, where he was accepted as king of York. Evidently the Northumbrian magnates preferred separatism under a Norseman to union under the house of Wessex. Eadred could not afford to tolerate this, however, and straight away marched north to subdue the dissidents on a journey of despoliation and destruction. When he eventually turned south again, a local war-band overtook the rearguard of his army at Castleford, and 'there was great slaughter'. Eadred was ready to turn about and harry Yorkshire a second time, but the Northumbrians quickly took action: they expelled Eirík and approached the king with peace-offerings for their misdeeds.

The next year the king allowed York to be taken over by Óláf Sihtricsson on his return from Dublin, and he maintained the north on friendly terms with the southern English; but in 952 Eirík returned and seized power once again, probably at the behest of Archbishop Wulfstān. Eadred had the churchman imprisoned for his part in spreading anti-Wessex feeling. When, in 954 Eirík was driven out a second time – and betrayed by his supporters and slain – Eadred allowed Wulfstān to hold office once again, but only as bishop of Dorchester, where he could have little contact with his homeland, and where he could be kept under the watchful eye of the king's most loyal supporters. The earldom of southern Northumbria was conferred on ealdorman Ōswulf, who was possibly involved in the betrayal of Eirík, and who joined the kingdom of York to his holdings in northern Northumbria to reunite the ancient kingdom.

On his death in 955, Eadred had done much to

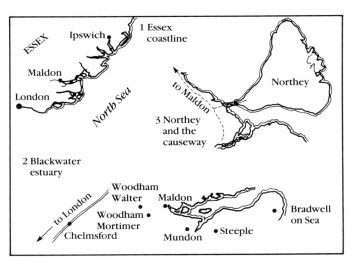

The Essex coastline.

reintegrate the Danelaw into the kingdom of the English. His adversary, Wulfstān, outlived him by just one year.

Byrhtnōth

In the year 956, the existing ealdorman of the East Saxons named Byrhtferth ceased to attest charters and was replaced by a thane of his named Byrhtnōth. The new dignitary lived through a period of great change in England, and his death foreshadowed greater change to come.

Unfortunately we have little reliable information concerning Byrhtnōth's birth or early years, nor of the family into which he was born. His father's name is known to have been Byrhtelm, though no record exists of any ealdorman or magnate of that name in the early tenth century. Of course, it is perfectly possible that Byrhtnōth's father was related to Byrhtferth, especially when one remembers that noble Saxon families had the custom of repeating the same initial sound or name-element in the children of the family; this is why all the kings of Wessex since Ecgfrith had names beginning with vowels (and, consequently, why they are so difficult to remember individually). The likelihood is that Byrhtelm was related to Byrhtferth the existing ealdorman, perhaps a son or younger brother. However that may be, the older man either died or became too ill to carry out his duties and Byrhtnōth stepped forward into his position.

The year of his birth cannot be precisely decided, but it is likely to have been around 930. We know that Essex was administered by an ealdorman Ælfgār from c.945 to the year 951. Byrhtnōth was married to one

Detail from the Ramsey Psalter, late tenth century, Latin. The psalter may have been designed for use by the Ramsey's founder Oswald, Bishop of Worcester and Archbishop of York, one of the great Church reformers in Edgar's reign.

Cohhanfeld (Cockfield, Surrey), Ceorlesworth (Chelsworth, Suffolk), Fingringahō (Fingringhoe, Essex), Polstede (Polstead, Suffolk), Strætford (Stratford St Mary, Suffolk), Lauanham (Lavenham, Suffolk), Byligesdyn (Balsdon Hall, Suffolk), Peltandun (Peldon, Essex), Myresig (Mersea, Essex), Grēnstede (Greenstead, Essex), Ylmesaeton (Elmsett, Suffolk) and Thorp (Thorpe Morieux, Suffolk). As is clear from this one bequest, the main holdings of the family were in Suffolk and northern Essex, though Byrhtnōth himself is known to have held lands throughout the south.

The terms of the queen's will specify that the land she left to her sister and brother-in-law were theirs for the duration of their lives, but afterwards were not to be assessed as private holdings: they were to pass to religious houses she favoured, such as Ely Abbey, Bury St Edmunds, Stoke-by-Nayland, and St Paul's, London. During the course of his long life, the ealdorman acquired many other estates as royal grants, and as inheritances through his family. He in turn made generous donations to religious institutions, notably Ely Abbey, which has records of land-grants he made to it of properties in Cambridgeshire, Huntingdonshire, Norfolk and Suffolk. In addition, mention is made of gifts from other members of his family: his daughter, Leofflæd; and her daughters Ælfwynn, Æthelswyth and Leofwaru, as well as a nobleman called Thūrstān who may be the son of one of these ladies. Other holy places Byrhtnōth favoured include Ramsey, Mersea (Essex), Abingdon, Christ Church in Canterbury and Barking Abbey. Apart from properties that he owned in such far-off places as Northampton and Worcester, he presumably also had extensive holdings in Essex itself, which he did not donate or dispose of, though he did make a wedding-gift to his wife of some land at Rettendon. Obviously the amount of property he accumulated during his lifetime in high office must have been vast for him to make charitable donations on this scale.

Byrhtnōth first signs documents as ealdorman in 956, at which time Essex was a satellite of East Anglia, of which the ealdorman from 932 to 956 was a certain Athelstān. This nobleman was known as Athelstān Half-King so great was his wealth, power and prestige. His son Athelwine took over this position in 962, and between him and Byrhtnōth there grew a warm and firm friendship which was to last the rest of their lives, prompted perhaps by their mutual interest and co-operation in the foundation of new monasteries and in establishing the Benedictine Reform in this country. Athelwine particularly favoured the monastic

of his daughters, named Ælfflæd; the other daughter Æthelflæd was married to King Edmund in 944. Ælfflæd's marriage must already have taken place when Ælfgār made his will, since he refers to Byrhtnōth in it as his son-in-law. The will was in all probability made out shortly before Ælfgār ceased to sign charters in 951 – perhaps in the year 950. Thus, if Byrhtnōth was already married in 950, we may put his birth at not much less than twenty years before, and this makes him more than sixty at his death in 991. At this period sixty was a very considerable age – especially for a warrior – and his great lifespan no doubt contributed to his almost unique position at court in his later life.

Byrhtnōth's father-in-law Ælfgār and his sister-in-law Queen Æthelflæd bequeathed many important and valuable properties to Byrhtnōth and his wife. Æthelflæd's will mentions lands and estates at Wudaham (Woodham, Essex), Hedham (Hadham, Wiltshire), Dictun (Fen Ditton, Cambridgeshire), centre of Ramsey, while Byrhtnōth endowed that at Ely. Interestingly, the first abbot of Ely was also called Byrhtnōth, and may possibly have been a member of the ealderman's family.

At the time of Byrhtnōth's promotion, there was a succession crisis looming due to King Eadred's having died childless. The two sons of his brother, King Edmund, were not yet of an age to rule: the elder, Edwȳ, was fourteen or fifteen; the younger, Edgār, only twelve. These brothers were able to rule only through the Witan, the king's council of wise men, church leaders and secular magnates. Foremost among the lay members of the Witan at this time were Ælfhere of Mercia, Byrhtnōth of Essex, Ælfheah of Hampshire and Athelwald of East Anglia, while the church contingent was headed by the formidable Archbishop (later Saint) Dunstān, whose overbearing character caused him to be at loggerheads with Edwȳ, the notional king. Edwȳ exercised his royal authority by having Dunstān exiled, though the archbishop later returned in response to Byrhtnōth's pressure on the king and Witan. The king married a noblewoman named Ælfgifu in 956, but the marriage was dissolved in 958 due to consanguinity. The king, meanwhile, was rejected by the Mercians, who preferred his younger brother, but a compromise was agreed whereby they could share the kingship. The possible fragmentation of the kingdom was avoided, however, by Edwȳ's death in 959 while still in his teens.

His brother's death paved the way for Edgār to become sole ruler of the English. Edgār recalled Dunstān and the elderly cleric effectively gained power through the young king, who was always anxious to please him: for example, he was not even crowned until 973 because of Dunstān's opposition.

The king was well-disposed towards Æthelwine and Byrhtnōth, having been brought up in the household of Athelstān Half-King, and his goodwill probably translated itself into handsome gifts and privileges for the two leading ealdormen. Byrhtnōth seems to have been the less important of the pair, at least during Athelwine's active lifetime. Normally, Ælfhere of Mercia witnessed documents first among the ealdormen, followed by Athelwine and Byrhtnōth in succession; after Ælfhere's death in 983, the East Anglian and Essex ealdormen sign first and second respectively. The title 'Ealdorman of Essex' carried with it responsibility for areas outside the modern county, which represents only part of the older East Saxon kingdom. This explains Byrhtnōth's land-holding throughout eastern England, and his endowment of Ely. The former kingdom had spread by

The Bosworth Psalter. Last quarter tenth century, with early eleventh-century additions. It is possible that the psalter was designed for St Dunstan himself. The text follows the Roman version which was probably introduced at the end of the sixth century by St Augustian's mission.

Viking horseman from the tapestry recovered from the Oseberg ship burial.

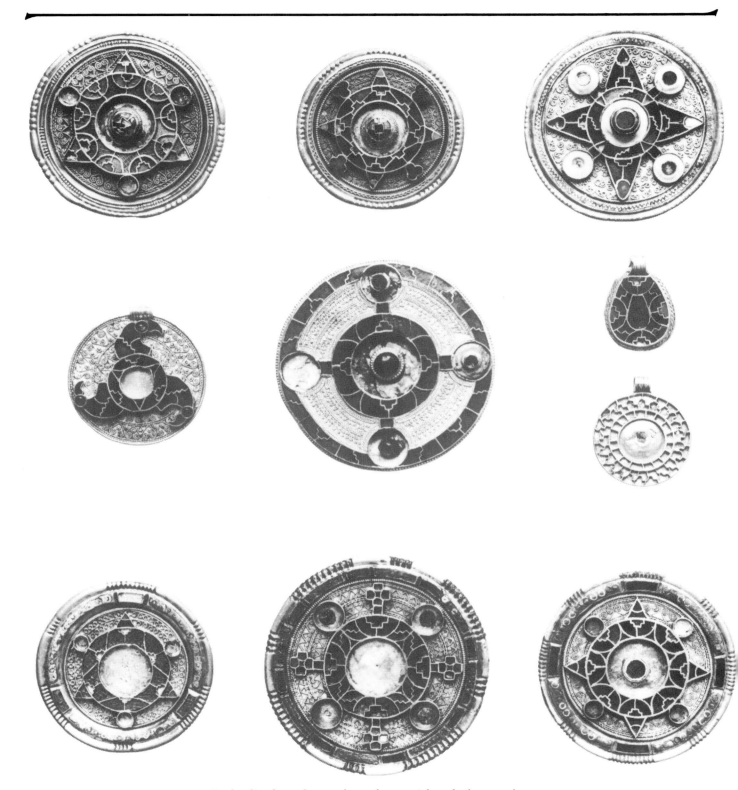

Early disc brooches and pendants with polychrome decor-
ation; the centre-left brooch features a triskele of stylised
birds' heads.

conquest and judicious expansion from a nucleus on the north bank of the Thames to include Middlesex, Hertfordshire, and probably Surrey as well, for a time. Surrey had been seized by the West Saxons during their earlier defence of southern England. The land north and west of London became Mercian territory, while the eastern section was regarded as an outlier of East Anglia. The ruler of Essex was therefore of lower status than that of East Anglia, since he was notionally subject to his authority and dependent on him for help.

edward, king and martyr

When King Edgār died unexpectedly in 975 at the age of thirty-two, once again, the king's sons were mere children. This time there was considerable civil unrest and many of the nobles took the opportunity of contesting the spread of church power which had been promoted under Edgār, probably under the influence of Dunstān. The most outspoken leader in this secular backlash was ealdorman Ælfhere of Mercia, who seems to have coerced many of the lay magnates into supporting his cause. With the monasteries growing in wealth and power, at the expense of their own influence, they were probably not unwilling to listen to him. The political opposition to Ælfhere was led by ealdormen Athelwine and Byrhtnōth, and it is almost certainly due to his siding with the church against the landed noblemen that the monastic historical records deal so favourably with Byrhtnōth, and that the poem concerning his last fight came to be recorded.

Edgār's elder son was called Edward; he was a surly, selfish youth for whom there was little popularity during his lifetime. His brother, Ethelred, was at this time just a boy. Dunstān favoured Edward. Edward's teenage years were characterised by a general worsening of affairs: famine and evil portents in the sky, and rumblings in Scandinavia, warning of further trouble to come from there. The last thing England needed was a petulant, headstrong youth on the throne, and some Englishmen determined to see that England need no longer suffer under so inappropriate a monarch. In 978, at Corfe Gap where the half-brothers were staying with Ethelred's mother, Edward was stabbed to death by one of the thanes, before Ethelred's eyes. That this could happen on one of the royal estates has been taken to suggest that Ethelred was involved in the plot, but it is more likely that the strong-willed queen disliked her stepson and took private steps to dispose of him in favour of her own son.

Three early belt buckles from Faversham, Kent; the outer two have stylised animal shapes in gold filigree, while the central buckle has a plainer, triangular motif as a border.

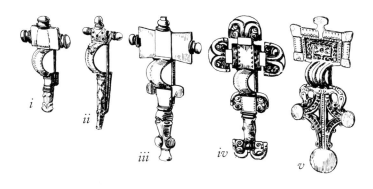

i. East-Anglian long brooch, made of bronze, probably fifth century. This pattern is also found in Scandinavia.

ii. Long brooch from the end of the fifth century. The actual brooch is now cast as a single piece. Found in Cambridgeshire, England.

iii. A cruciform brooch in bronze from Kenninghall, Norfolk, England.

iv. A cruciform brooch in bronze with silver panels on the arms of the cross. Seventh century, from Sleaford in Lincolnshire, England.

v. Square-headed brooch from Kenninghall, Norfolk. This resembles brooches found in Denmark. The Anglo-Saxons also used chased or jewelled circular brooches and quoit brooches, made of silver and gilt. The quoit brooches, which were shaped like an incomplete ring, were an elaborate development of the Early Iron Age penannular pattern. By the tenth century some quoit brooches had pins over two feet long.

The Edgar Window, Bath Abbey.

If Edward had been unsatisfactory as a king, however, he was even more troublesome now as a martyr. The church quickly took the initiative and declared him a representative of Christ on earth – as medieval kings were popularly regarded – and his murder an act of wanton opposition to the will of God, who had chosen Edward to rule. The young Ethelred could not help but appear to be implicated in the treachery, whether he actually took part in the plot or not. The effects on the young Ethelred of witnessing his half-brother's murder were to have damaging repercussions for English history well into the next century.

the vikings return

In 980, the Vikings were back — and with a vengeance! It was indeed welcome news in Scandinavia that a boy had come to the throne of one of Europe's richest nations; one, moreover, with long and indefensible coasts. The news was the more welcome since things had been rather uncomfortable at home. King Harald Bluetooth had unified much of the Danish areas under his rule, and towards the end of his reign he had even imposed Christianity on his subjects, and introduced it to the Norwegians. Viking power in the east was waning as horse-borne nomads established their hegemony over the Slavs and threatened the Byzantine Empire. But the period of the old Viking free-for-all system was soon over. Early raids were launched against English coastal towns, and at just this time, when the king was most in need of advice from experienced men, nearly a whole generation of councillors died. The king was not twenty years old till 988, by which time his reputation was irredeemably damaged in the eyes of the Vikings. Just as the large pirate raids were beginning to make inroads into the English economy, the nature of Viking activity altered. The royal house of Denmark saw the advantages of systematically plundering the English, and they determined to do the job properly. As the raids increased in frequency and audacity, the Danes constructed a series of military camps in which to house the legions of mercenaries recruited for the attacks on England. Sven Forkbeard, son of King Harald, led a band of professional soldiers whose aim was to plunder and extort as much wealth as possible from England, and especially from London.

At the same time, the English defences were increasingly indecisive and confused. The Danes took the initiative and kept it. The English responded too slowly, too feebly and in too few numbers to achieve anything. Their every enterprise was attended by the most appalling bad luck, and the *Anglo-Saxon Chronicle*'s entries for the period read like a series of national disasters and farcical blunders. The average Englishman of the time probably regarded the whole problem as stemming from the bloody, treacherous and entirely unholy way the king had been brought to the throne. The nation had incurred God's anger through the king and there was nothing to be done but ride out the storm. Steadfast resistance became a thing of the past – each shire would no longer help others repel Viking attacks and the more cynical leaders took to lining their own pockets by taking bribes from the Vikings.

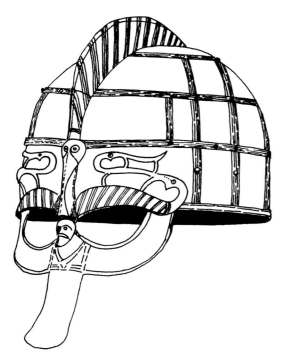

Helmet from Vendel, Sweden, of a type which may still have been in use in the later Viking Age.

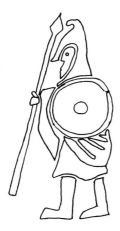

Figure of a warrior from the Franks casket (eighth century, Northumbrian) wearing a helmet with a hooked or beaked ridge, otherwise apparently similar to the Coppergate example.

An important feature in England's decline and humiliation is revealed by the *Chronicle*'s entries: the king's personality. His arrogance and lack of perseverance in the face of adversity shine through the *Chronicle*'s pages. Although an ineffective military leader, he was not above having his own subjects slaughtered wholesale, as when he ordered all the people of Danish extraction in the country to be mercilessly slain by their English neighbours in the infamous Saint Brice's Day massacre. It is unlikely that this order can have been carried out on any but the smallest scale, bearing in mind the conscience of the Christian English, not to mention the fact that in many places the Danes outnumbered them.

The king was manifestly cruel and ruthlessly dispassionate in this scheme, which was probably not of his own devising but which he had put into effect. He may well have been paranoid, and have regarded every Dane as an actual – rather than a potential – enemy. Yet when we recall the manner of his accession to the throne – at the expense of his brother's life – it becomes clear that he could hardly have been anything other than suspicious and distrustful.

In 991, ealdorman Athelwine fell ill, though he did not die until the following year. This made Byrhtnōth effectively the senior ealdorman of England, being the longest-serving and most experienced lay adviser upon whom the king could call. He also became the *de facto* military commander of the English army – an unenviable post at that time, when the Danes were proving themselves masters of the seaways again. *Liber Eliensis*, the Book of Ely, records that all the chiefs of the local English levies bound themselves by oath to serve him in his capacity as 'Army Chief of Staff', a responsibility that he seems to have taken very seriously, as we shall see.

In the same year a force of Vikings made its way along the southern coast towards London, harrying and raiding as it passed by. It was Byrhtnōth's intent to stop it and the story of how he went about this can be at least partially reconstructed from contemporary and slightly later sources; it is this that is attempted in the next chapter.

chapter 3

the Battle at maldon, ad 991

The primary reference for much of the course of early medieval English history is the *Anglo-Saxon Chronicle* (often abbreviated to ASC). This is not a single unified work, but rather a number of manuscripts sharing a common origin. It would not be overstating the case to say that it is the most important vernacular work for early northern European history.

The sources for the early entries, from the coming of the English to Britain in the fifth century, are probably vernacular tradition, Bede's *Ecclesiastical History of the English People*, and a variety of annals kept at monastic houses as marginal notes in the canonical tables. These, and several other works such as lists of kings, were collated into a single document some time in the eighth century; copies were then made and distributed to monasteries in central and southern England. Not unnaturally, the *Anglo-Saxon Chronicle* has been connected with the period of intellectual revival under King Alfred, particularly as the work is written in West Saxon rather than Latin, as was usual for such documents at that time. There is no comparable document for the period it covers anywhere in northern Europe.

Because the *Chronicle* was distributed to a variety of centres of learning, where the records were continued independently, often being copied again and the new document sent on to a different location, there exist several separate sets of *Chronicle* annals. The convoluted relationship between these has been worked out largely by establishing at what point the narratives begin to differ, and also by studying the works of medieval authors who used the *Chronicle* as source material for their own writings.

The *Parker Manuscript* entry sets out the following record for the reader:

> Here [at this point in the annals] in this year came Unlāf with ninety-three ships to Stone in the New Forest and ravaged it, and then went from there to Sandwich, and likewise from there to Ipswich and overran it all, and thus to Maldon. And there Ealdorman Byrhtnōth came against them with his Fyrd, and fought against them, and they slew the Ealdorman there and had control of the place of slaughter.

The events are described under the year 994 in this document, but the scribe, realising his mistake, inserted a caret mark indicating that the events referred to took place before that year.

The 'C' version of the *Chronicle* reads slightly differently:

> Here [at this point in the annals] was Ipswich plundered, and very quickly after that Ealdorman Brihtnōth was slain at Maldon. And in that year it was first advised that tribute should be paid to the Danish men, because of the great destruction they wrought along the coast. It was first ten thousand pounds. That advice was first given by Archbishop Syric.

From a study of these two entries we may deduce that the Viking fleet began its plundering expedition in England somewhere along the south coast where the New Forest extended to the sea – which it did until well into the high Middle Ages. Southampton would have been a very tempting target for a sea-borne raiding party. If the *Parker Manuscript* is accurate and the fleet did consist of ninety-three ships, this would

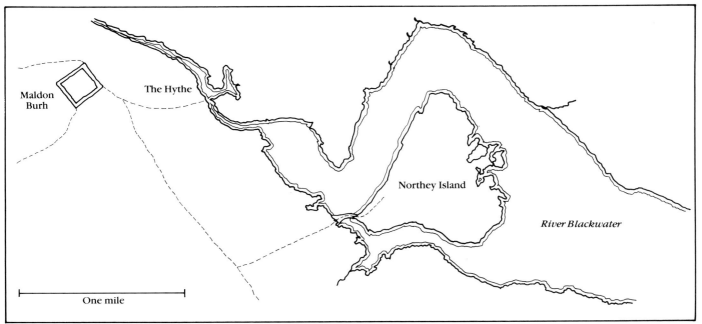

Maldon Burh.

indeed have been a mighty force for those days, with a total manpower not far short of four thousand men, even allowing for non-combatants. It is not necessary to place complete trust in the numbers mentioned in these records, however, since it is unlikely that the victims of a Viking attack stopped to count the vessels their foes came in; yet ninety-three does not appear to be an estimate – the clerk would be more likely to round the figure up to one hundred.

The name of the leader of the fleet, given as 'Unlāf', may be significant: we know from Norse sources that there was a famous Norseman named 'Ólāf' in England at this time. This was Ólāf Tryggvason, later king of Norway. His father, Tryggvi, had been a petty king over a small province who had been ousted by Harald the Fairhaired, and killed. Tryggvi's wife, Ástrid, had fled the country because she was pregnant with Tryggvi's child. She first took refuge with relatives in Sweden, but when the king sent messengers to the Swedish court demanding the extradition of Ástrid and her infant son, she decided it was no longer safe to live so near to the influence of her husband's enemies, so she set off with her son and a few servants to stay with her brother Sigurd at the court of the jarl of Kiev, in Russia.

She had no better luck here, however, for the ship she was travelling in was attacked by Estonian pirates who divided up the loot and took the women, children and young men as slaves. Ólāf was separated from his mother and spent the next six years as a serving-boy until, in 977, he was bought out of captivity by his uncle. His first act as a free person was to seek out the Viking who had first taken him prisoner, and kill him.

As the nephew of a court official, Ólāf spent a great deal of time with the royal family, and entered the army as a junior commander. However, he was not popular with the other officials due to his growing influence over the troops, and he soon turned his back on the courtly life and returned to the sea. He set himself up as a freelance pirate in the Baltic, and is believed to have married Queen Geyra of the Wends, according to later tradition. When his royal bride died in 990, he equipped a fleet of Wendish vessels and set off west. For the next four years he led raids on Saxland (Northern Germany), Frisia and Britain, which tallies well with the *Chronicle*'s information.

A fleet crossing from the Netherlands might well run along the Channel, travelling west while waiting for a favourable wind to take it north. The next point mentioned after Stone in the New Forest is Sandwich in Kent, where the land turns northwards into the West Sea (as the Vikings called our North Sea). If the intention was to harry London, one might have expected the raiders to turn into the Thames Estuary, but perhaps the southerly wind forced them to sail past – the alternative would be to row the ships for fifty miles along the Thames against the current. Whatever the case, they pressed on to Ipswich, where they overran the local resistance and plundered the

Viking weapons: battle axes and spearheads from Museum of London.

town. Perhaps while they were engaged in this the wind swung round to the east and they realised that they would now be in a good position to sail back down the coast to the Thames. On the way there, some or all the vessels entered the river Blackwater, and sailed up it far enough to threaten the town of Maldon, about ten miles from the sea.

Such is the evidence for the movements of the enemy fleet. There is a certain amount of other information in the *Chronicle*'s entries: that the fight at Maldon took place 'very quickly' after the plundering of Ipswich; that as a result of the Englishmen's failure to beat the Danes, the Danegeld was introduced, on the advice of the archbishop; and there is an alternative spelling for the name of the English leader – Brihtnōth. In fact, 'Brihtnōth' is only a variation, perhaps due to the local pronunciation of the manuscript's writer, on the more usual form 'Byrhtnōth'. In early times – in the reign of King Alfred, say – it would have been

spelt 'Beorhtnōth', and the later forms are due to linguistic changes. Even today, there is a difference between the word 'bright', and the same word in personal names: Al*bert*, Her*bert*, *Bert*rand. The poem commemorating the ealdorman's death consistently spells the name 'Byrhtnōth', so we may assume that this is the poet's own local pronunciation; and if the poet was a contemporary of Byrhtnōth (as I believe he was), it is reasonable to suppose that the poet used the same pronunciation of the name as the ealdorman himself used.

Besides the *Chronicle*, there are a number of other references to Byrhtnōth's death. Two 'obituaries' survive for him, one from an Ely calendar of the late twelfth century, the other from a Winchester calendar from the early eleventh century. Here the date of his death, and thus of the battle, is given as 11 August, while Ely's reference is a day earlier on 10 August. One would logically expect that the record nearer to the events it describes should be the more accurate, but the ealdorman and his family had very close links with Ely, and the monks there may have had access to more reliable information. After the battle, they carried his body away for burial on their premises.

Vita Oswaldi, the Life of Saint Oswald, is a Latin work written around the year 1000 at Ramsey Abbey. Although close to the battle in time and place, however, its record is not very reliable: for example, it places the events of 991 before the death of Saint Dunstān in 988. Its narration is a stilted and conventional description of the battle and the flight of part of the English army, and it suggests that the Danes had sustained such losses that there were scarcely enough left to man their ships. If this had been the case, there would have been little need for Archbishop Syric to advise paying them off with money rather than fighting them. Perhaps more trustworthy is the description of Byrhtnōth himself as unusually tall and with white hair; his poem also refers to him as *hār hilderinc*, 'a hoary-headed warrior'.

A number of chronicles in Latin, mostly dating from the twelfth century, mention the events of the year 991, but their accounts are believed to be based on the *Anglo-Saxon Chronicle*. The *Florenti Wigorniensis Monachi Chronicon ex Chronicis*, known as 'The Chronicle of Florence of Worcester', indicates that the Vikings were led by two men, whom it names as Justin and Gūthmund. Justin may be a misinterpretation of the Norse name 'Eystein'.

Another reference to Byrhtnōth and his death is in *Liber Eliensis*, the Book of Ely. As we have seen, Ely was the last resting place of the ealdorman's body, and was richly endowed by his family. It is all the more disappointing to learn, then, that where we should have expected traditions about Byrhtnōth to have survived longest, the chronicler's information is based on earlier written records. The 'earlier records' are presumed to be the *Anglo-Saxon Chronicle*, probably the same version as Florence of Worcester used, since here also the Vikings are said to be led by Justin and Gūthmund. However, it is possible that some outside tradition contributed to the Ely account, and it is even possible that the chronicler had the text of the poem set out below to work from, since some of his Latin phrases resemble terms used in the verse: for example, *unum passum pedis*, 'one foot of land' corresponds to *fōtmǣl landes* in the poem. Whatever his sources may have been, he expanded them into an epic struggle in which Byrhtnōth first routs the Danes, who return years later to challenge their conqueror to a return battle, which, through his great boldness, he fights for a fortnight before being slain along with his followers.

The source of the wide variation between the sober *Chronicle* entry and the Book of Ely's fantastic reconstruction is mentioned elsewhere within its pages: it records the donation by Ælfflǣd to the abbey of a tapestry commemorating her husband's deeds. After more than a century, when the book came to be written, it is quite possible that the exact significance of some of the scenes would have been forgotten. Exaggerated details thus came to surround the events shown in the pictures, and this more sensational account came to be accepted because it was so much more memorable and heroic than the plain facts. English needlework, represented by the Bayeux Tapestry, enjoyed a very high reputation throughout Europe at that time. Consider how difficult it would be to determine the sequence of events shown on it if there were none of the Latin captions to the scenes.

None of the works above is of unimpeachable authority: the late works must be treated with suspicion because they are so distant in time from the events they describe, as well as the inherent likelihood that they have been corrupted or their sources embellished. The *Chronicle*, though usually reliable, is necessarily brief, and is in any case mainly concerned with accessions and deaths of nobility and the appointments and deeds of churchmen. The *Vita Oswaldi*, though early, is not really concerned with the battle, which is peripheral to the theme of the work: hagiography.

There is one other work alluded to above, however, which deals specifically and in some detail

Slender Viking spearhead with inlaid decoration at the neck and a series of small lugs or studs along the sides.

with the battle and the ealdorman's death. This is the poem, usually called *The Battle of Maldon*.

The manuscript in which the poem occurs is first mentioned as belonging to the Cotton Collection; sadly, it was destroyed by fire in 1731; the same fire which caused the only surviving text of *Beowulf* to be singed at the edges, so close did it come to destruction in the flames. The poem had been transcribed some time before by a copyist named Elphinstone, so most of the work survives, although when he made his copy part of the manuscript was already missing. The leaves of parchment were bound in with a number of other documents relating to the Danish wars, but it is improbable that these various texts formed a single work before they came together in the Cotton Collection – in other words, the collection's owner, Sir Joseph Cotton, had bound together a number of originally separate documents with a common theme.

A wolf-warrior, in the company of a dancing youth, illustration from a Swedish helmet-plate. The ritual significance of the animal mask and the dance may once have formed part of the cult of the battle-god Wōden.

The cult of the wolf-warrior, as exemplified in an emblem from an early German sword scabbard featuring a wolf-headed warrior armed with a spear and a seax, and carrying a sword in its scabbard.

Any information taken from the poem is not, strictly speaking, from first-hand source material, since we do not have the original document from which Elphinstone made his copy. Therefore, there always exists the possibility that the copyist has introduced misspellings, or has misdivided words, or even omitted sections altogether. Indeed, this is known to be the case in some instances, where, for example, a warrior in the poem is named as 'Godrine'; no such name exists, nor is it thought possible that such a name could have existed. This must be a misreading of the manuscript's lettering, and may conceal either 'Godwine' or 'Godrinc', both English names of the period. Close examination of the copy by a variety of scholars for over a century has pointed out the failings of Elphinstone as a copyist, and the knowledge thus gained has been used to determine just where he would be likely to fall into error (and

what that error might be). Accordingly, we do know that there is a section of verse missing from the poem, where a line breaks off at the half-way point, but it is virtually impossible to tell how much of the text is missing: our only guide is to study the poet's style to acquire some idea of how many lines he would be likely to devote to a passage such as the one where the omission occurs, and to compare the number of lines the medieval copyist set out on his page, in order to determine if there appears to be any significant deviation from the pagination pattern, since Elphinstone did carefully note where the folios began. Neither of these measures is very precise, and together they can only act as 'rule-of-thumb' indications.

When new, the manuscript probably consisted of a quire of eight leaves, as was usual in the early Middle Ages. The outer leaf was already missing when the transcription was made. Since Elphinstone was working on behalf of the document's owner, it is reasonable to assume that this leaf was missing when the manuscript came into his possession. Indeed, the outer sheet, being subject to greater wear and tear, would be most likely to disintegrate, or may have been removed in medieval times due to decay or defacement.

As previously mentioned, Elphinstone was careful to note the original pagination, so we know that the poem was written out as prose, just like other Anglo-Saxon verse, with between twenty-five and twenty-nine lines to the page. The last remaining page contained thirty-two lines, presumably in an attempt to cram the text into the available space. If we assume that only one outer leaf was lost – that is, two sides of writing at each end of the poem – then roughly fifty to sixty lines are missing from the beginning, although this figure would be reduced if a versal or decorated capital had been used. Slightly more than this must be assumed to be missing from the end, perhaps as much as seventy lines. The fact that the scribe began to compress the writing towards the end of our fragment does, in itself, suggest that he was approaching the end of the text from which he was working.

the events of the poem

Before our text takes up the tale of Byrhtnōth's death, there had evidently been a landing by *Wīcingas* ('Vikings') which had been brought to the attention of the *eorl*, later identified as Byrhtnōth. In Old English, the word *eorl* does not mean the same as our word 'earl', but rather 'warrior, hero'. Byrhtnōth's rank and title is ealdorman, which means 'leader, governor, alderman', and I have used the Old English word throughout since there is no modern term which conveniently sums up the high position and the wide responsibilities which the old word implies. There was a contemporary word *earl*, which was an anglicised form of the Norse word *jarl*, meaning 'nobleman, leader'. Byrhtnōth could not be said to be an *earl*, which kept its very definite Danish overtones until much later (it is used to describe men in the Danelaw districts equivalent in rank to English ealdormen). Evidently the poet decided to use the native word *eorl* to give his poem some of the lustre of traditional heroic songs, whilst expecting his audience to make the equation *'eorl'* = *'earl'* = ealdorman.

A meeting had taken place, at which Byrhtnōth and some of the leading men were present, as well as a number of the thanes and fyrd-warriors – this is explicitly referred to later when Offa voices the misgivings he had felt then. As was traditional at such gatherings, the warriors all swore allegiance to their leader, and promised to perform great deeds of courage in his honour to repay him for the gifts he had given them. This kind of warrior-lord bond is of great antiquity among the Germanic peoples, and was commented upon by the Roman historian Tacitus in the first century. The tenor and colouring of the poem as a whole show that the poet was deliberately evoking the ancient customs in his verse, to suggest that Byrhtnōth and his troops had the kind of relationship that the old stories made clear existed between the legendary Germanic kings and their war-bands.

From the place where the meeting was held, the *meðelstede* or 'speaking-place' mentioned in line 199, the troops rode to a point within walking distance of the riverside. It is not known whether all the men of Essex who were liable for military service had been brought together (the so-called 'Great Fyrd'), or whether only the ealdorman's own followers, the hundred-men and the garrison of the *Burh* (stronghold) at Maldon were involved.

As the poem, or rather the fragment, begins the men had dismounted and collected their weapons; they may also have been blessed by a cleric and have attended Mass, as good Christian men preparing to meet their deaths.

the Battle of maldon

The modern English version given here of the Anglo-Saxon poem cannot, in any sense, be considered a 'poetic translation' of the original. Anglo-Saxon verse

King Athelstān presents the life of St Cuthbert to the saint, from Bede's Lives of St Cuthbert. *The illustration shows distinct English characteristics. The manuscript was presented by the king to the shrine of St Cuthbert in the summer of 934.*

is a highly-wrought form in which features such as alliteration, rhyme and assonance play an important part (see Appendix 1). If they occur in my version, they occur only by accident.

I have tried throughout to express the formal sense of each line of verse in as straightforward and intelligible a manner as possible. My search for fact in no way reflects the skill of the poet, nor the artistic quality of the original. There are a number of modern, very good verse renderings available for those wishing to acquire a notion of the 'flavour' of the original work.

In order to adhere to the 'line-by-line' formula it has occasionally been necessary to resort to some quite unnatural English. I have supplied pronouns where the context requires them, and have omitted many instances of the word *ðā* ('when' or 'then') which might confuse and weary today's reader.

. . . should be broken.
He then bade each of the warriors drive away his horse,
send it far away and go forwards,
think of his hands' work, and of good courage.

₅ *Then Offa's kinsman first found out*
that the eorl would not stand for slackness

— he let fly from his hands his dear one, then,
his hawk, to the woods, and he strode to the fight.
By means of that one could tell that the young man would not
₁₀ *weaken in the warfare when he took to his weapons.*
Eadric wished also to follow his leader,
his lord, to the battle; he then started to carry
his spear to the fray. He had a firm resolve
while with his hands he could yet hold
₁₅ *his shield and broad sword; he fulfilled his boast*
when he had to fight before his lord.
Then Byrhtnōth began to draw the warriors up there;
he rode along and advised them, showed the men
how they ought to stand and keep their place
₂₀ *and bade that they held their shields in the right way,*
firm with their fists, and that they should have no fear.
When he had correctly arrayed the Folc,
he alighted then among the men dearest to him
where he knew his hearthband were most steadfast.

LINES 1–4 The order to drive away the horses must have been intended to deny them to the enemy; neither the English nor the Danes used what we would term 'cavalry', but both would use horses to ride to the battlefield, as here, and perhaps also to send messages and to pursue a fleeing foe. Had the Danes been able to seize the English mounts, they would have promptly set off on a pillaging raid inland, while the Englishmen, deprived of their horses, would have been able merely to look on helplessly. Equally, a sudden stampede of riderless and uncontrollable horses through the battlefield would have benefited neither side.

LINES 5–6 Just who 'Offa's kinsman' was is impossible to know for certain: he was presumably named in the lost lines before our fragment begins. The fact that he was a *cniht* (youth) might identify him with Wulfmǣr the Young, who later stood beside Byrhtnōth in the shieldwall and was described as *cniht on gecampe*, 'a youth in warfare'. This Wulfmǣr (as opposed to Byrhtnōth's nephew of the same name) may have been a squire whom the ealdorman was training, and who was now seeing contemporary warfare from the front line. His kinsman, Offa, must have been of some considerable importance, as becomes clear later in the poem.

LINES 7–21 The release of the hawk was probably a sign that the day-to-day pleasures were to be put aside while the serious business of warfare was conducted; it is not necessarily a poetic fiction, since it was common for wealthy men to ride accompanied by a favourite bird of prey or hunting-dog, as well as an attendant to look after them while the owner was otherwise engaged. Meanwhile, Eadric (who is not mentioned again in the fragment) showed his determination to fulfil his vows to Byrhtnōth, which evidently concerned fighting before his lord – perhaps he had sworn to fight well alongside Byrhtnōth and not to flee even though his life depended on it. More is said later concerning the importance of the *beot* (boast, vow) among Anglo-Saxon warriors.

When his force reached the appropriate spot, Byrhtnōth arranged them as he thought best for the day, and then rode along the line speaking words of advice and encouragement, as many a good general has done before and since.

Some students of the poem have assumed from lines 18 to 21 that the English force did not know how to fight, or how to handle their weapons properly! This is, of course, not the case; nor is it a natural reading of the text. Byrhtnōth is probably pointing out the difficulties of the situation to his men: specifically, the terrain over which they must fight, the static, defensive manner of fighting, required and how they should adjust their posture to accommodate these. One gets the overall impression of an experienced leader showing his men that he is not daunted by the prospect of the fight, and that cunning warriors can adapt to difficult circumstances; . . . *and ne forhtedon nā*, 'and they should not be at all afraid', confirms that he had confidence in them to beat the Danes, and that they should share his confidence.

LINES 22–24 Having thus arrayed the fyrd along a defensive line, Byrhtnōth dismounted at the spot where he intended to remain during the fight, 'where he knew his hearthband were most steadfast'. This is certainly an ironic statement by the poet because the hearthband as a whole were very steadfast, as Byrhtnōth thought; yet, as we shall see, one of them was not at all steadfast and his flight had dire consequences later. Byrhtnōth was by now the only mounted member of the English force – which also told against him afterwards.

LINES 25–52 A Viking messenger hailed the ealdorman across the water and Byrhtnōth strode forward to hear what the marauders had to say. The messenger delivered his speech *on beot* which may mean 'threateningly', as I have rendered it, though it may mean no more than 'haughtily' or 'boastfully'. The Viking's insistence that the English should act speedily, and the messenger's condescending 'you may' (*đū mōst*) betoken a high-handed attitude, though later his tone is more respectful, even wheedling. It is conceivable that the poet was here trying to represent the kind of broken English that the Norsemen used and that *đū mōst* was a common idiom among the Danes representing the Norse *đū munt*, meaning 'you must'. Another possible Norse usage is at line 38 where the Danes demand to be given tribute 'according to their own judgement', which may refer to the Norse practice of *sjalfdómi* by which an aggrieved party could name his own compensation.

25 *Then at the shore stood, calling out sternly,*
the Vikings' messenger; he uttered words,
he who threateningly delivered the seafaring men's
message to the eorl, where he stood on the bank:
'Bold seafarers have sent me to you,
30 *have told me to tell you that you may quickly send*
rings for your protection; and it is better for you
that you buy off this clash of spears with your tribute,
than that we should share in so hard a battle.
We need not destroy each other if you are wealthy enough;
35 *in return for the gold we wish to make a firm peace.*
If you who are most powerful here so decide
that you wish to free your people by ransom,
give to the seafarers – according to their own judgement –
wealth in exchange for friendship and accept peace with us,
40 *then with the money we intend to go to our ships,*
put out to sea and leave you in peace.'

Byrhtnōth spoke out, he raised his shield
and shook his slender spear; he uttered words,
angry and single-minded, he gave him his answer:
45 *'Do you hear, seafarer, what this people says?*
They wish to send you spears as payment,
a deadly point and an ancient sword,
a heriot which will be of no use to you in battle.
Seamen's messenger – declare in reply,
50 *say to your people far more unwelcome tidings:*
that here stands an eorl of no ill-fame with his war troop
who means to defend this homeland.

It should be stressed, however, that all the direct speech in the poem is artificial, giving only the sense of what is said, not the actual words. Old English verse is a highly-wrought art form, entirely unsuited to the needs of a warrior communicating on the battlefield.

As the speech progressed and the overt threat of bloodshed was replaced by politer terms and warmer sentiments, the message was addressed directly to Byrhtnōth in person, suggesting either that his decision was binding on his men, or that they would follow their leader's example voluntarily. Whichever was the case, Byrhtnōth was not intending to treat with marauders demanding his gold and threatening the peace of his lands. He replied angrily and defiantly, with uplifted spear and shield, and spoke not merely for himself but for all his people – 'this folk', or even 'this nation'. The sarcasm in his reply was calculated to anger the Vikings, who were renowned for their lust to avenge any insult. Their messenger had taken pains to end his speech with friendly words, yet the Englishman showed them no such courtesy. 'They wish to send you spears as payment' is a very clear indication of his intentions, and the mention of heriot is a pun at the Danes' expense, for in late Old English 'heriot' (*heregeatu*) was a tax payment due from a landowner towards the provision of a soldier for the defence of the country. Originally, however, the duty had been to provide armour and weapons (*here-geatu*,

Illustration to a psalm from the Harley Psalter. Second and third decades of the eleventh century. The drawing shows not only examples of early medieval clothing but also weaponry. This is an early section of the psalter, and follows the pattern of the original Utrecht Psalter more closely than does the illustration on page 100.

'army equipment'). In Byrhtnōth's speech, the only tax payment the Danes will get from him would be war gear, but not of a kind to be of service to them in battle, because they will be the victims of the blades rather than the wielders.

He goes on to say of himself 'here stands a warrior of no ill-fame', actually using the word *unforcūd*, which is a typical poetic expression. The basis of the term is *cūd*, which means 'known, famous, familiar', and is related to our word 'uncouth', meaning 'strange, oddly-behaved' and thus 'badly-behaved' according to the rule which accepts only the familiar. The addition of the prefix *for-* modifies this meaning to 'notorious, infamous'; the further addition *un-*, gives the opposite meaning: 'not infamous, reputable' which I have tried to convey by 'of no ill-fame'. It is just this kind of twisting and modifying the basic elements of speech that gives the verse much of its distinctive character and charm, though it does nothing to increase its intelligibility.

Æthelred's country, my lord's
people and territory. They must fall
55 in battle, those heathens. It seems too shameful to me
that you should go to your ships with our wealth
unfought for, now that thus far to this place
you have travelled into our land.
Not so easily ought you to come by treasure:
60 point and edge ought first to decide the matter between us,
– grim war-play – before we give tribute.'

He then bade shields be raised and warriors go forwards
so that they all stood on the riverbank.
Because of the water, each troop could not reach the other:
65 the river came flowing there after the ebb-tide
– the waterways locked together. It seemed too long to them
until they could bear spears together.

They stood about the Pant's stream in their war-might,
the East Saxon battle-line and the Ash-army;

LINES 53–69 The ealdorman's reply to the Vikings was given in the name of the king, or so we may assume when he speaks of 'Ethelred's country'. In fact he seems to be defying the foe on behalf of the entire nation; in this light, his statement that it seemed 'too shameful' to him to give up the gold without a fight could be seen as the poet's indictment of Ethelred's policy of offering money to the Danes in return for peace – which lasted for no more than a few months. The ealdorman and his band showed great courage (losing their lives in so doing) in refusing to hand over protection money to the marauders; yet the king and his advisers lost no time in doing just what the men of Essex had refused to do. There seems to be a moral here, pointed out deliberately by the poet, who was probably living through the consequences of the archbishop's advice.

After this speech to the messenger, Byrhtnōth had his men carry their shields forward to the river's edge, presumably to deny a bridgehead to any Danes who might manage to get across the waterway, and to have a better defensive stance once the fighting started. Yet neither army could get to grips with the other due to the tidal in-flow in the channel between the island where the Danes were moored and the English-held mainland. Impatience to get at the foe was already overtaking Byrhtnōth's men, as we see from line 66.

The Vikings are here described as *æschere*, 'ash-army'. *Æsc* can mean 'spear' in Old English, so perhaps the reference is to an army of spear-carrying warriors. Alternatively, it can simply mean 'ash-wood' and may be descriptive of the Viking ships – in medieval Latin, Vikings are called *Ascomanni*, 'Ashmen'. The English force, on the other hand, is described as *Eastseaxena ord*, the *ord* being the point of a weapon, so the sense here is probably a transferred image of the point of a wedge-shaped battle formation. The 'van' of a medieval army derives its name from *avant*, 'before'. The idea is obviously that the best part of the army, comprising the biggest and bravest men, stands at the front of the wedge at the point, or, as we might say, 'up the sharp end'.

LINES 70–90 While the tidal streams converged in the channel separating the island from the mainland it was impossible for the two armies to get to grips; their only means of venting their feelings on each other was to shoot arrows across the sound. The stalemate was ended when at last the tide turned and the seafarers' renewed activity showed that they were preparing to force a crossing. Byrhtnōth accordingly set one of his men to hold the 'bridge' with the support of two *wīgan unforhte* (dauntless warriors), named as Maccus and Ælfhere, against the expected onslaught. The use of the word *bricg* (bridge) here is slightly unusual since the crossing is elsewhere called a ford. From the context of the poem it is clearly the only means by which the island and mainland were joined, but it was submerged – or at any rate, impassable – at high tide, which rules out a 'bridge' in the modern sense of the word. The most likely explanation is that it was a kind of causeway, a raised path which was passable at most times, but which was covered when the water was deepest at high tide.

Two types of English spearhead: the slender blade (below) from Thames Ditton is acutely pointed to puncture armour, while the other (provenance unknown) is provided with twin 'lugs' at the base to prevent the weapon piercing a wound so deeply that it could not be withdrawn (compare the illustrated spear on p.14).

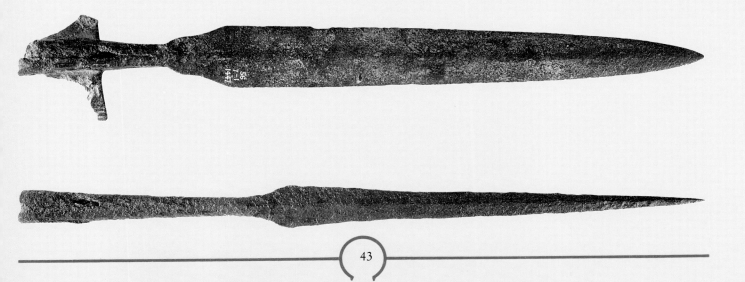

70 *none among either of them could harm the others*
except those who met their end through the arrow's flight.
The waters drove outwards. The sailors stood ready,
many Vikings, eager for war.
The heroes' protector then bade the bridge be held
75 *by a war-hardened fighter who was called Wulfstān,*
a bold man like his kinsmen – he was the son of Ceola –
who with his Franca killed the first man
who – the boldest there – stepped along the bridge.
With Wulfstān there stood undaunted warriors,
80 *Ælfhere and Maccus, two brave men*
who did not mean to take flight from the ford,
but rather they steadfastly fought against their foes
as long as they could wield their weapons.

When they recognised and clearly saw
85 *that the bridge-keepers they found there were fierce*
the hated strangers began to use guile:
they proposed that they should be allowed passage ashore,
to cross over the ford and to line the footmen up.

Then the eorl in his over-confidence began
90 *to allow too much land to the loathed people;*

The causeway was evidently of no great breadth since the three English warriors were able to hold it with ease, and the one Dane brave enough to cross was slain by Wulfstān with his weapon, called a 'Franca'. This is usually assumed to be some kind of spear, and the poet certainly suggests that it is a throwing-weapon: he says Wulfstān *ofsceat* the Dane – *sceat* means 'shot, threw' and *ofsceat* must mean 'killed by shooting or throwing'. It is conceivable, however, that the Franca was a kind of tomahawk or throwing-axe, of the type used by the people known as Franks, who derived their name from it. Such throwing-axes were certainly known and used in Anglo-Saxon England, though I can find no evidence of their use at so late a date, and it may simply be that 'Franca' has come to be a poetic word for any missile or throwing-weapon.

The English defence of the 'bridge' was evidently too successful for the Danes' liking. They soon set about using other means to overcome their lack of progress, and the poet uses strong language to show his contempt for the *lāðe gystas*, 'loathly strangers', who now fell back on their cunning to achieve what their military prowess could not. The Danes asked the ealdorman to make room for their army on the landward bank of the watercourse, which in the poet's opinion was treacherous and unmanly.

A great deal of ink has flowed over what happened next, and the poet's language in describing it. My rendering is fairly unemotional, but many scholars have read great criticism of Byrhtnōth into lines 89 and 90. The argument centres on the Old English phrase *for his ofermōde*, which some translate 'because of his great courage', and others 'through his excessive pride'. It is worthwhile noting here that *ofermōd* can have the meaning 'great pride', translating the Latin word for a simple excess of confidence, *superbia*, and that the assertion in line 90 that he began to allow the Danes too much land can be taken to imply that any land he allowed them would be too much, and that he should have denied them any land

at all. However, *ofermōd* is a word found chiefly in religious contexts, where it is often applied to Satan, and there are no exactly parallel examples of its use in heroic poetry. The word consists of *ofer* meaning 'over-, excessive', and *mōd*, which can mean 'mind, courage, spirit, pride, mood'; the earliest meaning seems to have been 'anger'.

Because of the many different nuances of the word it is difficult to be sure just what it meant for the poet, and in which way he intended it to be interpreted in this context. A word may have a narrow, specific meaning in religious or theological use which is quite separate from its meaning in secular speech – consider 'spirit', 'form', 'essence' in modern English, each with a religious significance which is almost comically distant from the everyday usage. Thus it may be that the poet was praising Byrhtnōth's 'great spirit', his courage in war and his generosity, which extended even to his enemies and allowed him to treat them fairly, as a Christian warrior should. *Mōd* has an adjectival form *mōdig* (the modern word 'moody') which occurs twice in the poem, each time with the meaning 'brave, bold, courageous', rather than 'proud, wanton' as we might have expected if an excess of *mōd* were a fault in a warrior. Furthermore, the poem as a whole is extremely generous in its praise of an English force which was, after all, defeated – even if it was with honour and some glory. If the poet had considered Byrhtnōth reckless, he could have made this clear long before now. Should we read blame into these two lines of the poem, when the other 323 lines are so laudatory? Perhaps the poet was deliberately using a multifaceted word here to point out the need for excessive courage from a warrior, and the need to temper this with caution when the warrior becomes a leader.

(I have thought it best to render my version of the text in as neutral a way as possible and allow readers to come to their own conclusions. I offer mine at the end of this chapter.)

he started to call out then over the cold water,
the son of Byrhtelm – the warriors listened:
'Now room has been made for you: come quickly to us,
men to the fight. Only God knows
95 *who shall be allowed to have control of the place of slaughter.'*
The war-wolves waded, did not worry about the water,
the troop of Vikings went westwards over the Pant,
across the bright stream they carried their shields,
the seamen bore the lindenwood to land.
100 *Against these fierce men there stood ready*
Byrhtnōth and his warriors. With shields he ordered
the war-wall be made and the troop to hold
firm against their foes. Then battle was nigh,
glory in fighting: the time had come
105 *when doomed men had to fall there.*
A shout went up in that place; ravens circled round,
the eagle, eager for carrion; the world was in uproar.

They sent file-hardened spears from their fists,
grimly-ground javelins flying forth.
110 *Bows were busy, shield clashed with point.*
Bitter was the battle rush – warriors fell
on either side, young men lay still.
Wulfmær was wounded, he chose war-death
that kinsman of Byrhtnōth – with swords he was
115 *fiercely cut down – his sister's son.*

LINES 91–106 Having drawn his force back from the riverbank, perhaps to its original position, the ealdorman called out to the Vikings that he was ready and put the outcome firmly in the hands of God, believing (despite the evidence of recent events) that God would naturally favour the Christians. At this the 'slaughterwolves' advanced westwards to the mainland against the waiting defenders, whom Byrhtnōth ordered to 'work the war-hedge', evidently a type of shieldwall formation. As the armies neared, a great shout went up from both sides to fill the men with courage and to focus their minds on the fighting.

The images of raven and eagle are probably no more than traditional poetic devices, dating back to the time when Wōden was worshipped by warrior-adventurers. The raven and the eagle figured largely in his cult, as did the wolf, and they became associated with battle-imagery in the verse.

LINES 107–115 Once within range 'they' – either Englishmen or Danes, or more probably both – sent a shower of arrows and spears into the enemy ranks, killing a few unfortunates, then 'bitter was the battle rush' as the first real face-to-face encounter got under way. Among the first casualties was Wulfmær, Byrhtnōth's nephew who must have been at the very front of the *ord*. There was a special relationship between a maternal uncle and his nephew (called *swustersunu*, 'sister-son' in line 115) which was traditionally associated with the great heroes of the old songs and stories, as for example Sigurd and Fjotli. The poet introduces it here for the same reason that he persists in calling Byrhtnōth an *eorl*, as a means of suggesting that Byrhtnōth and his men belong to the ancient Germanic culture, that they live in the traditional *comitatus* of lord and retainers and that they are brought down by events which conspire against them, as happened in many of the traditional tales.

A reward-in-kind was given to the Vikings then:
I heard that Eadweard struck one
mightily with his sword – he did not hold back the blow –
so that the doomed warrior fell at his feet;
120 for that his lord said his thanks to him,
to the bürthēn, when he had the chance.

So they stood firm, the single-minded
warriors in battle: they eagerly sought to see
who with his spearpoint could first
125 win the life from a doomed man,
a beweaponed warrior. The slain fell to earth.
They stood resolute – Byrhtnōth commanded them,
bade each man turn his thoughts to the struggle
who meant to win a good name against the Danes.
130 A war-hard Viking then strode up, raised his weapon,
and his shield for protection, and stepped forward to the warrior.
Just as resolutely went the eorl to the ceorl:
each of them intended harm to the other.
Then the seaman sent a southern spear
135 so that the warriors' lord became wounded.
He shoved with his shield so that the shaft shattered
and the spear shivered so that it sprang away.
The war-man became enraged: with his spear he stabbed
the proud Viking who had given him the wound.
140 The campaigner was old and wise: he let his Franca bite
through the young man's neck; his hand guided it
so that he took the life of the deadly attacker.

LINES 116–121 In vengeance for this attack, an Englishman called Eadweard, possibly the same Eadweard the Tall of whom we hear later, struck down a Viking and earned his lord's gratitude. Eadweard is said to be a *būrdēn*, a 'bowerthane' who had charge of the sleeping quarters in the ealdorman's household. As such he was a trusted officer of Byrhtnōth's entourage, and probably quite wealthy.

At this stage the battle was running in favour of the defenders, whose young men were vying with each other to see who could kill a Dane first, which Byrhtnōth encouraged them to do to increase their reputations by fighting Vikings. English morale was high, and the ealdorman's leadership effective; the Danes could not allow this to continue.

LINES 122–142 A Viking, 'hard in war', stepped up against Byrhtnōth with his spear and shield at the ready, while the Englishman went to meet him with equal determination. The poet says: *eorl to đām ceorle*, 'the hero against the churl'. 'Churl' does not mean 'surely lout', but is the Old English term for a class of freeman, and is perhaps equivalent to 'yeoman'. Nevertherless, the poet is drawing a distinction between the high-born ealdorman and the lowly warrior who faces him. Byrhtnōth was wounded by the Dane's 'southern spear', perhaps a Frankish-made weapon, which lodged in his armour, so that he had to shove against it with the rim of his shield, which caused the shaft of the weapon to break and the head to be dislodged by the violent jerk. Angered by his wound the leader stabbed back at his attacker with his own spear, and thrust his Franca through the opponent's neck. If the Franca is a spear, then this phrase is parallel to the action of stabbing mentioned in line 138, and the weapon pierced the Dane; if the Franca is an axe, as suggested above, then the phrase can equally well be rendered 'cut into' the Viking's neck.

One could just as well read the lines in sequence rather than in parallel: Byrhtnōth first stabbed the Dane with his spear, then, drawing on his experience of warfare, quickly followed this by hacking at him with his Franca, before the Viking had a chance to strike back or flee. The poet's practice generally in this epic is not to repeat a single action with parallel phrases in the battle scenes, though the habit of repetition is a prominent and influential feature of Old English verse as a whole.

Then another one he hastily hurled
so that the byrnie burst apart: he was wounded in his breast
145 *through the mailshirt; in his heart lodged*
the deadly point. The eorl was the gladder at this:

then the bold man laughed, said his thanks to God
for that day's work which the Lord allowed him.

Then a certain Dreng sent a dart from his hand,
150 *flying from his fist so that it sped forwards*
through the noble thane of Æthelred.
By his side stood a boy, not yet fully grown,
a youth in war who most hastily
drew the bloody spear out of the warrior –
155 *that was Wulfmǣr the young, the son of Wulfstān.*
He sent the hardened spear back again:
the point stuck in so that he lay on the ground,
he who had severely harmed the lord before.
Then a mail-coated warrior went to the eorl;
160 *he meant to take off the nobleman's rings,*
his war-gear and jewels and patterned sword.

LINES 143–146 Further ambiguity surrounds the next two lines: it is not clear from the verse whether Byrhtnōth 'hurled another spear', or 'shot down another warrior'. The wording *đā hē ōđerne ōfstlice ofsceat* can be interpreted with either sense. Yet I think that if the poet intended to introduce another attacker here, there would be some explanation of his presence: the first attacker gets two lines of verse devoted to his approach, so a subsequent opponent ought to merit at least a half-line of introduction before the deadly point lodged in his heart and frustrated his bid for fame.

LINES 147–161 The ealdorman's thankfulness and exultant laughter at having overcome his assailant were premature and short-lived. In the moment of his victory, a certain Dreng – a Viking hero – hurled a spear which pierced him through. Those who take the view that Byrhtnōth's arrogance (*ofermōd*) lost the English the battle are quick to point out that the poet shows him laid low by God, mentioned in the line before the attack, in the very moment of his triumph, because of his pride. *Hlōh đā mōdi man* is then rendered 'then the proud man laughed', though *mōdi(g)* is more often 'bold, brave, in war-like frame of mind'. As with the previous uncertainty over lines 89 and 90, one will read the text according to one's view of the propriety of the ealdorman's action.

The wound Byrhtnōth received from the Dreng's spear was obviously not fatal, which in itself suggests that the armour he wore was quite substantial, though the point pierced it and entered his flesh, to be quickly (or boldly) withdrawn by the youngster Wulfmǣr, who had been standing beside his lord. His quick reaction allowed him to avenge the ealdorman by throwing back the spear and so killing the Viking with it. It was a Norse curse that a man's weapons should turn against him, which is the reason that Germanic peoples swore their greatest oaths on their swords, as a token of good faith.

Byrhtnōth must by now have been in a sorry state, twice wounded by the spears of his enemies, and so it is not surprising that one of the Danes came forward to seize his armour and rings, thinking that the old warrior was finished. Stripping and robbing the dead was all part of medieval warfare, and is clearly shown on the Bayeux Tapestry.

Byrhtnōth drew his sword from the sheath,
broad and bright-edged, and struck at his byrnie.
One of the seafarers was too quick, hindered him
165 *when he wounded the eorl's arm.*
The golden-hilted sword fell to the earth:
nor could he hold the hard glaive,
wield the weapon. Yet he uttered words,
that grey-haired warrior – he emboldened the fighters –
170 *bade them go forwards, the good companions.*
No longer could he stand firm on his feet;
he looked to the heavens . . .

'I thank you, O Ruler of Nations,
for all those joys which I have experienced in life.
175 *Gentle Lord, I now have greatest need*
that you grant mercy to my spirit,
so that my soul may journey to you,
O Lord of Angels, and into your power
travel in peace. I beg of you
180 *that Hell's harmers may not take it from here.'*
Then the heathen warriors cut him down
and both the fighters who stood beside him;
Ælfnōth and Wulfmǣr both lay still,
who alongside their lord gave up their lives.
185 *Those who no longer wished to be there then turned from the fight:*
Odda's sons were first in flight from there,

LINES 162–172 The ealdorman was not dead yet, however: he drew his sword and hewed at the armoured coat of the seafarer, but another of the Danes was too quick for him and disabled his arm. 'The golden-hilted sword fell to the earth' says the poet, which is presumably literally true; yet *fealo* is the name of a colour denoting golden-yellow, an autumnal shade suggestive of decline and decay, and very appropriate for the downfall of the English leader. One might say that the sword's fall to earth is a symbol, an image both of the ealdorman's fall from greatness and power, and of his tumbling to the ground under the second Viking's blow. We are then told that he could no longer use his weapons. For Byrhtnōth, the days of fighting were over and he must have been aware of it as he reeled from the attack. Yet he was not, even then, utterly powerless – he could still play a part in fighting off the band of marauders by exhorting his men and shouting encouragement to his East Saxon comrades.

LINES 173–186 The hero was no longer able to stand firmly; he may have sat down, or he may have been supported on his feet by bystanders. His last conscious act was to gaze up to the sky and beg God to allow his soul to enter Heaven. Then the heathen attackers cut him down along with the two men beside him – perhaps, as mentioned before, the two warriors who were holding him up till the very end.

This was the turning-point in the fight for those close enough to see what had happened. Byrhtnōth had been ealdorman for as long as many could remember, indeed for longer than many had been alive. His fall was the destruction of the mainstay of their society, indeed of their world. For some this was too much, and they turned and fled.

Three late Anglo-Saxon swords, the outer pair with 'drooping' quillons after Viking taste, decorated with inlay on the blades.

Godric was away from the fray and abandoned the good man
who often in the past had given him a horse;
he leapt onto the steed – which his lord had owned –
190 in its trappings, which it was not right to do;
and with him his brothers both ran –
Godwine and Godwig – they did not care for fighting
but went away from the battle and sought the woods,
fled to the place of safety and saved their lives,
195 and more of the men than was in any way fitting
if they had taken thought of all the rewards
which he had bestowed upon them for their benefit.
Offa had said to him earlier that day
at the speaking-place when he held a meeting,
200 that many there spoke bravely
who later would not last out in the strife.
That folk's leader had then fallen,
Æthelred's warrior. They could all see
– the hearth-companions – that their leader was down.

205 Forward from there went the proud thanes,
the undaunted men eagerly made haste:
they all wished for one of these two things:
to give up their lives, or to avenge the dear man.

LINES 187–204 The first to flee was the thane Godric son of Odda for whom the poet reserves a particular feeling of loathing and contempt, because of the catastrophic consequences of his disloyalty. We are told that he deserted the good man who often made him a present of a horse, and we cannot fail to detect the bitter irony of Godric seizing Byrhtnōth's own horse and riding off on it, with his brothers running at its tail. The rest of the English army, unaware of the ealdorman's death, immediately supposed that this was their leader fleeing the battlefield, which filled them with so much dismay that they followed *en masse*. The fight was now lost for the remainder, who must have been hopelessly outnumbered.

Godric, in his panic, had taken the only horse on the field, as the others had been sent away (line 2). The natural conclusion for the fyrdmen to draw, probably the only one that they could draw under the circumstances, was that their leader had seen that the day was lost, or had just lost his nerve, and was deserting them. The poet says it was 'no proper thing' for the army to run, but although it may have been unfitting, it was hardly unnatural: the warriors' loyalty to their lord could hardly have been strengthened by the sight of him galloping to safety (as they thought) while they were left to face the Danes.

The fugitives were not just the farmers and yeomen, since the poem states that they should have borne in mind the wealth Byrhtnōth had bestowed upon them, suggesting that some at least were thanes and retainers of his. It is presumably no accident that, at the meeting earlier, Offa the nobleman had noticed the unease and lack of will among the men, despite the brave words which custom demanded of them before their countrymen. We should not forget that this was a very dark period in England's history, when things seldom ran smoothly for the English, and the East Saxon troops were almost certainly at a psychological disadvantage even before they strode on to the battlefield. Those brave men who stayed to die with Byrhtnōth did so out of personal conscience and loyalty to their dead leader, rather than through any belief in right winning out over injustice – which experience showed was seldom the case.

LINES 205–208 When it was plain to all who were left that the ealdorman was down, the resolve among the defenders stiffened: for the staunch warriors left there the duty of vengeance for the fallen lord overrode considerations of personal safety. This remainder did not consist exclusively of the hearth-troop: Dunnere, who addressed his countrymen later, was specifically called *unorne ceorl*, 'a humble yeoman', though he was hardly the less brave for that and his decision to stay must have been founded solely on personal sentiment since his duty to seek vengeance for Byrhtnōth cannot have been so binding as it was for the thanes and personal retainers of the ealdorman's household.

So Ælfric's son egged them forward,
210 a warrior young in winters, he uttered a speech,
he spoke of courage – Ælfwine said:
'Remember those words which we often spoke over our mead
when we put up boasts at the bench
about hard strife, we heroes in the hall:
215 now whoever is brave may prove it.
I wish to make my ancestry known to all:
that I come from a great family among the Mercians.
My grandfather was called Ealhelm,
a wise ealdorman, lucky in this world.
220 Thanes in the land shall not be able to blame me,
or say that I wished to leave this fyrd
to seek my homeland, now my leader lies
cut down in the fighting. It is the greatest of griefs to me:
he was both my kinsman and my lord.'
225 Then he went forward, remembered the feud,
so that he wounded a man with his point,
a seaman in the host, so that he fell to the ground
slain by his weapon. The friends began to encourage each other
– those comrades and brothers-in-arms – so that they went forwards.
230 Offa shook his ash-spear and spoke:
'You have emboldened us all indeed, O Ælfwine,
us thanes in time of danger. Now that our lord lies dead,
the eorl on the earth, it is necessary for us all
that each of us shall encourage the other
235 warrior to the warfare, while yet his weapons he can
have and hold: a hard blade,
a spear and a good sword. Godric has
completely betrayed us, the cowardly son of Odda:

LINES 208–254 The initiative seems to have been seized by the English remnant, who began to press forwards in order to obtain revenge or die fighting for it, and the poet now records a number of speeches of exhortation and encouragement made by certain men among the survivors. First young Ælfwine reminded them of the boasts they made while drinking mead in their hall, and took the opportunity to make his ancestry known to all present. Great importance was placed on the identity of the forebears of a man among the Anglo-Saxons, partly because family feuds tended to go on for generations and it was always useful to know whether there was any cause for taking revenge. Men also took very seriously the duty of not letting the family down, and Ælfwine was probably reminding himself of the nobility of his lineage so that he would be encouraged to live up to its glorious name. Interestingly, he claims that Byrhtnōth was both his lord and kinsman: on him, then, the duty to exact vengeance was doubly incumbent and it may be that the recalling of the ancestor Ealhelm had some significance in respect of Byrhtnōth's own forebears; unfortunately we do not have enough information about either family to be sure. He was, nevertheless, careful to avoid mentioning his father Ælfric, who was in disgrace, and whose brothers Ælfhere and Ælfheah had been political adversaries of Byrhtnōth. Ælfwine himself advanced and slew a Dane, though we are not told how he met his end.

While Ælfwine was still within the English ranks, Offa began to exhort the men to great deeds, addressing his remarks to the young nobleman. He brought the treachery of Godric and his brothers to the attention of all, to explain the desertion of their countrymen. Offa then pronounced a formal curse: *Abreoðe his angin* – 'may what he begins come to nothing' or 'may his enterprise fail'.

After Offa, Leofsunu made his declaration before the troops, that he would not flee, but would go forth for vengeance. He lived in Northern Essex, at the village of Sturmer, it seems, since he stated that the heroes there would not have cause to reproach him. The blame he feared was that he 'came back a lordless man', for in earlier times the warrior who left the field once his lord fell was reviled as a coward and a traitor, unless he first took vengeance on the slayers; for this reason, the survivor of a slain lord was often a friendless, homeless refugee who wandered the world searching for a new lord to provide a seat in his hall; yet any warrior who had no lord was regarded with suspicion as a potential traitor or deserter. Thus the poet has woven another ancient image into his verse. For his part, Leofsunu fought on with determination: his end is unrecorded.

Next to speak was Dunnere, the lowly yeoman. His words are perhaps a well-known maxim or proverb; they are, at any rate, general in application and very succinct. The weapon he uses is a *daroð*, a kind of javelin or throwing-spear, which was less substantial than the professional warrior's stabbing-spear. Interestingly, although perhaps only to be expected, the two noblemen make quite long speeches (thirteen lines apiece) while the thane Leofsunu is allocated seven and a half lines, and the churl gets just two lines. We can hardly doubt that the poet is making social distinctions between the classes, though we must not overlook his inclusion of the lower ranks — who are most often ignored in contemporary descriptions of warfare, although they must always have made up the bulk of an army. It says much for the poet that he did not ignore the support and help which the freemen gave to the nobles and thanes, who usually get all the credit and glory.

many a man believed, when he rode off on the horse
240 *– on the proud steed – that it was our lord;*
because of that the folc was split up in the field,
the shieldwall broken apart. Let what he may begin be destroyed!
– because he has caused so many men here to flee.'
Leofsunu spoke and raised up his lindenwood
245 *– his shield as protection – he said to the warriors:*
'I give my word that from this place I do not mean
to flee one foot's space; rather will I go forward
to avenge my friendly-lord in the fight.
Steadfast warriors around Sturmer need not
250 *blame me in their speech together, now my friend is fallen,*
that I am going home lordless
fleeing from the fight; rather shall a weapon take me,
a point and an iron sword.' He strode very angrily,
fought resolutely; he scorned flight.
255 *Then Dunnere spoke and shook his throwing-spear,*
the lowly ceorl called out over all,
bade that each of the warriors should avenge Byrhtnōth:
'He must not draw back who thinks to avenge
his lord on the foe, nor care for his life.'

260 *They moved forwards then, did not take heed for their lives;*
the war-band's men began to fight hard
– those fierce spear-bearers and prayed to God
that they should be allowed to avenge their friendly-lord
and bring death to their foes.
265 *The hostage began to help them eagerly;*
he was from a hard kindred of the Northumbrians,
his name was Æscferth, Ecglāf's son,

LINES 255–268 There seems next to have been a final advance by the English, an attack to take as many Danish lives as possible in revenge for Byrhtnōth. We now learn for the first time of the presence of a *gysel*, a 'hostage', from a leading Northumbrian family. It is not immediately clear what 'hostage' means in this context, until one recalls that the North and Midlands were heavily settled by Danes in the ninth century, and that the North was often more than ready to throw in its lot with any Scandinavian force which looked likely to overthrow the hated kings of Wessex. It was quite in character for the Northumbrian leaders to make common cause with the Viking leaders, and assist them in their harrying of the South. It was to avoid the Northumbrians succumbing to just this temptation that the leading families of the region, those who had most to gain from renewed independence in other words, were required to send their young men south as guarantees of their good faith and loyal conduct. Such hostages, for such they were, were sent to live with trusted nobles in the southern shires, where they could have little contact with their kinsmen. As a member of Byrhtnōth's household, the hostage was obliged to accompany his host. Whether the obligation extended to fighting alongside him or not is unclear, but probably good manners dictated that Æscferth should stand by the ealdorman in battle. It must have been something more deep-seated than mere urbanity that prompted the Northumbrian to stand fast when the fyrdmen fled: his 'hard kindred' had produced a noble scion whose personal conscience would not allow him to run from the fight.

An iron seax blade inlaid with bands of brass, its horn or wooden hilt having entirely decomposed, found at Honey Lane, London.

he did not shrink back at the war-play;

rather he sent forth arrows swiftly –
270 *sometimes he hit a shield, sometimes pierced a warrior;*
time and again he dealt out wounds
while he was able to wield his weapons.

Eadweard the Tall still stood at the forefront
ready and keen; he spoke boasting words
275 *that he did not mean to flee by a foot's length of land,*
to turn back while a better man than he lay dead.
He broke through the wall of shields and fought against the warriors
until his ring-giver on those seamen
he had worthily avenged, before he lay among the slain.
280 *Ætheric, the noble companion, did likewise –*
keen and eager to advance, he fought single-mindedly,
the brother of Sibyrht; and very many others
clove through the ridged shield – keenly they fought.

The shield's rim burst and the byrnie sang
285 *a song of fear. Then, in the fighting, struck*
Offa at the seafarer so that he fell to earth
and there Gadd's kinsman sought the ground.
Offa was quickly cut down in the battle,
yet he had carried out what his lord had ordered
290 *– just as he had boasted before his ring-giver:*
that they both would either ride into the fortress,
come safely home, or fall in the host,
die of wounds at the place of slaughter.
Loyally he lay beside his lord.

LINES 269–271 It is most unusual to find a nobleman using a bow in war, since this weapon was reserved for hunting by the upper ranks of society. It was normally considered unmanly to kill an adversary by shooting him from a distance – the honourable thing among the warrior classes was to fight it out face-to-face with sword, spear and shield. Although the ideal nobleman was expected to be skilled in the use of the bow, he was not supposed to use it in battle: this was a churl's way of fighting. Perhaps the clearly desperate circumstances prompted Æscferth to try to kill as many Danes as he could by any means possible. As we have noted above, warriors did not scruple to loot the dead, so he might easily have come by a bow and some arrows in this way. Alternatively, he may have been present at the fight as an observer only, not intending to enter the fighting, and as a hostage he may have been denied the right to carry weapons. Some Anglo-Saxon documents show a king in battle protected by a warrior who carries no weapon other than the shield which he holds up before the king as they both watch the progress of the combat; could such a figure also be a hostage? Becoming involved in the fighting as a member, if only an honorary one, of Byrhtnōth's household, Æscferth would have been forced to use whatever weapons came to hand; the distance from the Danish forces suggested using the bow, though he might later have taken a sword when he closed with the foe – the loss of the poem's conclusion means we do not know. As a Northumbrian, he may have been sufficiently influenced by Norse practice to have less prejudice against archery.

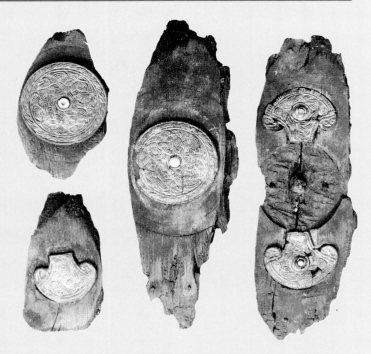

Bronze ornamental shield mounts from Caenby, Lincolnshire, England; the roundels feature a complex interlace design while the outer 'crescents' terminate in stylised eagles' heads.

must mean something akin to 'provided with a ridge', while *cellæs* probably then means 'ridge-less'. That a shield should have a strengthening ridge is not unlikely: certainly more likely than that the meaning is 'boat-shaped', which has been proposed in the past.

LINES 273–283 One Eadweard, presumably the same as he who slew the Dane earlier, stood at the forefront and joined in the general resolve not to flee; when he rushed forward he 'broke the shieldwall' – that is to say, he thrust himself through the line of Viking warriors – and avenged his lord before he was slain, as did another English hero named Ætheric.

We read at line 283 that the English *clūfon cellod bord*, clove through a *cellod* shield. The meaning of the word *cellod* is disputed, because it occurs only here, though another battle poem has the related phrase *cellæs bord*. It seems probable on prima-facie grounds that *cellod* is the past participle of a verb *cellian*, and that *cellæs* is a formation with the same root, and the element *-laes*. *Cel* seems to be related to the word *ceol* (Norse *kjol*) meaning 'a ship', originally 'a keel'. Since a keel is essentially a wooden ridge beneath a ship, one may reasonably assume that *cellod*

LINES 284–294 The shield's *lærig* – presumably its rim or edge-binding – burst, while the warcoat sang, or groaned, as metal clashed with metal. Offa slew one of the seamen, who fell to the earth; then 'Gadd's kinsman sought the ground'. Gadd's kinsman is Offa, mentioned in the previous line; though what we are to make of the phrase 'sought the ground' is less certain. Perhaps he tumbled to the ground off-balance while striking the Dane; alternatively, he may have lunged at the invader as he fell, then leapt on top of him to finish him off; or again, perhaps the phrase means 'sought a final resting-place in the ground, refused to flee, sought death in battle'. Whether he sought it or not, death is what he received in fulfilment of his earlier boast that either both he and Byrhtnōth would ride back safely, or neither would. Line 294 may be read 'he lay like a good thane beside his lord': the contrast with Godric is implicit.

295 *Then came the clash of shields. The seamen strode up*
angered by war. Often a spear went through
a doomed man's body. Wīstān then went forward,
the son of Thūrstān, and fought against the foemen.
He was the slayer of three of them in the throng
300 *before Wīgelm's kinsman lay among the slain.*
It was a hard encounter there. They stood fast,
those warriors in the strife. Fighting men fell
weary from their wounds. Gore fell to the ground.

All the while, Ōswold and Eadwold
305 *– both those brothers – encouraged the fighting men,*
bade in their speech their beloved kinsmen
that they must hold out in their time of need there,
use their weapons without weakening.
Byrhtwold spoke up, he raised his shield
310 *and brandished his spear – he was an old retainer;*
with great courage he addressed the troop:
'Mind shall be the harder, heart the keener,
courage the greater as our strength dwindles.
Here lies our leader, cut down,
315 *the good man in the dirt. May he ever grieve,*
who now thinks to turn from this war-play.
I am old in life: I do not wish to leave,
but rather beside my lord
– beside so dear a man – do I think to lie.'
320 *Likewise they were encouraged by Æthelgār's son*
Godric, onward to the struggle. Often he sent a spear,
a slaughter-shaft, spinning into the Vikings;
thus he led the fighting in the battle,
hewed and slew, till he fell in the fight.
325 *That was not the Godric who turned away from the strife . . .*

LINES 295–303 The Danish attack was renewed in response to the greater activity among the English. There follows a confusing episode concerning Wīstān, who is said to be the son of Thūrstān in line 298, yet two lines later we read that Wīgelm's son is among the slain at the end of the section dealing with Wīstān's fight. It seems, therefore, that either Thūrstān and Wīgelm are the same man, or the relationship is not father : son, or that the text is slightly awry here. To take the first possibility: there are instances of Anglo-Saxon men with two names, but these are usually churchmen who adopt a religious identity and name separate from their secular lives – as monks and nuns do, even today – or they are laymen whose name is shortened for ease of use, as when Folcbeorht becomes Fobba; in such a case the shortened form is really only a nickname. Neither of these conditions seems to apply here. Wīstān is actually said to be *Đūrstānes suna* (son of Thūrstān) and *Wīgelmes bearn* (child of Wīgelm), so that it is conceivable that Wīgelm is not specifically the father, but some more distant relative: grandfather, foster-father, perhaps even mother's brother (see Wulfmǣr at line 115).

An alternative solution of the problem would be a slight emendation of the text, and the least violent change would be to insert '7', the Anglo-Saxon scribal shorthand for 'and' (known as *Tyronian et*), at the very beginning of line 297. The form of the word for 'son' found there, *suna*, is usually the plural, though in very late texts it can appear as the singular also. If the copyist is assumed to have omitted this mark, and we reinstate it, the line can then read 'forwards then went Wīstān / and the sons of Thūrstān'. The verbs are in the singular still, but this is conventional Old English usage, and parallels are numerous.

LINES 304–325 By this stage in the battle so many of the English warriors had fallen in the 'harsh meeting' that leadership had passed to the two brothers named Ōswold and Eadwold, who persisted in the encouragement of the English with brave words, as many before them had done. The last man to deliver a speech in this fragment was the *eald geneat* (old retainer) of Byrhtnōth's household, named as Byrhtwold. His magnificent speech has a bitter, defiant ring, and these verses are among the most often-quoted of all Old English poetry, for they sum up the English fighting spirit of determined resistance in the face of insuperable odds. The poet uses great economy in the first part of the speech, as well as a symmetrical structure to achieve the effect of naked courage; or, as Professor Tolkien puts it: 'The words of Byrhtwold were made for a man's last and hopeless day' ('Beowulf: The Monsters and the Critics').

As those who had spoken before had done Byrhtwold wished ill to anyone who intended to flee the field, and declared his own intention of dying with his lord. Again the Germanic warrior-code is revealed through the mouth of an East Saxon warrior centuries after it was believed to be a futile anachronism. The last image in the text is of the warrior Gōdric son of Æthelgār being spurred on by Byrhtwold's speech to seek battle-death against the foe. The poet reminds his audience – if any reminder were necessary – that this Gōdric was not the same as the one who turned away from the fighting.

And there, for the modern reader the poem ends – abruptly – because the end of the fragment still available was not the end of the original poem. There is a great deal more historians would like to know: how the battle ended, according to the poet; what the immediate and long-term consequences of the battle were; and how the local people fared in Maldon after the Viking's victory; what brought the Danes to London; and many other things besides. The answers to some of these questions may at least be guessed from our knowledge of the *Chronicle*, and we shall look at this evidence in the next chapter.

As becomes clear from examining glosses to the text, the leadership of Byrhtnōth has often been criticised for his handling of the battle. He has been charged with wantonly sacrificing his men's lives in pursuit of the ideal of chivalrous valour and the aggrandisement of his own reputation, neither of which, supposedly, had any part in modern (tenth-century) warfare. For many people, the ealdorman appears either as a weak-minded idealist, or as a foolish old man determined to achieve a last blaze of glory at any price. But can these views be reconciled with the documentary records? How did his contemporaries view his actions? There was evidently considerable interest in Byrhtnōth and in his last battle after his death. Yet nowhere do we meet any feelings of bitterness against him on the part of his countrymen. The ecclesiastics of Ely took great pains to squeeze every last ounce of kudos out of having taken over his mortal remains, which may have been granted to them by his widow. They were almost certainly used to exploit the medieval 'tourist' industry, which centred on the graves of saints and famous men.

The principal case against Byrhtnōth lies in the use of the word *ofermōd* in the poem – one word in one document, not clearly defined as a rebuke, and in any case far from proof of gross misconduct. Had the poet wished to indulge in criticism of the ealdorman, surely there ought to be some evidence for it in the surviving 325 lines of the poem, or elsewhere in our sources, if there were a popular feeling of resentment against the leader. The text may be interpreted in a variety of ways, according to the view of Byrhtnōth one favours. I would offer the following explanation, which may clarify some of the apparent inconsistencies.

The Viking fleet sailed northwards before a favourable wind, intending to head towards London. Rather than wait at the Thames estuary indefinitely for a change of wind-direction or, alternatively, row the fifty miles upstream, they decided to make their way to Ipswich, which they reached on, say, 8 August. Word was brought by mounted messenger to the ealdorman, who was travelling southwards from the Midlands where he had accepted a number of hostages from leading Northumbrian families. The message for the thanes to assemble was sent out the same day, arranging to meet at a given point on the Essex-Suffolk border, there to rally forces and ride to Ipswich in good order. In the meantime, the Danes had managed to overcome the local defences, and had sacked the main part of the town on 9 August. Fugitives from the town fled past the mustering English force, with news of their defeat and the town's capture.

Loading their booty aboard their ships that evening, the Vikings found that the wind had veered enough to enable them to set a southerly course, down the Essex seaboard. During 10 August, the ships travelled on while a small contingent sailed into the Blackwater River, where there would be safe harbour among the many shallow creeks and islets. A group of a dozen or so vessels sailed further upstream to Northey Island, to within sight of the walls of Maldon. There they encamped to make minor repairs to their crafts, and to share out the booty they had taken at Ipswich.

Byrhtnōth had not been idle. His force of retainers was travelling south, gathering warriors as it went, and despatching messengers to his deputies further afield. When word came that the Vikings had left Ipswich and set off south, he was taken off guard, unsure of his next move, until late on 10 August a messenger from Maldon brought news of the fleet's arrival there. Losing no time, he rode hard to an estate that he owned a few miles from the town, and held his meeting with the thanes of Essex whom he had bidden to meet him there. That evening, a feast was held at which the leading warriors made vows of loyalty to their lord, although Offa expressed his doubts about their ability to live up to the undertakings they were making over their mead.

Scouts had been sent to the river to establish what the Vikings' intentions were, and these returned at dawn with the news that the Danes appeared to be encamped dangerously close to the town. Rather than wait to see what the attackers would do next, Byrhtnōth bade his men get ready their horses and ride with him to the river. By taking the initiative, he hoped to be able to deprive the Danes of the opportunity of sacking the town. Leading a force of mounted Essex fyrdmen, Essex and Suffolk thanes (some of whom had expected to defend Ipswich rather than attack a camp), and his own personal retinue of warriors, he rode the remaining distance to the river, just below the stronghold. From this position on the bend of the river, the English could see a number of foreign vessels riding at anchor off the outward shore of the island, on which were pitched tents and several plumes of smoke from cooking-pits where the Danes were roasting sheep. Byrhtnōth realised at once that this was no raiding party, and in the same second realised that he could use this against them, for it had been impossible hitherto to get the Vikings to stand and fight, but here if the situation were properly handled, he might be able to get them to do just that.

The ealdorman could not afford to hold back until the full militia arrived, for if the Danes saw a large English army assembling, they could easily sail away without giving battle at all, and sack and burn another town before he could get his forces there by land. Equally if he delayed overlong some of his own men would eventually realise that their homes were under threat because only part of the fleet was actually present; and these would soon steal away to get their families to safety rather than remain with the fyrd.

More pressing was the question: how could he be sure the Danes would be willing to fight? After all, they had already taken a good deal of plunder, so even the rank-and-file warriors were now relatively wealthy, and might prefer to live to enjoy their riches rather than risk everything in a fight which they could easily avoid, for the English could not reach them on the island because of the narrow ford which linked it to the mainland and prevented the passage of large numbers of men except in single file. Byrhtnōth would never be able to attack across so unsuitable a route. His only weapon against the Vikings was their natural puerile pride and impetuosity – he felt sure, however, that that would be enough.

The ealdorman decided to risk a challenge. He advanced his men to the heathland which spread down to the water's edge, and here he had them dismount, and ordered some of the older warriors, who might not stand up to fighting on such a hot day, to take the horses back into the wood and watch over them there. He kept his own mount so that the Danes would be able to see the leader of the troops coming towards them. Then, riding near the bank of the stream as his men formed their battle-line, he was hailed by one of the seamen, who very pointedly threatened him in broken English, and promised destruction for Byrhtnōth and his men unless some payment were forthcoming – and not too slowly. Changing tack, the seaman went on to say that the Danes wished only for peace with their English cousins, and good friendship, if only the friends who were richer would share a little of their wealth with poor seamen from across the ocean.

Byrhtnōth was not thinking of peace, however, and his reply, which was cast in the most calculatingly insulting terms, was intended to sting the pride of every Viking who heard it; sure enough, they were soon howling for English blood in revenge for the haughty, arrogant manner of the greybeard who dared make fun of them, in the shadow of their spears.

The raiders wanted to fight; part of Byrhtnōth's plan was under way. Unfortunately, he had not been able to think of any way of overcoming the obstacle of the ford, which neither side wanted to cross in the face of enemy weapons. The berserk who had tried to dash across had been easily despatched by the warriors that Byrhtnōth had set at his end of the causeway, and the Danes could see that it would be suicidal to force their way over. It looked like stalemate, with the two forces glowering at each other across the ebbing stream, until the messenger again called out, this time with a request that they should be allowed safe passage across and room to form up on the English bank.

Byrhtnōth was loath to let the marauders on to English soil if he could prevent their passage. Yet he had come this far with his scheme successfully: the Danes were ready – eager, even – to fight, and that was no small achievement in itself, since they would not normally give battle unless they could do so on their own terms. To refuse their request would be to throw away a rare opportunity, and in light of that, he would have to see it through, and allow them across, sacrificing a tactical advantage in order to achieve a strategic success.

With the benefit of hindsight it is obvious that the gamble was too great, the chance of succeeding too slim, to make it worthwhile. We know that the enemy took advantage of his courageous acceptance of a dangerous situation, and that the old warrior paid for his error with his life.

This defeat was only one in a series of disasters about this time, but there was a popular feeling that there was something different about the great fight outside the town of Maldon. Although the Danes won the day, in another sense the ealdorman and his followers were not beaten. His friends and followers did not flee and hide, but faced their enemies with only their loyalty and love of their fallen leader to sustain them when all hope of victory had gone. They continued to resist when only slavery or death remained to them. It was not in itself enough to overcome hired killers such as these Vikings were, yet neither was it the spirit of defeat, that loses battles and surrenders to a cruel foe. On that summer's day a thousand years ago, the East Saxon warriors rose above the petty intrigues and treacheries of their times, and for once the English could feel a measure, if not of pride, at least of self-respect, no matter how short-lived or wasted.

Having examined the poem thus closely, it is legitimate at this point to speculate upon the poem's meaning:

that is, the poet's purpose in writing it. For some, the matter is clear: the poet's intention was to set down the folly of an old man, to publicise the ealdorman's rash and wanton waste of human life. The argument for this centres, as previously noted, on lines 89 and 90:

Đā se eorl ongan, for his ofermōde,
alȳfan landes tō fela lāđere deode

Ever since the 1950s, when he published his critical essay on this section of the poem, the views of the late Professor Tolkien have been widely regarded as the definitive statement on the subject, and no treatment of the poem is complete without some reference to the professor and his paper. Briefly stated, Tolkien's view was that *ofermōd* was necessarily a word implying sin and its use by the poet indicated disapproval. This, coupled with the sarcastic use of the phrase 'too much land' in the next line, was thought by Tolkien to imply the severest criticism of Byrhtnōth's action.

I think it is fair to say, however, that Tolkien's reading of the text has been coloured by his private views on personal morality. The paper (*Essays and Studies*, 1953) was composed at the same time as he was evolving a new 'heroic ethic' in his work, *The Lord of the Rings*. When we apply the principle of altruistic self-denial to our tenth-century nobleman, we should not be surprised if he falls somewhat short of the ideal; an ideal which, though profoundly encouraging for late twentieth-century man, would have been entirely incongruous when measured against notions of heroism and proper conduct a thousand years ago – not because right and wrong are different now, but because England's need was then for strong, determined action against an equally strong and determined foe. Taken as a whole, the English leaders were an ineffectual and lack-lustre group, and Byrhtnōth shone among them.

On balance, however, it is perhaps wrong to see the old ealdorman as the hero of the piece; for the point of the poem, is, surely, not that Byrhtnōth was over-bold, recklessly arrogant, or simply too brave for his own or his men's good: it is rather that his men were unfalteringly and, at last, hopelessly courageous in their decision to outface the despair of certain death, and to die with the man they had loved in life. These determined Essex warriors – thanes and churls alike – are the real heroes of the poem. Only when read with this in mind does the action make sense. It is very uncommon for a poet to take such pains to name so many of the fighting men (some of whom were not even gentry) on the English side. What motive could there be for his doing so, other than the commemoration of a noble deed of self-sacrifice? And what could be more welcome in Ethelred's reign, with its treachery and intrigues, than for Englishmen to be reminded of the ancient values of the Germanic warrior: loyalty, courage, and generosity? To know that these ideals lived on in men's hearts, and still moved them to do what they believed to be right, must indeed have been welcome news to a nation accustomed to hearing only of pirate raids and ignominious defeats.

Chapter 4

Byrhtnōth's Legacy

The sequence of events following the premature close of the poem cited in Chapter 3 is shrouded in mystery, but a few intelligent guesses may be made.

The Book of Ely records that when the monks arrived at the battlefield to claim the ealdorman's cadaver, they discovered that the Danes had hacked off the head and borne it away as a grisly trophy of their victory. The rest of the remains were carried back to the abbey for Christian burial with honour, and these remains were later removed – or 'translated' – in the reign of King Stephen to a new Norman building, along with those of other celebrated men whose bodies had been taken over by Ely, including archbishop Wulfstān the homilist. They were moved again during Edward III's time, and carvings were made to commemorate the lives of those whose bones lay within the building; these carvings were mentioned by James Bentham, who was present at the rebuilding of the abbey choir in 1769. According to his report, vestiges of the images were detectable then, with the name of each man inscribed above. Unfortunately, the reconstruction destroyed both the representations and the coffins, but Bentham goes on to report that he examined the bones found beneath the name Byrhtnōth, and could find no trace of the skull, even though most of the other bones were intact – except the collar bone, which had been hacked so deeply that it was nearly split in two, tending to confirm that the head had been removed by a hefty blow while the corpse was still undecayed. Bentham estimated the height of the skeleton at 2 m (6 ft 9 in), although all the estimates of height he made for the skeletons interred at Ely exceed 1.8 m (6 ft).

We may be confident that after the battle the English arrived and took their kinsmen's bodies for due burial; it is possible, though less certain, that the Norsemen made a funeral pyre for their fallen comrades, decked with the weapons of the slain from both sides. The Danes probably looted the dead, took what plunder they could extort from anyone foolhardy enough to remain within striking distance of their ships, and retired to their camp.

The site of the Danish camp is usually considered to be Northey Island in the Blackwater, a short distance downstream from the town of Maldon itself. This spot was first suggested by E. D. Laborde in 1925, in defiance of previous claims that the battle took place below the medieval defences at Maldon, where there is a bridge over the Blackwater to Heybridge. Attempts have been made to prove (and disprove) this theory by examining details in the poem and applying the data to maps of this part of Essex. Yet a poem, as we have seen, cannot be an exact record of an event in the way that a photograph is. A poet deals in images, tableaux, and intense, moving actions and emotions – and at the period we are concerned with, he used the spoken word of the oral poetic tradition.

There is a great deal of Old English 'heroic' style in the poem, which leads some readers to see it as a virtuoso performance, a deliberately archaic piece drawing together elements from heroic lays which were still popular at that time. Phrases from this poem occur elsewhere in Old English poetry – that is to say, half-lines are found in other poems, for example the words *hār hilderinc*, which is the first half of line 169, occur in at least three other poems. This is not unusual, for in the poetic tradition of the time half-lines formed the base material from which verses were

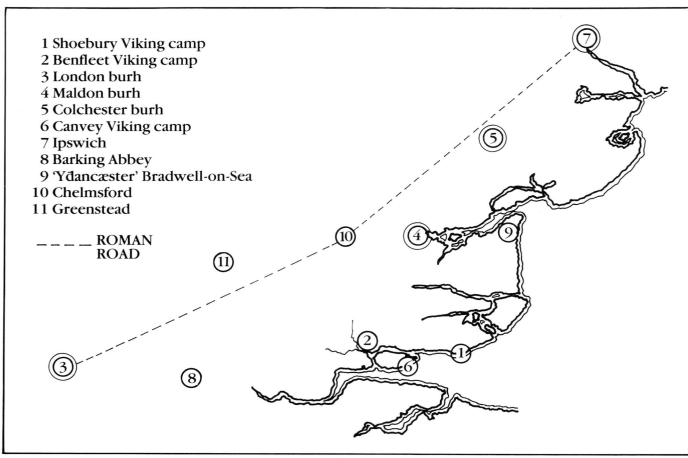

1 Shoebury Viking camp
2 Benfleet Viking camp
3 London burh
4 Maldon burh
5 Colchester burh
6 Canvey Viking camp
7 Ipswich
8 Barking Abbey
9 'Yđancæster' Bradwell-on-Sea
10 Chelmsford
11 Greenstead

— — — — ROMAN ROAD

Essex in the Viking age.

composed by skilfully arranging and adapting the ancient formulae. Our poem has a very marked narrative quality, avoiding much of the paraphrasing and 'harking back' which can make Old English poetry as a whole so tedious to modern readers. This is mainly due to the poet's having a very clear idea of what happened and who did what to whom, and his wish to set it down lucidly, though suitably embellished with words of praise where appropriate.

Using the poem as a guide, what can be said about the action and site of the battle? First and most obvious is that it took place next to the Pant, which is the old name for the Blackwater River. Secondly, a crossing (called both 'bridge' and 'ford') figures in the action. Thirdly, the Viking force, when crossing, went *west ofer Pantan* (west across the Pant), as we read at line 97. Last, the existing fragment does not mention the town of Maldon, although the *Chronicle* explicitly places the battle there in both versions cited.

Taking the last point first, it seems unlikely that the battle would have taken place immediately outside

the town stronghold without this fact being alluded to, however obliquely, in the narrative. The evidence of the 'crossing' is inconclusive, since it is not precisely described, and even if we could guarantee 'bridge' to have its modern meaning, it is by no means certain that the bridge at Maldon today is located where its medieval counterpart would have been. Anyone crossing from Heybridge across the modern bridge will be travelling slightly west of *southwards*, while the poet says the Vikings were crossing *westwards*. At Northey, however, there is a link to the mainland by means of a causeway, and this is slightly curved, so that its first part runs due west, then bends south-west to the shore. Doubts that the causeway has always followed that path have been allayed by geological research, which suggests that it has not altered much in the past thousand years, except that it is now longer due to the erosion of the channel, which is much wider than formerly. That the causeway existed at the time of the battle tells in its favour, and it would certainly have been wiser for the Vikings to have their

base on an easily-defended island than on the mainland across from the stronghold.

To date, no significant archaeological finds have been made in the area, so it seems preferable to reserve judgement on the question. If one rejects Northey as the probable site, there are many other small tidal islands in the Blackwater and its creeks, though few are suitable for mooring a small fleet of Viking vessels.

The battle at Maldon seems to have been regarded as the turning-point in the wave of Viking assaults against the kingdom of Ethelred. The English felt that if Byrhtnōth, with his long experience, could not stop the Danes, then probably no one could. The Danes, for their part, realised that they had overcome a great leader of the English, and lost no time in taking advantage of the dismay this caused. They headed for London, where the king agreed, on the advice of his archbishop, to pay ten thousand pounds of silver to them in return for pledges of peace and goodwill. The archbishop was presumably following historical precedent, recalling the occasion when the noble King Alfred had been forced to buy off the invaders when he no longer had any army to fight them with.

There were several important differences between the Vikings Alfred faced and those who now menaced Ethelred. The earlier armies had consisted of men

Harvesting in August, from an early Anglo-Saxon calendar; scythes and a pitchfork are used by labourers, while at left, a man uses a hone to sharpen his blade.

whose ultimate goal was the amassing of a fortune with which to acquire and enjoy a plot of land. The later Vikings were professional soldiers hired for the duration of the campaign by the leaders, who were magnates and noblemen. Moreover, Alfred had made the best possible use of the peace he bought with his gold, using the time to reorganise the military structure of the country, in order to be ready for the Danes when they returned. Ethelred seems to have attempted to do something similar – we read of him issuing commands for the building of fleets – but he was never really able to control the magnates on whose support he relied and whom he obviously feared greatly, remembering what they had done to his brother.

In 995, a comet was sighted over England – throughout medieval times this was considered a very bad omen, portending disasters to come. The English did not have long to wait for proof. Viking activity flourished, attracted by the promise of generous payments of silver by the English king. Ethelred responded by restructuring the army under the

A nobleman issues orders to shipwrights for the construction of a vessel; the double-prowed design is based on English or Viking prototypes.

command of two lay ealdormen and two bishops. The idea seems to have been to provide a standing 'task force' capable of striking at the Danes wherever they landed. Whatever the theoretical benefits of the scheme, it proved utterly useless in practice due to the leader: ealdorman Ælfric of Mercia decided to keep his options open, and sent word to the Danes before a proposed attack; they escaped, but returned later and inflicted a severe defeat on the bewildered English force. Ælfric himself stole away.

One can imagine how a king such as Athelstān or Alfred would have dealt with such a man, yet he apparently remained not only unpunished, but also in office as a military commander. In 1003, a Viking army devastated Wilton, and the men of Wiltshire and Hampshire mustered under Ælfric's command and marched against them. Having reached striking distance, Ælfric feigned illness, so that the English force (now effectively leaderless) withdrew rather than face the heathen host. An army does not need many men of Ælfric's calibre to lose its morale and become an intractable rabble.

Further disappointments were to follow as Ethelred's reign dragged on. In 1008 a fleet was raised by the king, requiring every landowner with a holding above three hundred and ten hides to provide a ship for the land's defence, while every landowner with more than eight hides had to provide armour and a helmet for the soldiers. The fleet was moored at Sandwich in Kent, so that it was capable of patrolling both the eastern and southern coasts from the same base. A dispute among the leaders of the fleet caused one of them, a Sussex thane named Wilnōth, to sail off with twenty of the ships as his own private 'Viking' force with which he set out to plunder southern England. His adversary, Brihtric, set off after him with a further eighty ships, but a storm in the Channel forced them to run too close to the shore and they went aground. Wilnōth took full advantage of his foe's misfortune, and burnt Brihtric's ships. After this, the king presumably saw the way things were going with his idea and lost interest in the scheme. The few remaining vessels were brought back to London.

No sooner were the English forces removed from Kent than the Danes came and ravaged it, sacking Canterbury. Seeing that there was little hope of the king coming to their rescue, the local leaders met the Danish chiefs and agreed to pay them 3,000 pounds of silver in return for their prompt departure. Once a small area such as east Kent is obliged to enter into negotiations for its safety, the purpose of national kingship is negated, and the cohesive structure of a single church and a single ruler loses its meaning.

England's fortune seemed to be locked into a downward spiral: every year the king raised taxes to pay for his anti-Viking measures; then, when these failed, he came back for more money to buy off the marauders.

It was probably at about this time, when the wealth which had been so carefully built up in England was being systematically drained through Viking activity, that a Danish prince evolved the most audacious plan yet: the conquest of the country. This noble was Sven Forkbeard, eldest legitimate son of the reigning king Harald Bluetooth. Harald was a long-lived monarch, who discovered late in life the benefits of Christianity. That is to say, he saw the benefits of not remaining heathen when his southern neighbour, the Holy Roman Empire, was continually looking for new territory to expand into on the pretext of converting the pagans to the true faith. Harald accepted Christ, and allowed churches and missions to be founded throughout his kingdom, which then included parts of southern Sweden (Skane), and a nominal claim to overlordship in Norway, ruled by Jarl Hákon, whom Harald had brought to power.

Sven remained heathen, and since his father showed no signs of dying and leaving him the throne in the near future he spent much of his life out west marauding. He amassed a considerable fortune from this, in company with Óláf Tryggvason, although the latter was converted to Christianity in the Scilly Isles (so the story goes) and returned to England, where King Ethelred stood as godfather at his baptism. In England he acquired a wife, an estate, and a magic dog, according to a saga concerning him.

Sven came back with monotonous regularity, and overcame every force which went out against him. This was probably due to his strategy of hiring out of entire armies of mercenaries from all the northern nations. He picked the cream of the warriors of the Viking world to serve under him, trained them, equipped them, housed them in great circular fort-resses such as Trelleborg and Fyrkat, and ferried them west in his great fleets of warships. He ravaged at will in southern England, though he seems to have been careful to avoid the northern counties where public opinion tended to side with the Viking armies against the southern English. He campaigned in East Anglia, however, and on into Mercia, until in 1013 he felt himself strong enough to make his intention known. He brought a fresh force of mercenaries over from Denmark, and accepted the submission of northern England; gradually the midland districts followed, and then the south, so that when at last he confronted London late in the year he was the *de facto* ruler of the nation, and was accepted as king. Ethelred fled over the Channel to the court of the Count of Normandy.

Unfortunately for Sven, though perhaps not for England, the old Viking did not enjoy his new authority for long: he died early the next year. His son Knut was still a youth and could not be sure whether his father's generals would support him or try to seize power for themselves. On the death of Harald Bluetooth, Sven had held the throne of

King by God's grace: Knut and his queen Ælfgifu dedicate a gold cross to the high altar of Winchester Cathedral.

Denmark as well as that of England, and Knut realised that he would have to establish his power at home before he could expect to lead an army to reconquer England, where Ethelred was already on his way back to London. With uncharacteristic vigour, Ethelred marched north to Gainsborough, where Knut was vacillating about his next move, and drove the Danes back to their ships. They set sail and, pausing only to harry Sandwich, journeyed back to Denmark.

Knut (known to later generations as Canute) came to an agreement with his brother Harald whereby the latter surrendered his interest in the claim to the throne of England. Returning in 1015, Knut found that Ethelred was already dead and his adversary was now the old king's elder son Edmund (later known as Ironside) – who conducted a campaign of armed resistance far superior to anything his father had carried out. Ethelred did his country a greater favour in leaving the way open to his more able kinsman than remaining in ineffective opposition to Knut.

Ethelred had reigned for thirty-eight years, no short span for a medieval king, especially in a country under permanent attack. His nickname, 'the Unready', was given to him shortly after his death, though it may have been coined during his reign. 'Unready' does not really convey the sense of the Saxon word *unræd*, meaning 'ill-advised' or 'clueless', or possibly 'evil advice'; these are all puns on his name, which means 'noble advice' – a misnomer if ever there was one. 'Ill-advised' he certainly was, in allowing men such as Ælfric of Mercia, and the equally odious Eadric Streona, to acquire and retain high office in the nation; 'ill-advised' also to make huge payments to his enemies, effectively paying for his country's destruction.

It is perhaps worthwhile to ask what were the consequences of Byrhtnōth's action, and of the battle in which he lost his life.

For the English the battle was a military disaster. After it, the Danes felt themselves strong enough to menace the king with impunity. Their morale was boosted by their victory, and they soon stepped up their activity in order to take advantage of their position as masters of England. They were as unrelenting in their raiding and pillaging as ever before, although they now had a supplementary source of regular income: the taxes the king raised in order to buy them off. Not surprisingly, such a convenient source of revenue proved very popular and attracted men from all over northern Europe; runic memorials to Swedish warriors mention their having taken gold in England, while Ólaf Tryggvason was supported by a band of Wendish sailors, if we accept the evidence of his saga.

The English of the day saw the gallant 'last stand' at Maldon as a moral victory for them, but there is little suggestion that any others decided to follow the example. Leaders such as Ælfric and Eadric Streona

probably inspired such a lack of trust in their men that the bonds of fellowship never developed in their armies.

It is interesting to speculate on what might have happened if the battle had not been fought. If Byrhtnōth had lived a few years more, would he have been able to guide the king into wiser policies? Such a forthright and forceful character as he was might well have been able to browbeat the young king into a course of action more in keeping with his own inclinations, but would the king have learnt from this? Or would he, as seems more likely, have been dominated by his bishops and councillors, as after Byrhtnōth's death?

It is probably fair to say that the king's character was largely responsible for the ineffective way in which the English tried to deal with the Vikings at this time. In view of Ethelred's failure to remove known traitors from office, this may be true; yet the suspicion remains that if he had early come under better influences, and had been allowed to mature in kingship before facing the Danish marauders, he might have made a better stand against them. We cannot attribute to Byrhtnōth's decision to fight the Danes at Maldon the poor quality of Ethelred as a king – that would be too large a claim – but it is possible that the death of the ealdorman was a factor in the king and kingdom's decline.

In contrast with Ethelred's reign, the reign of Knut Svensson (King Canute) came as a long-overdue time of relative peace for England. Edmund Ironside fought a long and bitter campaign against Knut, until it became clear that negotiation was the only sensible course – warfare having failed to give either side a satisfactory result. Under the terms of their agreement Edmund was to be instated as king of Wessex, ceding the rest of the country to Knut. This was less than Edmund desired, since he was reluctant to allow the Danes any territory he had inherited from his father, yet it was no disgrace to him in view of his lack of real military success against them. The Treaty of Alney, sealed in 1016, formalised the arrangement; later the same year, Edmund died. Almost immediately, in an effort to prevent further civil strife, Knut was

The initial I from Gospels. Before 1012, Latin and Anglo-Saxon. Tradition has it that the manuscript was given to Christ Church, Canterbury, by Knut as the manuscript contains a deed of Knut's confirming the rights of Christ Church. It seems likely, however, that the Gospels were already at Christ Church at the time of the king's visit.

accepted as king across the nation. Within two years he had raised a further Danegeld which he used to pay off his army of mercenaries, most of whom he sent back to Denmark, retaining only a small standing force known as the king's house-carls. These men were armed with the fearsome long-bladed axes so often associated with Viking armies. They constituted the first private royal army – as distinct from bodyguards – in Anglo-Saxon England. At first their function was to provide Knut with a trusted military force against possible uprising by the English; in time, however, they became a part of the royal retinue and were kept on by subsequent kings as a useful counter to the ambitiousness of noblemen.

Knut evidently relished the title 'King of England', and was careful to do as little as possible to alienate himself from his subjects. He supported the English church, even though his father had been a notorious heathen, and did all he could to heal the rift between the English and the Danes who had settled in England. He had had to fight a bloody and protracted campaign to become king, and he was consequently determined to ensure that nothing stood between him and his continued enjoyment of the throne he had won.

With one eye to potential disaffection, particularly in the south, where there was little sympathy for the Danes, Knut divided the country into four great earldoms. He kept Wessex for himself, believing that it would be from there that the first threat would come; East Anglia he allocated to earl Thorkel; Mercia to Eadric Streona; and Northumbria to earl Eric. Eadric misjudged the king badly: he advised him to have Edmund Ironside's brother and young sons secretly murdered. Knut seems to have calculated what sort of man he was dealing with: in the summer of 1017 he married Emma, widow of King Ethelred, and at Christmas the same year had Eadric and some other leading men of dubious trustworthiness slain at his command, so that there should be no further uncertainty about their loyalty.

On the death of his brother Harald in 1019, Knut also became king of Denmark, and spent the next two

A helmet from Vendel in Sweden. The brow of the helmet shows warriors fighting, with broken spears at their feet. A row of spearmen line the edge of the helmet. The ability to catch an enemy's spear in mid flight and return it without pause was a feat especially valued by the Vikings.

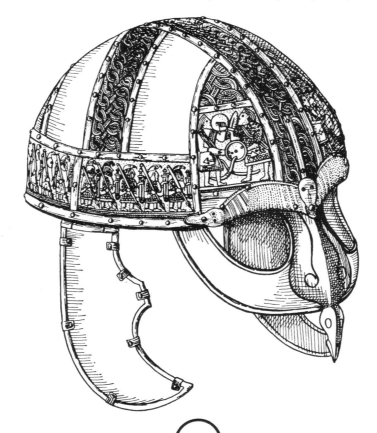

years there with an Anglo-Danish army, consolidating his position as hereditary ruler. During his enforced absence the king maintained contact with the English Witan by means of relays of messengers carrying royal despatches, drawn up by a team of English scribes he had taken along with him for that purpose. Some of his subjects feared that he would now rule England from Denmark, taking his taxes but playing no further part in English life; or, worse still, that he would use England as a recruiting centre for his armies of conquest in Scandinavia; yet from the letters we possess there is no suggestion that he intended to stay away from England for longer than it would take to settle the matter of claiming his inheritance and appointing men to rule in his stead.

As king of two Christian countries, Knut made his way to Rome for the investiture of Emperor Konrad in 1027, where he took his place alongside the other respected rulers of Europe. It is possible to view Knut's kingdom as a kind of empire centred on the North Sea, comprising England, Denmark (including part of southern Sweden) and Norway. At this time, England looked north-east to Scandinavia rather than, as now, south-east to Continental Europe.

In the years of Knut's reign England had little further trouble with Viking marauders, who evidently considered it unwise to provoke a king whose power was spread so widely among the northern peoples. The house-carls remained the king's private army, but attracted increasing numbers of young Englishmen into their ranks. Although he had been a foreign conqueror, and the son of one of the nation's most hated foes, Knut was at pains not to humiliate the country he had striven so long to rule, nor to estrange himself from English life and customs. He became a benefactor of the church, thus ensuring sympathetic treatment in monastic records of his reign, and took great care to uphold the law and promote peaceful relations through trade. To this end he issued his own law code, as many English kings before him had done; this was a balance of English and Danish practice, resorting to biblical precedents where necessary.

As a consequence of his thoughtful attention to the problems of the nation, England throve and regained some of its lost prestige. Traitors and wrongdoers were seen to be punished; the king's fleet was reduced in numbers of vessels; the ship tax was reduced as the threat of foreign invasion diminished with the passing years. The contrast between Knut's policies and those carried out under Ethelred is significant of the contrasting personalities and

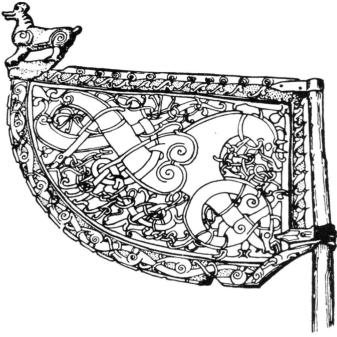

A carved weather vane. Most seafarers of the time were capable only of coastal navigation. This method was certainly used by the Vikings, but Viking raiders also made direct crossings over the North Sea.

demeanour of the two kings. In short, if the English groaned under the reign of Ethelred, they sighed with relief under Knut.

One unforeseen consequence of Knut's reign was that the king of Denmark acquired a notional right to the throne of England. In the eleventh century, while England remained strong and Denmark declined, the Danish kings had enough troubles at home without looking for further problems trying to enforce dubious claims abroad. By the middle of the century, Denmark was administered by a regent whose authority derived from the crown of Norway. When the Norwegian Harald Harðraða (the Ruthless) returned c.1045 from his career in the Byzantine Empire, he took over half his nephew Magnus's kingship, which included Denmark, and he therefore also acquired a nominal claim to the English throne. Though this sounds a feeble reason for invading, it was more than enough of a pretext for an old Viking like Harald, whose appetite for warfare had found little satisfaction in the relatively stable northlands.

Accordingly, Harald set out in 1066 with a fleet to dethrone and kill the usurper Harold Godwinesson, who had only been allowed to become king of

David faces a heavily-armed Norman Goliath. A manuscript illustration reflecting the uneasy relationship between the conquering Normans and the conquered.

England through being the most able and acceptable claimant to the throne. Harold had problems himself: not only was Harald Hardrada after his crown, but so was William of Normandy. Each was a grim opponent. The Norwegian was arguably the most experienced military commander in Christendom. Apart from being personally daunting, he commanded a force of Viking troops, and the English had learnt to their cost how difficult such men could be to defeat. William was known to be just as fierce, and led the most advanced military force in Europe, consisting of heavily armoured cavalrymen supported by bowmen. For its part, the English army under Harold was a successful and cohesive force, well-trained and well-armed, and better led than it had been for generations.

The English army was perfectly capable of defeating even the most powerful foe under the leadership of Harold Godwinesson. It was not, however, equal to the task of defeating two such fearsome foes at opposite ends of the kingdom within days of each other. It is unlikely that any contemporary army could have dealt with both threats, coming as they did so close together.

With Harold's death and William's victory, history closes the book on Anglo-Saxon England; the country enters the European Middle Ages from the point where William accepts the crown. In fact Anglo-Saxon England continued more or less unchanged for many more years, but the Normans' task of destroying the evidence of the nation's former greatness was carried out with characteristic efficiency. Minor local rebellions, and even attempted re-invasion from Scandinavia, were as thorns in the side of the Norman administration, which was geared to the occupation of the land and the suppression of the inhabitants. Winchester-standard English was immediately replaced by Latin as the language of official documents, and English was replaced by Norman French as the speech at court. Norman rebuilding was carried out in the Romanesque styles of the Continent, rather than in the native styles, and gradually the Norman warlords settled into their vast estates across the Channel, remaining strangers in a foreign land until the end of their days. The splendours of the pre-Conquest past were gradually forgotten, and England assumed its later medieval identity.

chapter 5

king ethelred's england

Old English conventional wisdom states that: 'Britain island is eight hundred miles long and two hundred miles broad, and here in the island are five languages – English, British, Scottish, Pictish and Book-Latin'. 'English' includes the dialects of the various Anglian, Saxon and Jutish areas of the country, which correspond to modern England and lowland Scotland; 'British' means the language of the pre-English inhabitants, whom we would today call Welsh (the word is the Anglo-Saxon term for 'foreigner'); 'Scottish' in this context means the Gaelic speech introduced by Irish settlers in the fifth century; 'Pictish' corresponds to the now lost native speech of the Caledonian tribes, a unique tongue belonging to pre-Celtic times which was spoken in eastern and northern Scotland; 'Book-Latin' presumably refers to the literary Roman language of the church, not used for practical purposes except in official, ecclesiastical or royal contexts, where it was soon the preferred medium for important documentary records.

Alfred the Great, among his many other achievements, introduced the spread of vernacular literacy in England. In his time, the widespread understanding of Latin, even among the clergy, had declined to such an extent that important and valuable books were being neglected. Alfred saw the futility of insisting that the entire nation should be taught Latin. He perceived how much more easily the goal of literacy might be attained if the English language were used as the basis of English literature, and he realised how much more efficient the administration of the country would be if the leading men of each region could read and understand the king's directives through letters and codices rather than having them interpreted from

Latin by clerks whose skill might not be equal to the task. Equally, the value of having legal statutes and documentary records such as wills, charters, manumissions and so on available to all free men in an accessible form would greatly reduce the possibility of error in interpretation, or indeed fraudulent misrepresentation by unscrupulous clerics. He therefore decreed that all thanes and men in positions of responsibility should learn both to read and write.

In order to get the programme of instruction off to a flying start, the king and his advisers spent many hours translating standard works of pious scholarship such as Boethius's *On the Consolation of Philosophy* and Orosius's *Historia Adversus Paganos* (a history of the world) into the Old English of Alfred's court. Rather than follow the originals slavishly, the translators introduced a certain amount of material which was intended to be of greater interest to the expected audience of well-informed, inquisitive English freemen.

One such intrusion is the famous passage of the *Journeys of Ohthere and Wulfstān*, describing reports made to the king by merchant traders who traversed contemporary sea-routes in search of markets for their goods, and commodities not available elsewhere. Wulfstān seems to be a native Englishman (judging by his name alone), while Ohthere is evidently Norwegian (his name in Norse would be Ottar). His report reminds us that dealings between the English nobility and their Norse counterparts could take the form of peaceful trade and exchange of information as well as violence and rapine.

Contemporary geography was a blend of native English lore concerning the lands bordering the Baltic (from where the English had originally come), Christian teachings concerning the topography of the Near

English quest for knowledge of the world at large, which distinguishes the court of Alfred. Wulfstān's account includes sailing directions to the mart he visited, and a long account of the funeral customs he observed among the Wends. Opportunities for recording this kind of material were perhaps less frequent at the courts of subsequent monarchs, who may have had less intellectual curiosity than Alfred.

Conventional Christian geography insisted that Calvary was the central point of the world, reminiscent of the Greeks 'omphalos'; the world-navel, the central point from which the many lands radiate. This view was difficult to reconcile with what the English knew, and were discovering, about the extent of land to the north. Norse tradition, however, held that the world was a land mass ringed about with sea, on the outer shores of which dwelt the Etinns (giants) of Norse mythology. Because of this, the Vikings were confident of reaching land no matter which direction they sailed in, which may have caused them to journey further and with greater confidence on the outer ocean; equally important were their ships, which were well suited to withstanding the rigours of the open sea, while contemporary European craft were usually little more than rowing boats and coastal barges equipped with sails.

King and young, unarmed warrior who appears to be protecting his lord with his own shield. The king has a forked beard without a moustache (characteristic of the nobility), and wears his crown even in battle. He wields a large lobe-pommelled sword and wears a mail-shirt, split to the crotch to allow him to ride a horse. The younger man is clean-shaven and wears the strange ridged cap typical of Saxon warriors. His shield is studded and decorated, while the king's is apparently plain.

East, the writings of classical geographers on the regions surrounding the Mediterranean, and the discoveries of the Viking merchants and land-seekers who pushed even further back the limits of knowledge of the more northerly latitudes. Ohthere's description of his voyage north along the coast of Norway gives details of his discovery of the White Sea, far to the north-east, and of his trading there with the locals who produced, among other commodities, excellent ships' ropes of seal hide. Although this information can have been of little practical use to the English – who had no intention of voyaging to the White Sea themselves – its inclusion is characteristic of the

The king and councillor in discussion. Each has a cloak with a brooch fastened at the right shoulder and the king appears to be seated in a folding chair.

From the writings which have survived from the Anglo-Saxon period, the reader will form the impression of a prudent, practical and reflective people, well adjusted to acceptance of life's inherent injustice, and whose moral outlook saw virtue mainly as the outfacing of despair. Such a view of life may owe more than a little to attitudes inherited from their pre-Christian forebears, yet almost all Old English writings are piously Christian, presumably due to the editing out by monastic scribes of anything flagrantly non-Christian. Consequently, many poems on religious themes survive and precious little secular verse, though this must at the time have been more common and more popular with the nobles and warriors it commemorated. Elegies are also well represented in the manuscripts which survive, as well as spells and charms, gnomic verse and riddles. Gnomic and preceptual statements often appear in poems of quite different types, as for example Dunnere's speech in *The Battle of Maldon*, or the following passage in *The Wanderer*:

A wise man must be patient,
must not be too hotheaded, nor too hasty in speech,
not too bashful in battle, nor too blindly reckless,
nor too craven, nor too carefree, nor too keen for wealth,
nor ever too fond of boasting before he fully understands.

Such timeless statements, which sum up generations of observation of human behaviour, had a profound appeal to the minds of the people of that time. As adages and maxims, these old saws live on into our own day, folk-wisdom conveniently packaged in a memorable and useful form.

The Anglo-Saxon poet knew how to tackle other matters of importance apart from religious themes. And beside the poems there was a great deal of prose literature produced in the Old English period, much of which consisted of saints' lives and similar uplifting material. More interesting, from a modern point of view, are some homilies which give brief insights into the ordinary lives of the poorer folk, who go largely unrecorded in the *Chronicle* and similar records. Perhaps most interesting of all is the *Sermo Lupi ad Anglos*, or *Wulfstān's Address to the English*. This dates from 1014, just after the death of Sven Forkbeard, at the time when Ethelred returned and drove Knut out of the country.

Archbishop Wulfstān echoes at some length the concern of the men of this time for their future, which must have seemed uncertain and bleak to them, for Wulfstān's picture of contemporary England is far

The church tower, Sompting, Sussex. Although now unique, this style, in which each face of the tower is gabled, may once have been typical of the period among English timber churches.

from promising. He begins by reminding his audience of the approaching doomsday – which had been widely forecast as likely to occur at around the time of the millennium, that is the year AD 1000 – and the advent of the Antichrist; he then moves on to the theme of the sins and iniquities of the English nation – that they had been led astray by the devil, that good faith was a thing of the past even though men used fair words in their dealings together, and that men devoted too little attention to the correction of vices, but increased evil after evil. Wulfstān reminds them that the remedy for their hurts and insults can be found only with God, and that God's mercy would

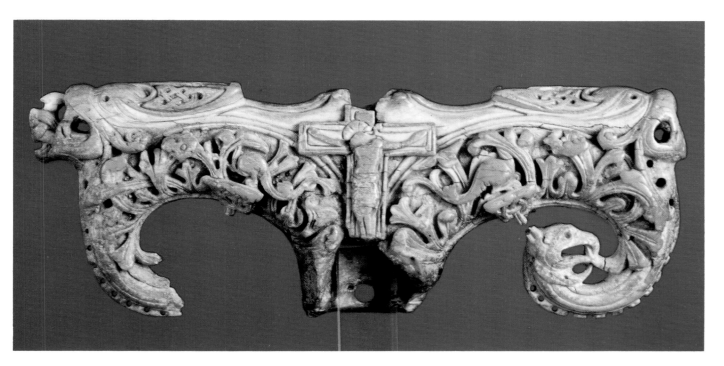

The Alcester Tau Cross (above). Anglo-Saxon. Early eleventh century. The Tau Cross is a form of crozier head, named after the Greek letter T. *The Alcester Tau is one of the finest examples of Anglo-Saxon carving, and the decoration with its extensive ornamentation closer to manuscript decoration than is usual.*

St Benedict and the monks of Christ Church, Canterbury, from the Eadui Psalter, probably before 1023. Latin and Anglo-Saxon. The monk nearest the saint holds an open book inscribed with the opening words of Benedict's Rule. The miniature is the best surviving marriage between the use of full-colour painting and line drawing.

have to be earned by better behaviour than had been the norm hitherto. He goes on to draw an interesting parallel from his own times: that among the 'heathen' (presumably the Vikings) men dared not withhold any gift that was set aside for the honour of their false gods, while the English were only too ready to withhold the church's dues. As an ecclesiastic he would naturally regard any diminution of the church's income with horror, but he seems also to have had reliable knowledge of the dues given to heathen temples established by the Danes.

Wulfstān then goes on to contrast the richness of adornment of pagan sanctuaries with the churches which sometimes had their costly treasures taken and sold to pay the Danes; and the English practice of depriving God's servants of honour and protection, while the heathen priests were bound not to ill-use each other in any way. He then declares that 'hardship is the remedy' for this unrighteousness, because God's (i.e. the church's) receipts have been diminishing for so long throughout the land; secular laws have degenerated so that now God's houses are deprived of their ancient dues and of their costly fittings; widows are given to men in marriage without their consent (this had previously been prohibited), and many of them were reduced to poverty and humiliation; poor people are cruelly oppressed and defrauded and sold into slavery abroad (also prohibited by earlier laws); young children are sent down into servitude for a small misdemeanour (previously forbidden); the rights of freemen are negated while the rights of slaves are even further reduced – freemen prevented from looking after their own affairs, going where they wish, and disposing of their own property as they wish, and slaves not able to gain their freedom through working on their own account to acquire enough money to buy it, nor to achieve it through their master's gift as an act of charity. All such alms-giving is diminished or withheld outright through the unrighteousness and lawlessness of the nation.

Thus, Wulfstān continues, God's law is hateful to men and his teachings are despised, and therefore the English are humiliated through God's anger. Nothing has been of any use against the 'raiding and hunger,

&equitate   ;   fuum fctm & terribile   omnibus facientibuf ei ;
R edemptionem mifit po I   nomen eiuf   L audatio eiuf. man& in
pulo fuo. mandauit ine   I nitium fapientiæ timor   feculum feculi   ;
ternum. teftamentum O   dni . intellectuf bonuf

B ALLELVIA REVERSI   ONIS AGGEI ETZACHARIÆ .   · CXI ·
E ATUS UIR   lumen rectif corde :   Paratum eft coreiuf fpe
q uia m& dnm. in   mifericorf &miferator   rare indno. confirmatu
mandauf eiuf cupit   & iuftuf dnf   ;   eft cor eiuf noncommo
nimif   ;   I ocunduf homo qui mife   uebitur. donec uideat
P otenf interra erit fem   retur & commodat dif   inimicof fuof ingla ;
eiuf. generatio rectoru   pon& fermonef fuof in   D ifpfit dedit pauperibuf.
bene dicetur   ;   iudicio. quia inæternu   iuftitia el man& infcm
G loria & diuitiæ indomo   non commouebitur   ;   feculi. cornu eiuf exaltabit
eiuf. & iuftitia eiuf ma   I nmemoria eterna erit   P eccator uidebit & irafcet
n& infeculum feculi ;   iuftuf. abauditione ma   dentibuf fuif fremebit &ta
E xortum eft intenebrif   la nontimebit   ;   befc& · defideriu peccatox p
                                                             ibit ;

A murderous 'stiletto' style dagger found in London (above), its grip is studded and bound with a metal strip.

Almsgiving at a lord's house: even when dispensing charity to the poor, the wealthy man (seated) is attended by warriors with spears and shields. The hand of God blesses the giver for his act of charity.

burning and bloodshed' across the land, as well as the other evils of 'stealing and killing, sedition and death, cattle-murrain and disease, envy and hatred and the plundering of marauders' which have harmed the English greatly, not to mention the unfair taxes, bad weather bringing crop-failure, many injustices and wavering faith. It has come to the point that a kinsman will no more protect his kindred than a stranger, nor a father his son, nor a son his father, nor one brother another – nor has any one, either layman or clergy, lived his life as he ought to. Loyalty towards one's fellow men has disappeared and most people will stoop to cutting down other men from behind in shameful attacks, for many have betrayed their lords in various ways, the greatest betrayal being that a man shall 'Betray his lord's soul' (perhaps meaning to encourage one's lord in defying the church), although it is also a great betrayal that a man should treacherously kill his lord, or drive him from the land while still alive (compare the ideal conduct of Byrhtnōth's men, who protected their lord and saved his body for Christian burial; compare also the situation of the exile in Old English tradition). Wulfstān states that both evils have been perpetrated in England: King Edward was treacherously slain by men whom he trusted, and King Ethelred was driven overseas by those who turned to Sven Forkbeard.

Godparents and godsons have been slain, Wulfstān continues, and holy places have been allowed to deteriorate because men who do not honour God's peace have been put in charge, while Christian people have been sold out of this country into foreign servitude, contrary to God's law. And a further evil practice occurs widely: that poor men join their money together to buy a woman whom they hold in common, against whom 'they carry out their foulness, one by one and each after the others', then sell her abroad (perhaps to foreign slave-merchants). The poverty of the lowly increases so that a father is forced to sell his son for money and a son his mother, and a brother his sibling. A greater evil still is that good faith and trustworthiness have declined, so that oaths are broken and often men are perjured and forsworn (the basis of English society rested in part on people's desire to earn the praise of their neighbours and friends, which previously had prevented most people from acting with open dishonesty).

Wulfstān adds that it is evident that God's anger rests on the nation, but that few worse things could happen through God's displeasure than the English are dedicated to bringing upon themselves through their own behaviour. He cites the case of a thrall

St Peter-at-Gowts church tower, Lincoln, with long-and-short quoining (cornerstones which alternate). See p. 127 for another view.

running away from his lord to join the Viking army, whom he then leads back to the lord's house for vengeance; if, in the ensuing fight, the thrall kills the thane his kinsmen are unable to obtain compensation for him under the law, while under the same law if the thane kills the thrall he must pay a full thane's wergild for the slaying of his former slave. Through such shameful laws the English have been deprived of victory and greatly disheartened, so that one seafarer may put to flight ten or more Englishmen in a fight; and ten or twelve raiders will 'shame and harass' a thane's wife and daughter in turn while he is forced to look on, even though the thane considered himself powerful and worthy; and it may even happen that a thrall captures and binds his former lord, and makes him his own slave in turn. The English repay the insults they endure by honouring those who harm them – they yield constantly to the marauders and are humiliated by them each day; the Vikings harry and burn, plunder and rob and carry goods off to their ships. What can this be but God's anger against us? he asks.

Wulfstān goes on to point out that, according to the monk Gildas, the British saw the arrival and conquest of the English as God's punishment on them for having failed to live righteously. It has now come about that the English nation itself is Christian, and

similarly oppressed by a heathen power due to its failure to live up to God's teachings. He concludes by stressing the urgent need for the nation to turn back to Christ again, and to do all in its power to reverse the wrongs which had been committed in the past, so that divine favour might again allow England strength and success.

I have presented Wulfstān's text at length, though still only in summary, for it shows very clearly the situation that had come about in his day, and also what he considered should be done about it. It is not a very comfortable picture of late Saxon England, but it is worth remembering that the archbishop's purpose was to shock and shame his audience into better behaviour, and not to present an unbiased view of events. Nevertheless, it is interesting to pick up on his claim that English slaves would sometimes run away to seek a better life among the Vikings rather than help their masters to fight against them. The contemporary English could only view this behaviour with horror, as the worst kind of betrayal by men who should have been striving to drive off the Danes with their countrymen. A thousand years later, we feel more sympathy with the hopeless bondsman who was prepared to risk everything in escaping from his master and taking his chances with a band of cut-throats. Similarly, Wulfstān's insistence that the nation is given over to faithlessness is an indication that the accepted standards of behaviour were declining under the pressure of the constant threat of Danish attack, as is the reference to the poverty of the lower orders causing them to ignore the bonds of kinship and respect for women, which had been mainstays of the Anglo-Saxon moral outlook.

If Wulfstān's *Address* seems long on doom and gloom, it is worth bearing in mind that Knut later took over the Old English practice almost unchanged into his legal system, only altering it to accommodate the Danelaw practices which he considered should have full legal status. If a man as exacting as Knut Svensson was content with the practices of the English as enacted in their laws, then we may assume that by the time his law code was drawn up things were back on a relatively even keel.

As previously mentioned, little is said about the lives of ordinary people in the literature which survives, and the scarcity of information is made the more irritating by the lack of surviving examples of the everyday things of the period, except in chance finds of such trivial items as combs, loom-weights, and cheap, mass-produced trinkets. Nowhere is this sense of ignorance more acute than in the matter of housing. For the most part we have only the vaguest of ideas concerning the sorts of houses the English (the poorer ones, at least) lived in. A few well-known habitation sites of the wealthy, such as the royal 'palaces' of Cheddar and Yeavering, give some impression of the appearance of a nobleman's hall, although the danger here is that chance resemblances and odd details may give a false idea of the similarity of appearance of the halls of thanes and kings from early times to late.

It seems likely, however, that the timber aisled hall was the standard Anglo-Saxon design of dwelling for the wealthy man and his family. The hall at Cheddar was 110 feet long and 60 feet wide, and thus the largest known example of this type of building in England. It had a further set of 2-feet-square arcade posts set into pits outside, which may have allowed for a structure up to 60 feet high. At the eastern end a foundation for what may have been a gallery or balcony was discovered. The normal arrangement, as far as can be determined, was that the main entrance to the hall was sited either on one of the gabled end-walls supporting the pitched roof, or centrally along the long side wall, sometimes opposite another door, separated from it by a screen across the centre of the building to prevent the unavoidable cross-draught from the two openings making life more uncomfortable than necessary for those within. Usually the side walls were supplied with benches on their inner faces for the retainers to use as seats when feasting, and as beds when the feast ended.

The hearth was placed centrally along the longitudinal axis of the building; between it and the benches, tables were erected for the use of the diners, and later taken down and folded away when not required. At one end of the hall, but still along a side wall, was a raised dais upon which stood the *Yppe*, the high seat of the lord; this was probably a fairly ornate affair with carvings and a high back to emphasise the occupant's importance. In later times, the table in front of the high seat became a fixed feature, and so a mark of high rank, while in Viking halls, the high seat was virtually a sacred object, and many early settlers voyaging to Iceland took the trouble to dismantle the high seats of their halls, and take both the seats and the earth beneath along to their new homes over the sea.

Some aisled halls probably had a kind of vestibule, a sheltered porch attached to the building where visitors could remove their travelling clothes and deposit their weapons, which were strictly banned (from royal halls at least). These porches may be

English fyrd-warrior armed with axe and seax or sword, but otherwise without protection of any kind.

related to the surrounding 'arcade' found at other sites. The walls of the building itself were made up of jointed planks (a slot on each plank accepting a tongue on its neighbour) thus increasing the integrity of the construction, and excluding wind and rain. The planks were set into wooden sills, themselves set into trenches dug into the ground to some depth, so that the walls were capable of taking the weight of a substantial roof. Notwithstanding this, a double row of posts ran the length of the building (either side of the hearth) supporting the transverse timbers of the roof's framework. This, in addition to the external arcading, made the structure very resistant to high winds. For the same reason, some halls had the gable ends tapered inwards, so that the overall plan was similar to the shape of a ship.

It is not clear whether the timber hall was left in its natural state or plastered and painted (as were some other buildings); *Beowulf* mentions that the splendid hall Heorot was bound about with iron, suggesting that the construction featured some form of metal strapping around the timbers, which would have been obscured by any applied daubing or caulkings.

Roofing was probably mainly of thatched straw, although the use of shingles (wooden tiles) was common towards the end of the Saxon period, due to the immense fire risk involved with dry straw, which became greater as towns grew in size. Reed, rush or straw thatch could be made fireproof by the simple measure of applying plaster to it; and this later became a legal requirement for such roofs. Shingles of square shape are shown in contemporary manuscript illustration, and this may have been the preferred method of roofing in the later period. The roof summit may have been decorated with knobs, scrolls and spurs (as shown in the Bayeux Tapestry), or even with stag's horns, as mentioned in *Beowulf*, where

Heorot is described as *horngeap*, which may mean 'horn-adorned and steep' (though it need mean no more than 'steep of gable').

In some areas, chiefly the more remote parts of the north-west, a different arrangement was used for supporting the roof-ridge; this is the noted cruck frame, whereby two curved baulks of timber are set at each end of the house so that they meet at a given height, at which point they are jointed together with the roof-ridge itself.

The flooring of the hall in early times was simply rammed earth, and when later constructions began to have wooden plank flooring on a large scale, further earth was sometimes spread over this according to the ancient practice. Common in smaller dwellings were floors of pebbles and even of stone slabs; the finer buildings may perhaps have had paved entrances, though little evidence now exists.

Even less is known about the houses of the peasantry than the great halls, which do at least tend to be noticed by the excavator. The simplest form of house was the sunken-floored hut, a hole in the ground covered over with a roof supported by small posts set at either end of the ridge. Whether the inhabitants lived in the hole itself or erected a wooden raised floor over it is not certain, though it is quite likely that by the time of Ethelred's reign any such rudimentary structures would have served for work-shops only. The common building material was timber, which was then in plentiful abundance in the great forests. Thus the crudest huts may have been intended to serve only for a short while, until the construction of a permanent dwelling was completed. The walls of these houses were of wattle and daub: that is, they consisted of stout stakes set in the ground through which were interwoven supple withies (willows), and the whole wall was then covered with the 'daub' – a mixture of clay, dung, and animal hair which was sufficiently hard and tough on drying to exclude the worst of the weather.

Small, low, rectangular buildings of this kind cluster about the great halls and probably represent the guest-houses and bowers of the nobles and the store-houses for the foodstuffs to be consumed in the hall itself. Freemen and peasants who lived away from hall-dominated settlements presumably had similar dwellings. In regions where timber was less common, houses made of undressed stone, or of stones faced with turfs, are common.

Some Saxon houses were two-storeyed, as is clear from contemporary literature: for example the meeting-house at Calne in Wiltshire of which the upper floor collapsed leaving Saint Dunstān miraculously preserved by standing on a cross-beam. 'Lofthouse' is a common place-name in northern England, and probably refers to just such a building. What arrange-ments were made for ventilation is not clear; the Bayeux Tapestry and some English manuscript illus-trations show round-headed windows, apparently without any form of shutter. Windows of this kind are known from Saxon stone churches, the only buildings from Saxon times to have survived. In Alfred's time, we are told that the king ordered stone houses to be taken down and re-erected where they might be of more service, so the building of royal dwellings in stone was evidently practised in his time, and may later have been widespread. Unfortunately the Norman practice of dismantling Saxon stonework and incorporating it into their own constructions has robbed us of all but a few Saxon buildings.

INTERIOR FITTINGS

As far as the internal fittings and furnishings of the period are concerned, there is a scarcity of evidence corresponding to the accident of survival of perishable material. Ordinary people sat on benches ranged along the walls, and used collapsible tressle tables. Free-standing chairs and solid tables (known as 'boards') were the prerogative of the wealthy and a visible symbol of status – even today, the men who sit on the board of a company enjoy high standing, while the most important of them is the chairman, a relic of the pecking order in Anglo-Saxon halls.

The walls of the better sorts of building were decorated with carvings (at least among the Norsemen, but presumably also among the English), and were hung with tapestries and decorated fabrics. The Bayeux Tapestry (actually an embroidery) is probably the best known of these, though other such work survives from elsewhere in northern Europe. Apart from brightening what may have been quite sombre chambers, the hangings also served to exclude the worst of the draughts. The central hearth served to provide both heat and light, and was also used for cooking, though in the later period food was prepared in a kitchen separate from the hall, to reduce the risk of fire destroying the entire settlement. Cauldrons probably would have hung from the rafters over the fire for the purpose of heating water: the provision of warm water and a towel for a newly-arrived guest was the first duty of the host among the Vikings.

From the Oseberg ship-burial comes a great wooden free-standing bedstead with decorated headboard ends – although nothing directly similar is known from this country, it is perfectly possible that such furniture was used here. For the warriors who followed war-leaders, 'bed' meant just the hall bench strewn with blankets or furs, and with a bolster for the head. Slaves may have slept on the floor around the hearth. Privacy was the prerogative of the owner and his immediate family, who seem to have had separate sleeping quarters; as a general rule, high-born women also slept in separate bowers with their handmaidens, where their chastity could be preserved. The office of *Būrthegn* is believed to refer to the responsibility for the safe-keeping of the bower and women inside.

For the peasantry, home was the hut or house in which they ate and slept, perhaps upon straw mattresses on the floor. Their furniture seems, likewise, to have been sparse, perhaps comprising only low wooden stools, since the smallest huts do not seem to have been provided with benches of any sort. Indeed, such buildings usually yield only a hearth and loom-weights, which suggests that they may have been weaving-sheds rather than houses for habitation. Loom-weights are evidence of the widespread craft of wool-making and weaving which must have been carried on as a real 'cottage industry', providing a useful source of income for the poorer households.

Cupboards and closets being unknown, the storage of household objects was probably on wooden shelving, while clothing and precious items were kept in chests, many of which were lockable. Similar containers, such as reliquaries, which have survived attest to the craftsmanship that went into the production of the fine quality metal-bound, carved wooden boxes.

Tableware for the poor was probably just a wooden platter each, off which were eaten the porridges and stews that were their principal kind of food. Cutlery consisted of the knife that hung at their belts, which served a hundred and one other purposes. For those with the wealth to acquire them, there were many kinds of fine vessels available: glass beakers and cups, mainly imported from the Rhineland; silver dishes, of Frankish or even Roman work, or of native production; silver spoons and table-knives, ladles and wine-strainers, imported from the Mediterranean countries. Drink was served from pitchers, from French amphorae, or in less wealthy households from decorated pottery jugs and bottles. Native English pottery was usually not wheel-turned, and looks rather crude to us today, but it must have been very common, and very expendable, in its day. Some pottery was used for the burial of the ashes from cremations, though it is not clear whether this was always purpose-made, or simply convenient containers reused.

Animals which were kept for food were the pig, sheep, ox, cow, goat and various types of poultry. By hunting, deer and boar might also be acquired; by snares, various birds and the hare (the rabbit had not then been introduced); fishing was also a very important means of supplementing the diet. Milk was obtained mainly from sheep, and cheeses were made from this, and also from goats' and cows' milk. In fenland districts, eels were trapped and boiled; in other regions shellfish, and crayfish were eaten, as well as whelks, mussels and oysters.

Bees were kept both for their wax and honey, and honey was also gathered from the hives of bees in the woods. Apart from its use as a sweetener – at that time the only sweetener available – it could also be transformed into mead. It was therefore doubly agreeable to men, and swarms of bees were accredited with supernatural powers.

Loaves of bread were either 'wheaten' or 'clean'; the distinction was between what would now be called 'wholemeal' bread and the sifted and refined ('clean') flour which goes into the production of white bread. This was required in particular by the Church for the wafers used in services. Cakes, probably of the sort we would call 'griddle-cakes' or scones, were made. Oats were boiled in water to make a thin porridge or gruel, and were also used as animal fodder. Barley was ground into meal, from which bread was made, or else made into malt for brewing beer. The commonest vegetable seems to have been the bean, which may have been the staple diet of the poor. Fruits were popular, though probably not cultivated on a large scale; among the most popular were apples, medlars, cherries, mulberries, plums, damsons, pears and strawberries. The gathering of nuts and berries was presumably a popular practice in the summer months.

Evidence for Viking and Anglo-Saxon costume comes mainly from manuscripts and sources such as the Bayeux Tapestry and carvings of the period. The quantity of evidence increases as the period approaches the Middle Ages, and the scarcity of illustrations for earlier times may lead us astray in interpreting what remains. However, in any era dress habits from earlier times tend to persist among certain sections of society (for example in the starched periwigs of the legal profession and the medieval robes of some clergymen)

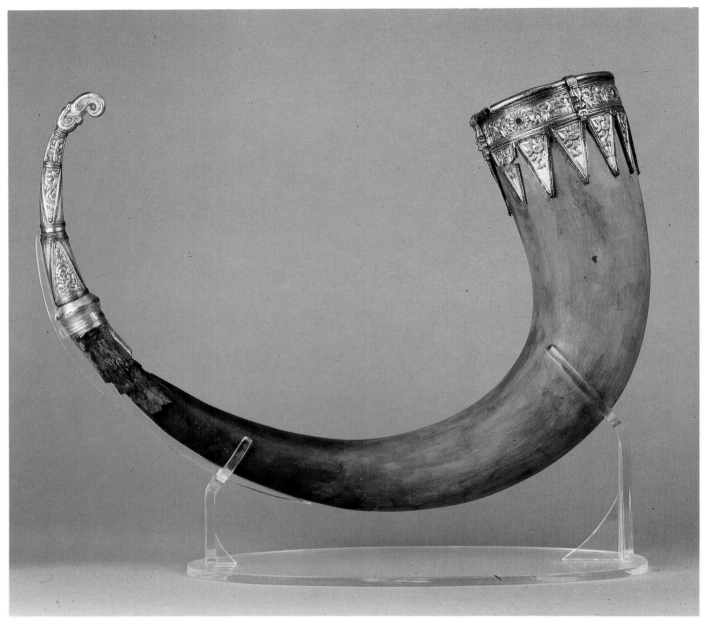

Spectacularly decorated Taplow Drinking Horn, with ornate silver gilt fittings.

A medieval view of the conqueror: William, seated, grants land to one of his Counts. The dress, armour and weapons are all proper to the (later) high middle ages. The caption begins 'I, William, known as the Bastard, King of England . . .'.

so what follows is only a guide to the aggregate dress habits of the ninth, tenth and eleventh centuries as pieced together from the available evidence.

Men's dress consisted of a number of separate garments worn in layers, which were added or removed as circumstances dictated. The basic dress of all men was the tunic in a number of slightly different forms: it resembled a combined shirt and skirt, and was either knee-length and slit at the sides for convenience, or ankle-length, though this may have been a kind of ceremonial dress for noblemen. Its neck opening was either round and big enough for the head to pass through, or round and narrow with a vertical slit extending down the chest, or again square. The sleeves were most often close-fitting and rolled or tucked back from the wrist, or alternatively loose and open (most often on ankle-length tunics).

About the waist there was almost always a sash or thin belt, though this was often hidden by a fold of the material, where the garment was hitched up for comfort. The material used was probably usually wool, though linen may have been preferred by the wealthy. By the eleventh century, the tunic tended to fit closer to the body and have a more pronounced flair to the skirt. Embroidered bands at the wrists, neck, hem and waist became more common, and fabrics with simple geometric designs appeared more frequently. Embroidered bands on the upper arm or shoulder, not found earlier, also came into fashion.

Above the tunic was worn the *roc* or over-tunic; this could be long, with open sleeves, or short, but in either case it revealed the tunic beneath at the wrists and hem. Again, embroidered or different-coloured bands were common on this garment, as was the wearing of a girdle or belt. By the eleventh century, under first Danish and then Norman influence, the *roc*'s sleeves became bell-shaped, or else impracticably long, and were turned back to form a definite cuff.

The outer garment was the cloak, which was a square-cut length of heavier fabric, worn above both tunic and *roc*. The length of the cloak may have been a symbol of wealth, or perhaps of social status. Cloaks were most often fastened by a brooch or a clasp at the right shoulder, thus leaving the right arm (the 'sword arm') free; some men seem to have fastened the cloak at the left shoulder, however, which may indicate that they were left-handed. An alternative was to fix the top corners together, with a brooch or specially attached ties, centrally beneath the chin. Later examples of cloaks were sometimes cut as semicircles, and were knee- or ankle-length.

A variant of the cloak used by the highest ranks of laymen and clergy was the mantle, a square 'poncho' with a central hole or slit for the head. No fastening was necessary for this garment, which hung down over the shoulders by its own weight. Mantles were also worn by high-ranking women, and some seem to have been lined with fabric of a different colour from the exterior. Later types of mantle look as if they are lined with fur, and have small metal rings sewn to the edges of the neck to tie them close together. The poor wore a rustic type of mantle, known as a brat. After the Norman Conquest, hooded cloaks made of coarse wool or skins appeared, worn by wayfarers and workmen.

Headgear seems to have been neither fashionable nor popular in Anglo-Saxon times, though some men are shown wearing the curious, ridged Phrygian cap, with its low, forward-pointing crown; others wore small round caps, perhaps made of felt. Kings are conventionally shown crowned, while some classes wear a narrow, presumably metal, fillet about the brow. The hair itself, for younger men, was combed back in waves from the temples, often with a centre parting, and was worn collar-length or slightly longer. For older men a centre parting was normal, but with the hair flowing down to the neck or shoulders; fringes were also more popular with them.

Many men are shown clean-shaven (though they were probably not on a daily basis), but moustaches were common with young warriors and nobles. Beards were popular, also, and were sometimes worn without a moustache (Abraham Lincoln-style). In the Bayeux Tapestry, the older warriors have beards and moustaches, while the younger men are shown mainly with moustaches only or clean-shaven. After the Conquest, the 'moustache only' became rare, and the peculiar Norman haircut began to appear: this consisted of shaving the head from the nape of the neck up almost to the crown, and combing the hair forward into a thick fringe. Within a couple of decades, however, this fashion seems to have died out, and all men seem to have grown their hair as long as possible and to have had it crimped and curled. Among the Vikings, the fashionable man wore his beard either combed forward or forked, or else plaited into a braid.

Legwear consisted of a number of different items of clothing, which could be worn separately or in

An eleventh-century seal die of Godwin – the inscription reads '+ Sigillum: Godwini Ministri' (the seal of Thane Godwin); the reverse of the roundel has been later re-cut with the seal die of the nun Godcyda.

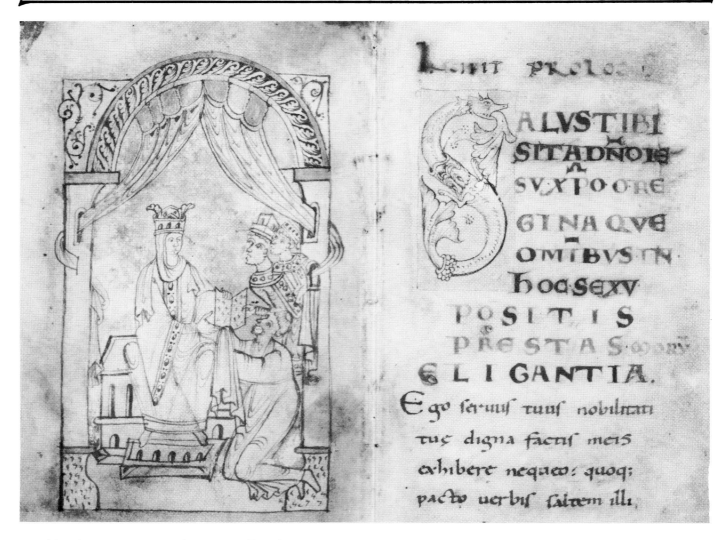

combination. *Braies* were loose woollen drawers, tied at the waist and legs by draw-strings. They frequently ended just below the knee. There are illustrations of longer examples which extend to the ankle, where they are often slit at the side; these are often bound by ties. All classes seem to have worn this garment, though fabrics varied with the wealth and rank of the wearer. Hose or stockings were loose woollen bags, extending to the thigh for the wealthy or to the knee for the poor. They were often brightly coloured, and were worn with socks, which differed from them in being much shorter, though often decorated. All legwear was kept in place by means of bindings, known in later times as *Yorkies*, resembling Indian puttees. These were lengths of decorated or coloured cloth which were wound spirally round the leg, though kings and certain holders of high ecclesiastical office are shown with criss-cross patterns. They

Emma, Queen to Æðelred and Knut in succession, receives the book Encomium Emmae Reginae *from its writer.*

St Ætheldreda from the Benedictional of St Æthelwold, Bishop of Winchester from 963 to 984. With twenty-eight full-page miniatures (with a further fifteen probably missing), the benedictional is the only surviving example with such an incredible wealth of decoration and illustration. As a young man Æthelwold was at the Court of the King Athelstān (reigned 924 – 939).

served to prevent the trouser-legs becoming torn, and often replaced the hose and socks. The ends of the cloth were often left dangling, in which case they could be finished with tassels.

Later trousers were much narrower beneath the knee, especially for the nobility, while the poor seem

to have worn longer garments with slits at the back of the legs. The puttees went out of fashion after the conquest, but were still used by workmen and rustics. Stockings also appeared, with a curious ornamental border, either a form of garter, or an embroidered edging. They sometimes ended in a full 'foot' as before, but may also have had a 'stirrup' extending beneath the sole to keep them in place.

Shoes seem to have been purpose-made for the left and right foot, and are slightly pointed at the big toe. There is no evidence of any built-up heel on shoes at this time. They featured either a wide ankle opening, often turned out or splayed back, or close fitting at the ankle with a slit along the top or side of the foot. The fastening could be by means of a thong tied over the instep, but in the majority of cases there is no suggestion of any closure at all. They seem to be fashioned mainly from leather, with soles of leather or wood, sometimes studded. Once the sole wore through, it could be pared away and a replacement sewn on. Boots were also worn, reaching to the calf, and either open-topped, or thong-tied with a decorated border. Wooden clogs appear in some illustrations, as well as slippers which have no back to the upper part; these are usually worn by women or clerics, who perhaps spent more time indoors.

Common accessories were belts and girdles, either plain or ornamented, from which were suspended a pouch and a small knife. Gloves were certainly known, although not illustrated; they took the form of cloth bags, like modern mittens, though whether they featured separate thumbs or not is not known. Aprons were used by workmen and may well have been of leather. Keys were worn attached to the ties of the *braies*, it seems, since one riddle refers to the lifting of the tunic to bring out the key.

Women's clothing was layered in the same way as men's, and the form of the tunic seems to have been little different from that worn by men. Above this was worn the kirtle, a ground-length frock with narrow sleeves, often embroidered or patterned. The *roc* was of similar length, but usually hitched up to knee-length; this was round-necked and lined, its sleeves either loose and cylindrical or bell-shaped. Embroidery was added at the neck, wrist, hem, and often down the front as well. It was tied by the girdle, a wide sash often of the same material as the main gown. Women's mantles were square and much larger than men's, nearly as large as the kirtle. Fastening was usually under the chin by means of a brooch or tie, though the closure was often hidden under the headgear. Sometimes the mantle was folded and worn like a shawl. Their footwear was similar to that worn by men, and included slippers and clogs.

The head-rail or veil was a distinctive garment worn by all classes of women, apparently even in bed, though probably not in intimate domestic life. It consisted of a long scarf, sufficiently wide to cover the head from the brow to the back of the skull, and extending down on to the shoulders, covering the hair. Its ends crossed on the chest, from which one hung loose while the other was draped back over the shoulder, covering the neck. A queen's crown was worn over the head-rail; this was often of ornamented fabric, according to the wealth of the wearer. The hair was thus covered, but there are references to plaits and hair-ties.

Later female dress differed slightly in that the sleeves of the kirtle sometimes extended over the hands in wide flared ends. The later mantle resembled the male garment except that it seems never to have had fastenings at the neck, and stockings began to appear in women's costume, held up by ties or garters. Female footwear still matched men's in style, but whereas men's shoes were always very dark colours, women's shoes could be red, orange, blue or tan. The later head-rail was also sometimes cut as a section of a circle or as a rectangle, with a straight edge across the forehead and the rest wound like a scarf. Women's hair was still always covered, but girls seem to have let their hair grow long and worn it loose and flowing.

Accessories usually consisted of headbands of cloth, fillets, diadems and metal neckbands. Viking women were particularly proud of possessing the keys to the household chests, and displayed them as a symbol of their status, by attaching them by a fine chain to a small brooch worn on the upper chest.

Jewellery in the form of finger-rings, neck-rings, arm-rings, necklaces, bracelets and bangles were common adornments for both sexes. Women sometimes seem to have worn ear-rings, which may also have been worn by men.

Common colours for clothing in illustrations are bright red, blue, green, pink, violet, purple and orange-yellow (this may of course reflect the availability of pigments for inks and paint rather than preferences in dress). Black is almost always shown as the colour of shoes, perhaps because leather shoes were treated with lard to waterproof them and keep them supple. Although blue dye can be obtained from woad, it is very unlikely that it was common due to the difficulty of stabilising the colour. Indeed, all dyes would fade quickly in strong sunlight or heavy rain, leaving the clothing looking bleached.

chapter 6

the land of the english

the modern concept of England did not exist in the early medieval period. The nearest meaning to present-day 'England' is expressed by the word *Angelcynn*, which means the 'English nation', the 'race of the Angles'. This is not a geographical term so much as an ethnographical or cultural one. The physical limits of the *Angelcynn* were therefore the perimeters of the area where the English king (or kings) held sway. In the centuries immediately after Roman rule ceased in Britain there had been a multitude of small tribes, often no larger in extent than a small modern town, the identity of many of which are preserved in England's place-names to this day. These tribes, though more or less successful locally, quickly came under the overall influence of larger groupings, whenever several lesser tribal units combined.

Associated with this movement towards unity under a single chieftainship is the astonishing growth of kingship in England; for kingship and the monarchical system of government were established relatively early, even among peoples such as the Saxons who, in their continental homelands, were 'republican' in constitution and steadfastly resisted the imposition of royal authority on their society.

By the seventh century, a number of independent kingdoms are known to have existed within the English part of Britain. In the course of the next century the number was fixed at seven – the so-called heptarchy of Wessex, Sussex, Kent, Essex, East Anglia, Mercia, and Northumbria. The advent of the Vikings changed the picture so radically, however, that the map of Britain in the ninth century bears little resemblance to the former situation. Scandinavian seafarers landed first along the eastern seaboard, so

that Northumbria (the land north of the Humber) was soon severely destabilised by their attacks. East Anglia (approximately all the eastern counties south of the Humber down to Essex) suffered the same fate soon afterwards. Essex (the modern counties of Essex, Middlesex and Hertfordshire) had already been made a dependency of the Mercian kings by the time the first Norse prow drove on to a British beach, so that, although relatively small and weak, the kingdom's fate was bound up with the dynasty of kings who ruled from the Midlands. The relative wealth and importance of Mercia (which at this time encompassed all England north of the Thames, apart from the regions just mentioned) marked it out as a prime target for raiding and plundering, though the kingdom put up a very stiff resistance.

Kent had always been the gateway to the Continent, and had prospered accordingly since harbours such as Dover offered a convenient and safe passage across the relatively narrow stretch of the straits there to the coast of northern France. Kent had been the home of the Catholic Christian mission to the English, and enjoyed considerable importance as the homeland of the archbishop; continental influence was at work in that kingdom from the very earliest times, and it remained a culturally distinct area even after it was taken over by the Mercian kings. Sussex formed a compact and separate kingdom of relatively little importance in later times, when it fell under the dominion of Wessex, which had itself begun as an outward-looking state based on the upper Thames, where it was ideally placed for expansion in every direction. Having extended their power to the Severn, the Channel coast, and the border (probably the Thames itself) with Mercia, the West Saxon kings set

Anglo-Saxon settlement (above). Timber hall, with timber and wattle-and-daub huts. The buildings were easy to burn and gave little protection.

King David playing the harp, from an eighth-century illuminated miniature, showing a number of musical instruments in use. The central 'harp' is not unlike the lyre found at the Sutton Hoo burial.

about dividing up the land south of the Thames among the various members of the family.

When the Danes finally overcame and overran Mercia, it was left to Wessex to safeguard the future fate of the *Angelcynn* as a sovereign people, for the kings of the other dynasties had largely been murdered and replaced with puppet rulers obedient to the Vikings. If there was any hope of victory over their foes, there was little chance of it coming from anywhere but Wessex. As we know, the West Saxons under the brilliant King Alfred did secure a toehold for the freedom of the English, which successive monarchs of that line were able to build upon. In the process of first ceding territory to the Danes, then reconquering that territory for the English, kings such as Alfred, Edgār and Athelstān also greatly enlarged the areas directly under their own control. Thus by the reign of Edgār all southern and midland England had been subsumed under the blanket-name of Wessex, as far as political power was concerned. The old names lived on – and indeed still do in some cases – but there was never any doubt that the mind that guided the running of these regions was based at Winchester.

In consideration of the feelings of the Mercians, who were at times bitter enemies of the West Saxons, there remained for a while a degree of self-government

for that people, under a ruler chosen not by the Mercians themselves, nor even by the king's advisers, the Witan, but by the king himself, and presumably because the situation demanded it. As we have seen in Ethelred's time, the leader (now styled ealdorman) of the Mercians was a man of some power – albeit notionally derived from the king – and men such as Ælfric could not lightly be taken to task for their actions, however ignominious.

Thus the English became a tripartite people: the southern region, ruled from Winchester but increasingly dominated by the sheer economic importance of London; the midland region, source of much of the nation's wealth – at this time due to its sheep – and retaining the embers of its former independence, and indeed dominance; and the northern region, heavily settled by Vikings and centred around the sometimes-independent kingdom of York, and resentful of outside interference in northern matters.

It is a curious fact that even King Alfred, the great and good king of the West Saxons, calls his speech *Englisc*, and his people *Angelcynn*, never *Seaxisc*, or Saxon. It is worth considering why this should be, when the Saxon part of the nation was no less important than the Anglian, or English.

As we saw at the opening of Chapter 5, there were in Britain five languages according to West Saxon reckoning: English, British, Scottish, Pictish, and 'Book-Latin'. The author of that text probably already had names for the Celtic tongues, and knew that the language of Church and government documents was called Latin; but what of the other languages of Britain, the Germanic tongues of the

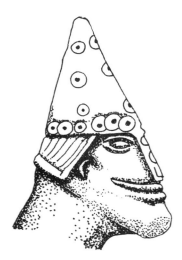

Carved antler from Sigtuna, Sweden, showing the Viking love of personal neatness – a trim hairstyle and moustache, and a conical Norman style of helmet.

lowlands, the south and the east? There was not just one standard speech throughout the Anglo-Saxon lands: every kingdom, every hundred, every village had its peculiar dialect, as they do even today, and the relative isolation of settlements from even their not-too-distant neighbours must have tended to preserve the special characteristics of each local dialect.

Notwithstanding all this, there is no reason to suppose that the language of Wiltshire was so different from that of Warwickshire or Durham that communication was only possible through interpreters. In fact, although there were distinctions of grammar and vocabulary between the various areas, there appears never to have been any real difficulty in communicating, by spoken or written word, between men of the far northern shires and the southern. Alfred himself entertained the Norwegian, Ohthere, and questioned him about circumstances in his homeland, and there is no suggestion that an interpreter was necessary for this conversation. If a West Saxon could make himself understood by a Norseman, and understand him in turn, there is every chance that the divergences in the Anglo-Saxon languages were not inconvenient to the degree that a careful listener could not understand, nor a careful speaker make himself understood.

It seems that the speech of the various peoples who made up the Anglo-Saxon nations was effectively a single language. Why, then, was it called English and the nation known as the 'English people'? The answer is bound up with politics and religion, for while the Anglo-Saxons had long been Christian, and militantly

so, their continental kinsmen the Saxons (often called the Old Saxons to distinguish them from the British Saxons in their newly-won territory) were still a pagan people. Indeed, so stubbornly loyal were they to their heathen gods that the noble Christian king Charles the Great, or Charlemagne, had to resort to offering them the choice between continued heathen-dom and continued life, in order to teach them the Christian message; and so few would bow to this pressure that his men are reported to have beheaded ten thousand Saxons in a single day. For the Christian Anglo-Saxons, it was unthinkable that they should commemorate their kinship with such unmitigated pagans, so the term *Seaxisc* was unfashionable, since to the popular Christian mind it was synonymous with 'pagan' and 'idolatrous'.

The only other major tribes represented in Germanic Britain were the Jutes, who were confined to Kent and the territory stretching from the New Forest to the Isle of Wight. As a term for all the Germanic nations, Jutish was too narrow, for the Jutes were not a major part of the nation as a whole. That left only *Englisc* (i.e. Anglian) as a possible contender, and it had much to recommend it. Firstly, it had no unpleasant overtones of devil-worship and the like. Secondly, according to Bede, writing in the eighth century, the continental Angles had all but disappeared due to the settlement of Britain, which had left their homeland almost deserted, so the likelihood of confusion with continental tribes was negligible. And thirdly, the Angles had, from the earliest days of the settlement of Britain, been numerous and powerful, so that the term was not altogether unfitting as a description of the new nation, the English.

Thus it came about that West Saxon kings were happy to style themselves *Rex Anglorum*, 'King of the English'.

Having thus examined the internal situation of England, the rest of Britain and its neighbours can be inspected.

When the English first came to the island of Britain, they did not drive out or annihilate the prevous inhabitants. They took over the estates and opened up new areas of forest to cultivation, and generally lived side by side with what must have been a more numerous native population of Celtic-speaking peoples. The English had a word for the Celts, *walh*.

The Crundale Sword pommel (seventh century, restored); simple interlace and a pair of opposed animals have ancestors in pagan Germanic art.

E t memoref sunt mandatoz
ipsiuf ad facuendum ea ;

tef uerbu illuif ad au
da uoce fermonum

CIII IPSI O AUTO·

B
ENEDICANIMA
mea dno. dne df meuf

tuum . quiambulaf
pennaf uentozum

Illustration to Psalm 103, from the Harley Psalter, second and third decades of the eleventh century. The Psalter is one of the most significant of all pre-Conquest illuminated manuscripts, an early copy of the Utrecht Psalter, made at Reims. The intention of the illustration for the psalter was to translate the contents of each psalm into visual form.

monti loco dominationef
ei benedic Anima mea dno;

ftabunt aquae
A bincrepatione tua fugi

and the plural of the word, *wealas*, gives the modern name for the Celtic area of southern Britain – 'Wales'. Of course, the *wealas*, the Welshmen, who continued to live among the English soon lost their distinctive Celtic culture, though it is true to say that a great many folk customs found in England today originated with the Celts, or their predecessors: such things as Morris dancing, veneration of wells (as when a coin is thrown in for 'good luck'), veneration of trees (as when the action of 'touching wood' is used to avert some evil), and so on.

As late as the ninth century, communities of Welsh-speakers were living among the, by then, predominantly English-speaking peoples of southern Britain. But as the English drove west, conquering through battles and sieges, or just enlarging their lands into the untilled no-man's-land, the Welsh tongue retreated before them. By the time of Alfred Wales consisted of the lands west of Offa's Dyke, and the lands west of Alfred's own kingdom, so that Devon and Cornwall were still foreign territory, not in the hands of a friendly power. Gradually, during the next century, the border was fixed between England and West Wales, as it was known, at the Tamar, and finally the *Cornwalas*, the Celtic people called *Cornovii*, were absorbed into England politically, though their Celtic speech did not die out until the 1700s, and has been artificially revived in modern times.

The more numerous and more stubborn Welshmen in the great western bulge of Britain constituted a more intractable problem than the *Cornwalas*. Not only were they secure enough in their mountainous country against any but an all-out invasion, for which the English had neither the resources nor the will, they also had sufficient strength and political will for some of their kingdoms to form alliances under a single leader. One such was the Welsh King Cadwallon, who formed an unexpected federation with the ruthless pagan King Penda of Mercia, and played no small part in the Mercian campaigns against Northumbria.

It is likely that the early history of the Welsh kingdoms contained many such episodes, where changing political conditions caused unlikely co-operations between peoples who might be expected to be deadly enemies. The Welsh example of uniting in the face of attack was not followed by the English, however, when the Danish menace first appeared. Indeed, the various English kingdoms seem to have shown precious little resolve to repel the Danes, merely to deflect their attentions towards neighbours.

Winnowing the corn with flails – the month of December from a late Anglo-Saxon calendar.

Once the consequences of this lack of concerted effort for the common good became clear, and only a small stronghold in the Somerset marshes stood between England and the Vikings, there still persisted the feeling that the preservation of Wessex was enough – though fortunately Alfred's descendants had the perspicacity to understand that real security for Wessex depended upon the incorporation of the Danes into England.

Wales was affected by the Danish invasions much less than her neighbours, and there is scant trace of the Viking presence in the history of Wales: much less than in Scotland, England, Ireland, or northern France. It is hard to account for this, but the fact remains that the Vikings had less impact upon the Welsh than upon the other peoples they came into contact with. Certainly, there are examples of Viking activity along the coast of Wales, for example the Norse pirates Broðir and Ōspākr who raided along the coasts of the Irish sea in the eleventh century. Somehow the natural resilience of the Celts was distilled into the Cymry in more than usual measure, and they reaped the benefit. Yet all was not plain sailing for them: the English, under a fresh impulse for political expansion with the concentration of their whole strength into one king's rule, were not content to allow the Welsh freedom to harbour the enemy, and in the end came to see Welsh independence as a threat to English security.

However, it did not come to a trial of strength, for from the 920s the Welsh came under the rule of King Hywel Dda, an exceptional ruler with a strong respect for English kingship, which he used as a model for reform in his own dominions. His attitude seems to have disarmed his English critics, and left the way open for friendly relations to develop with Athelstān's government. This did not prevent Athelstān from effectively ending Cornish independence, however, which suggests that by his time the two Welsh regions were not conceived of as a single entity, a larger kingdom of the Welsh straddling the Severn.

Later English kings could call on the kings of Wales for military aid, and not infrequently did so; there must have been some treaty or pact between the two royal lines which gave the Welsh kings some claim on the English monarchy. The last vestiges of Welsh autonomy did not disappear until the high Middle Ages, after the Welsh campaigns of the

Edwardian kings, and the defiant struggle of Owen Glendower.

The history of Scotland during this period is somewhat obscure; that is to say, the history of the lands to the north of the English is often difficult to discern. The very name 'Scotland' tells a story: the Scoti were an Irish tribe, who began to have increased contact with mainland Britain during the last years of Roman rule. Like the Saxons, the Scoti came as raiders and plunderers, and also like the Saxons they began to take over parts of the island as their own territory. Legend has it that the Saxons had first been called into the country to help defend it against this menace from the north. The first settlements were in the western isles, until a bridgehead was established on the mainland, the kingdom of Dal Riada. This expanded slowly into Caledonia, which was inhabited by Picts, an ancient and enigmatic people who had been partly Celticised during the preceding thousand years of domination of Britain by Celtic tribes, but who nevertheless retained echoes of an older culture. Thus it came about that there were two separate and dissimilar nations inhabiting the land north of England, while a native British enclave persisted west of the Pennines in the Kingdoms of Galloway and Strathclyde.

What might have been the outcome if this state had persisted is questionable, though the history of Scotland (if there had been a 'Scotland' to have such a history) would undoubtedly have been very different. But a new element entered the equation, and from an unexpected direction: Norse farmers who had settled in the Orkneys began spreading south, and came at last to Sutherland, the 'Southern land' – which, of course, it is to Norwegians approaching by way of the Atlantic islands, though from a British viewpoint it is the northernmost region of the mainland. In the centuries of Norse expansion, the various Norwegian possessions were consolidated into a district, a jarldom administered by jarls who were at least notionally dependant on Norwegian authority, though many of them had other ideas. Thus the political map of Britain in the time of Ethelred shows Saxon Wessex, Anglian Mercia and Northumbria; to their west were the Welsh of Wales, Strathclyde (and, arguably, also of Cornwall); to the east were the ex-Danelaw territorities of East Anglia; and the kingdom of York, and to the north the Pictish-Scottish kingdom of Alban. To the north of Alban was the Norse area of Sutherland (though probably nominally still part of Pictland), and Norsemen also

Few representations exist from the Viking Age of men in horned helmets. This figure from Birka was probably an amulet. A similar figure occurs in the Oseberg Tapestry and it is likely that horned figures were symbols of power drawn from Scandinavia.

infested most of the Irish Sea coasts, including the Isle of Man, Cumbria and Lancashire.

The varying political situations between these groups seem not to have hampered freedom of movement – for the wealthy at least – nor to have inhibited trade and administrative intercourse between them. Welsh merchants are recorded as having their own section of the city of Exeter, suggesting long-term and lucrative commercial contact requiring a permanent presence in the city. Irishmen, or perhaps Irish-Norse, seem to have had an equally important presence in other parts of the country. The picture is one of close and continuing contact.

Mention of Irishmen brings us to the situation in Ireland, which was seldom peaceful after the advent of the Vikings, until the Normans imposed their own brand of law and order in the 1100s. In fact, in 1014 – the year England received its first Danish king – the Celtic Irish fought a great battle against the Norsemen at Clontarf, outside Dublin, which was supposed to break the power of the Vikings forever in Ireland. The Irish gained a great propaganda victory, but little really changed and Dublin, the centre of Irish commerce, remained in Viking hands. Intermarriage, or more probably miscegenation, between the Vikings and the natives introduced a new element into Irish history, the Gaill Gaedhil, a sort of half-caste group with considerable nuisance value; they seem to have been in disfavour with both sides and to have formed a warrior society of mercenaries.

Beyond Ireland the 'English world' extended out into the boundless sea, on which supposedly existed such marvels as floating islands, and the like; but aside from the tall tales of seafarers, Norse expansion brought knowledge of Iceland – which had strong trade links with the West Country – and Greenland.

Beyond there lay the almost unexplored lands of Markland, Helluland and Vīnland, areas of the North American Atlantic seaboard. Though no Englishman ventured so far, Icelanders certainly visited England, and possibly some English monastics may have journeyed in the opposite direction after the conversion of Iceland to Christianity in the year 1000.

Travelling eastwards from Britain, the English knew of the various Baltic lands; as noted earlier, a ship's captain called Wulfstān visited the southern Baltic coasts during King Alfred's reign. Although the Baltic was many days' sailing distant, precise and detailed information was available on how to get there, which cargoes could be obtained, where the most convenient ports were, and so on. The English originated in the Jutland peninsula and evidently kept contact with their ancient homeland and its neighbours. English churchmen succeeded in bringing the art of the manuscript to Norway, and Anglo-Saxon letters and spelling had some influence in early Norwegian written records.

Soon after the conversion of the major English kingdoms, and while the minor ones were still heathen for the most part, the English church began the work of bringing the Christian faith to Germany, to the peoples with whom they shared a common tradition: the tribes dwelling along the lower reaches of the Rhine. Contact with this region had never been severed, and peoples such as the Frisians played a larger part than is generally realised in English history. Frisian seamen were used by King Alfred to man and run his fleet of ships against the Danes; Frisian traders and merchants were common in the southern and eastern towns, such as London and Lincoln. Frisian slave-merchants bought up the surplus captives taken in the early wars between the English kingdoms. For good or ill, the men of

Agricultural tools: an iron pick-axe head (above) and scythe-blade, tenth century, from County Durham, England. Compare the harvesters' scythes on p.69.

Monstrous serpents and a centaur from Marvels of the East. *One of thirty-seven illustrations with accompanying text in Latin and Old English. Second quarter of the eleventh century. One of the most lavish of surviving non-liturgical books from the early Middle Ages.*

Flanders and the Frisian islands played a major part in the economic life of England, particularly in overseas trade, which relied on Frisian vessels. Indeed, they dominated shipping in the North Sea and traded as far east as Birka in Sweden, until the combined attentions of the Vikings and the Holy Roman Empire reduced their influence.

Ranging even further afield, Englishmen were familiar with France and Italy, and English pilgrims journeying to Rome were a familiar sight on the Continent. Many early kings made the trip, which evidently carried with it a good deal of glory, as well as the presumed spiritual advantages of making an arduous trip to the Holy City. The young Alfred visited it twice, and saw much among a widely-literate and well-regulated people to open his eyes to the possibilities for good government. He established a voluntary payment to the church in Rome from his private income, and undoubtedly his future career was influenced by the knowledge he gained, particularly the wider perspective of a European rather than parochial British outlook. King Knut also visited Rome during his reign over England, and negotiated a better deal for his subjects travelling there.

English churchmen had contacts with the church in Greece, and probably other more distant lands; for example, Coptic influence has been suggested in some

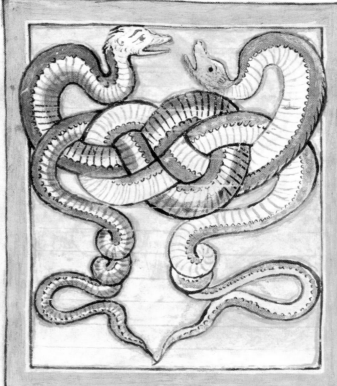

ȝyr hi þyltne mon ondam landū oriʒiað
odde ȝe reod þonne reonpuað hi irleod꞉~

Post hunc locum alia est regio oceano dex
teriore parte· stadia· cccxxii· quæ faciunt
leuuas· cci· ii· & miliariū unū ubi nascuntur
homodubii quisq̄· ad umbilicū hominis spe
cie habent reliq̄ corpore onagro similes· lon
gis pedib·: ut aues· lena uoce sed hominē cum
uiderint longe fugiunt· ∴

þa hyrre stope ir oðer pice on ða ruðhalre
þær ȝypsecʒes· þir ȝeteald þær læppan
milʒe teler rtadia· ccc· ȝþireo irþenuȝ þær
midan ðe leuua hatte· cci· u· ȝanimil· þær
beoð kende homodubii þat byð tpylice hi
beoð oððene napelan onmennircū ȝercape
rryðdan on eorcler ȝercape hihabbað lonʒ
reranican rpa pugelas ȝliðelice ræprne

Est & alius locus hominū barbarorum ha
bens sub se regem numero· cx· gem pessimū
& barbarorū est· Sunt & alibi loci duo· Unus
solis & alius lunæ qui solis est die calidus
nocte frigidus q̄ lunæ· e· nocte calidus die
frigidus longitudo eorum· cc· stadia st q̄ faciunt
leuuas· cxxxii· & dimidiū miliarium· ∴

Don ir oðer rtop ellreoðre menbeoð on þa
habbað kyninʒar under him ðæra ir ȝeteald
cx· þ ryndon ða þyrstan men ȝþa ellreon
drȝeftan þær ryndan· ii· readar oðer · ȝ unnan
ȝ oðer monan· Se ðe punnan ir re biȝ dæȝer
hat ȝ nihrer ceald· ȝ re ðe monan ir

aspects of Anglo-Saxon manuscript design. These contacts may have been through Italy, however, since there is little evidence for English travellers journeying so far off, though after the Norman Conquest a good many Englishmen took service with the Varangian Guard, the Eastern Roman Emperor's private bodyguard which had hitherto consisted exclusively of Scandinavians. The countries bordering the Mediterranean were familiar, in name at least, due to the translation of various books of classical learning into Old English and from Bible stories. There also seems to have been a body of folk-knowledge concerning the overthrow of the Roman Empire by the Goths, which dealt with events known to have occurred on the other side of the Alps.

Exactly what the average English ploughmen or neat-herds understood of all this geography is not

An Old Testament story in Anglo-Saxon guise: a shepherd with a staff guards his flock (centre) while farm labourers dig with one-sided spades (top left).

certain. For the most part, they probably retained the world-view of their forefathers: above them was Heofon, the home of the world's creator, in the sky; beneath was hell, the region of darkness and monsters. The geographical world, that men knew, was a part of Middangeard (the Middle Enclosure) about which lay the Outer Sea, on whose further shores dwelt giants and devils. The Middle Enclosure was in the middle, therefore, of a 'sandwich' of Heaven and Hell, as well as being in the middle of the surrounding sea. This cosmography predates Christianity – the heathen Vikings knew a broadly similar conception – and was little affected by the discovery of new lands further east or north, south or west, because these additions required only the extension of the notional distances within Middangeard; the system as a whole could accommodate the new knowledge without any fundamental change. Indeed, the general image of the lands of men existing above the realms of the dead, and beneath the heavenly dwellings persisted into relatively recent times.

chapter 7

the classes of men

It is a truism that English society of the period was composed of a number of different grades or classes of people, each of whom had specific and particular rights and duties under the law. Unfortunately, Old English terminology is unhelpful in defining and describing these classes, and so it is unwise to conclude that what we consider to have been the situation in the south-east in the eighth century, for example, would have been the same as in the north in the tenth century.

Broadly speaking, the social system consisted of three main grades: nobles, freemen and slaves. The origins of these classes will be looked at in the following sections, but it is well to bear in mind that the divisions between even these three groups was never precisely determined; social mobility seems to have been a factor also, with some men rising in status with accumulated wealth, and others becoming impoverished by the wars.

I have chosen to start the examination of the system at the top with the kings and their families, for it is of them that we know most.

the kings

The office of kingship among the Anglo-Saxons was very different from the office which has inherited the name today. For a king was expected – indeed, required – to rule as well as reign, and a king who lacked the power or ability to control his kingdom was not tolerated for long.

The Saxon 'gnomic verse' preserved in *The Exeter Book* begins with the words: *Cyning sceal rice healdan*, 'a king must hold his domain': his first duty was to protect and maintain his lands and all they contained. To help him do this the king had a network of local representatives, known variously as thanes, reeves, sheriffs, portreeves and ealdormen (although this list is not exhaustive). As the focal point of his people's hopes, and the figurehead of the nation's pride, the king was also responsible for conducting their military campaigns and (in the heathen period at least) for seeing that the gods and lesser spirits were favourably disposed to men. The earliest Germanic kings are believed to have been priests, and certainly something of the majesty and awe which surrounds priests, magicians and healers attached itself to the concept of kingship.

I have implied above that a kingdom had only one king at any time, but this was far from the case. *Cyning*, the word for king, describes any adult male member of the royal family, and the monarch could be chosen from any of those who were eligible. It may seem strange that kings should need to be chosen, because the tradition and rules of succession now dictate who will succeed the current monarch on his or her death. But in earlier times, uncontested accession to the throne was the exception rather than the rule. Even when a king had been enthroned there were often unelected relatives waiting for a chance to sieze power. Sometimes brothers ruled jointly, though how this worked in practice is unclear: did the elder brother take precedence over his kinsmen, or did they simply share out the royal revenue between them, and still live relatively well? King Alfred's brothers succeeded to their father's patrimony in order of seniority, and it was merely the working of chance – or perhaps the hand of God – that allowed him to come to the throne in time to save his kingdom.

Royal power was founded on a variety of things:

tradition, wealth, and personality were among the most important. The impulse to choose the son or nearest adult male relative of the former ruler as king was established early, yet this was never a formally encoded practice. The very act of 'election', which in practical terms meant the acceptance of the would-be monarch by the rich and powerful men he hoped to govern, was also seen as a mandate for rule. With the growth in church power, the idea grew up that the king was in some special way 'chosen by God' for the kingship. This notion spawned the doctrine of the Divine Right of Kings, by which, since God had chosen him to rule, the king's will must coincide with that of the Almighty.

The wealth that a king might accumulate was derived from a number of sources, chief of which was the tax that every landowner owed him, known as the 'king's farm', which notionally represented provisions for one night's lodging for the king and his retinue. This was a payment of food for the consumption of the royal party on the nearest estate belonging to the king. He also had a right to a proportion of all legal fines imposed under his law, and as head of the military he had the opportunity to acquire a great deal of plunder if his campaigns were successful. Merchants and foreigners entering the country paid a levy to the king's reeve which went into the royal coffers, as did certain sales taxes.

A man could sometimes become king by sheer force of personality, through being the 'right man for the job' at the time. One such was Athelstan, who was an illegitimate son of Edward; another example is Edmund Ironside, whom the nation preferred to his father and to his rival, Knut. Knut himself only managed to hold together his possessions in England and Scandinavia through his great energy and masterful character; his North Sea empire fell apart on his death because it had been too narrowly based on the king's personality.

To the king were owed, aside from taxes, the three duties to which exceptions were not granted: service in the army, construction of strongholds and repair of bridges. Locally he might have other specific rights, such as in coastal regions, where his subjects should keep a watch on the seas for enemy fleets. Even monasteries were expected to play a full role in the essential public duties.

It was one of the king's duties to ensure that the legal system was administered fairly, and anyone who thought that he or she had been unjustly or harshly dealt with could appeal to the king as a higher authority. In this role, it became the accepted practice

A tenth-century English ring, in which a Roman gem has been re-set in a new mount. The Roman empire held a fascination for the early medieval mind, due to its former glory and its unique place in Christian tradition.

for kings to issue law codes detailing what might or might not be done, and what fines or punishments should apply if the law was broken. Thus royal authority was bound up firmly with the rule of law, and both the kingship and the law benefited. We hear little of the workings of the legal system until comparatively late, but it is known that the prisons were situated on royal estates, and that men held in prison were fed by their kinsmen or friends, and so not provided for out of royal expenditure.

At the far-off time of the English arrival in Britain, the king was the leader of a group of warriors who contended with other such war-bands for wealth and prestige. Under this system, the giving of presents to followers, particularly the public bestowal of jewellery and gold, played an important part. On the king's favour rested the fighting man's status, while the king's own status among his peers rested on the warriors' readiness to fight for him. This complex relationship between warrior and ruler remained, at least vestigially, into much later times. It was reflected

Eleventh-century English weapons (above): an iron spear or dart-head, characteristic of the Anglo-Saxon warrior of all periods, and (right) a broad-edged axe blade associated with Knut's housecarls, the first English Royal Household Troops.

lower down the social scale in the practice of local leaders banqueting their retainers and handing out gifts, as we have already noted in connection with ealdorman Byrhtnōth, whose ungrateful follower Godric should have remembered the gifts of fine horses made to him by the eorl.

How did an English king regard his duty to rule? Fortunately, we have King Alfred's words on this subject:

> . . . the greed and the ambition of this earthly rule never pleased me overmuch, nor did I yearn too greatly for this earthly kingdom, though I wished for tools and materials for the work which I was bidden to carry out, which was that I should guide and rule, fittingly and honourably, the dominion which has been entrusted to me. Look! You know that no man can bring forth any skill, nor rule nor steer any dominion, without tools and materials. It is the material of any craft without which one cannot carry out that craft. It is, then, the material and tools of a king with which to rule, that he should have his land properly staffed. He must have prayer-men, and military men, and workmen. Thus, you know that without these tools no king can make his skill known. Also, his material is the sustenance of the three orders which are his tools. This, then, is their sustenance: land to dwell in, and gifts, and weapons, and food, and ale, and clothes, and every [other] thing which the three orders need. He cannot wield the tools without these things, nor without these tools carry out any of the things which he is ordered to bring about. For this reason, I wished for materials with which to rule, so that my skills would not be hidden and forgotten. Therefore each craft and each power will soon to be worn out and passed over without remark if it is without wisdom; for no man can bring forth any skill without wisdom, because what is done in folly may never be thought a skill. It should now be said at once that I wished to live honourably while I was alive, and after my life to leave to the men who come after me my memory in good works.

When not actively involved in the exercise of royal authority, the king's time was spent in feasting and hunting and in entertaining guests. Religion seems to have played a considerably larger part in some kings' lives than others.

the noblemen

As in later society, the nobles were divided into grades according to wealth and favours enjoyed. For the purposes of classification, I have split the land-owning classes into 'noblemen' and 'thanes', who are dealt with later. The noblemen include the minor members of the royal family, high-ranking church-men and local governors. The last group also includes *sub-reguli*, men who retain the title 'king', but whose authority is dependant on some outside power.

The mark of the class of noblemen was their vast and widespread ownership of estates; ealdorman Byrhtnōth is an example of this, and not an extreme one. His land-holdings were centred on the south-east and East Anglia. His properties were managed by reeves, who supervised the running of the farms, looked after the ealdorman's interests locally, and acted on his behalf. The ealdorman moved around from one estate to the next, consuming the foods which were his due as lord of the district and settling any disputes arising on his land.

In many ways, the life of the nobleman was little different from that of the king, though on a smaller scale. Noblemen had no direct connection with law-making, however, and enjoyed less legal protection than kings.

The main contribution of the upper strata of society to the rule of the king was through the body known as the Witan ('wise men') who were the king's councillors, ministers and governors. The Witan had to formally accept a new king as their lord, and were directly responsible for the management of affairs within their allotted regions. The leading men of the church were also members of the Witan, and men such as Dunstān, whom Byrhtnōth persuaded King Edgār to recall from exile, played a leading part in contemporary life at court. The royal advisers some-times acted in the national interest against the king: for example, in having Edwȳ deposed in favour of his brother Edgār. But generally they seem to have constituted a body of experienced, skilful and powerful men whose co-operation would be needed for the king to rule effectively, and whose views the king could ignore only at great peril to himself.

The councillors convened regularly at a royal estate for a *witenagemōt* ('meeting of wise men') to discuss affairs of state and propose measures to deal with threats from within or without. These meetings constituted an opportunity for leaders from all over the country to settle differences and to make the king aware of matters of particular concern to them. Yet the suggestion that this was some sort of early Parliament is misleading. Ealdormen were chosen by the king and his Witan, not elected through the ballot-box, and they served the interests of the men of their districts only in so far as these coincided with their own. Cynical readers may argue that this is still the case, but the Witan had no electorate to please, no party-line to adhere to, and no theory of social reconstruction to advance.

Whatever may have been the benefits of the advisers in curbing the excesses of this or that king, their most obvious and tangible legacy to us is the patronage of artists and craftsmen. Only when there is a multitude of works can some small part survive for a thousand years. Though we have seemingly few manuscripts, few really good pieces of fine jewellery, and fewer still fine buildings, the fact of the survival of the little we possess points to a profusion at the time

A bronze amulet in the shape of Thor from Iceland. Sagas mention that it was not uncommon for men sometimes carried such amulets in their purses. By far the most common amulet found is the Hammer of Thor.

The buddha from Helgo in Sweden is a sign of Scandinavia's links with the East. It was a search for new trade routes that led to the Swedish expansion along the Russian waterways and the establishment of the Viking kingdoms in Russia.

when these things were made. Some periods were apparently better suited to the production of such artefacts than others, and of course very little survives from the earliest years of Anglo-Saxon England – due as much to the covetousness of the descendants of the Anglo-Saxons, who were the more ready to melt down and reuse the precious materials of their

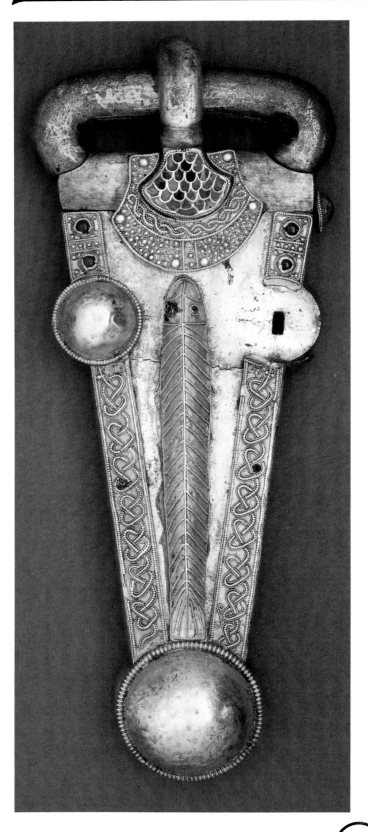

Beautifully wrought, inlaid buckle from Crundale Down. Anglo-Saxon.

ancestors because the artefacts did not suit their new tastes, as to the raiding of the Vikings and the wilful ignorance of the Normans.

the thanes

The word 'thane' (Old English *đegn*) strictly means 'servant', and has a common source with the Greek *teknon*, (boy, assistant). Its use as a title of honour derives from the early English kingdoms, when the king would give land to one of his followers, who became his servant in accepting it. Thus the name 'servant (of the king)' came to be used for 'landowner, leader'; another Saxon word *ombeht* shows a similar development from 'servant' to 'king's official'.

The common qualification for the office of thane was the possession of five 'hides' of land; that is the thane owned enough land for five families to earn their livelihood from. This does not necessarily mean that he was of enormous wealth otherwise, but rather that he had a specific and customary stake in the well-being of the kingdom. Landowners, above all other sorts of wealthy men, dislike unrest and civil disturbances of any sort, and they have everything to lose if their district is overrun by foreigners or devastated by disease or natural disaster. Thus, the custom was that no amount of movable property, even if it was of the same kind as a thane had to possess, could make a freeman into a thane, unless he had the five hides as well. Equally, the son of a thane who no longer possessed the land entitlement had only 'freeman' status.

An eleventh-century source gives the following list of things a freeman must acquire in order to move up the social scale: five hides of land; a church; a kitchen; a bell-tower; a fortified gate; a seat in the king's hall and a particular duty. Another means of acquiring the status was if a merchant made three voyages abroad as master of his own vessel.

The English reconquest of the Danelaw was achieved in part by the militarisation of the whole class of thanes; instead of being simply landed gentry, they formed a group comparable with the later medieval class of 'knights'. The mention of 'fortified gate' suggests that their residences were seen as strongholds; indeed, the thane's hall and attendant buildings, including a church and bell-house, surrounded by a defensive palisade, constituted the Saxon *burh*, or 'fort', which was used as a local

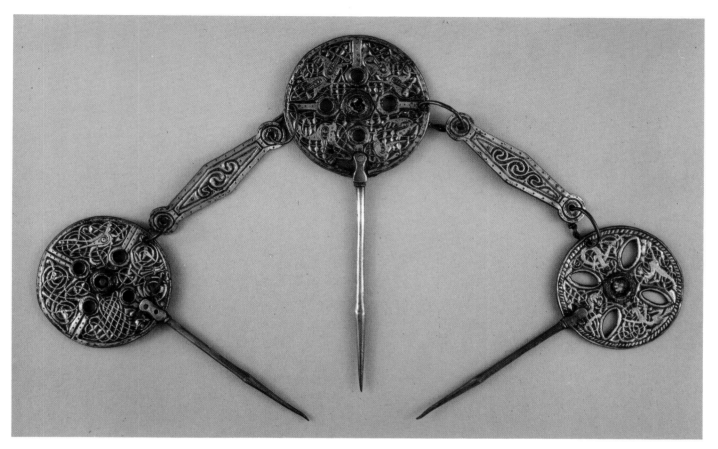

Three pins taken from the River Witham.

fortification in time of attack. Such forts could also act as garrison points for the warriors in the thanes' retinue, and they generally grew in economic importance. Many are still towns today.

On inheriting or acquiring his rank, the thane of the king or an ealdorman became liable to the king for four helmets, which suggests that he was expected to maintain his own force of soldiers within the fyrd, the national army. According to a statute dating to 1008, each man owning eight or more hides (all but the poorest thanes) had to present himself for military service wearing a helmet and a mail-coat, another indication that the rank of thane was primarily military in character by then. They were the backbone of the English military force, for at this time it was found to be impractical to keep large numbers of men supplied with food and accommodation for the duration of a campaign. The simplest and best solution of the problem was to reduce the numbers of men under arms while ensuring that each one was well-equipped and trained. Smaller armies are faster, more manoeuvrable and more easily controlled.

The wealthier members of the thane class were probably no less wealthy than the noblemen themselves; one Wulfric is known to have owned no less than seventy-two estates outside his holdings in south Lancashire and the Wirral. Though he was clearly a rich and powerful man, and a member of a vastly wealthy family, his possessions could probably have been matched by others in his day below the rank of ealdorman. Women could also own land in their own right, and many no doubt had sufficient to rival the thanes and churchmen; as we have seen, Byrhtnōth's sister-in-law disposed of a good many estates in her will.

As commanders of local militia and upholders of the law on the lands they owned, the thanes performed the function of town-governors. In Saxon law, each class had a wergild ('man-price'), which was the amount a murderer had to pay to the relatives of a man he had killed in atonement for his crime. For an ordinary freeman this sum was fixed at six hundred shillings; for a thane it was twelve hundred; the only evidence we have suggests that for an ealdorman or earl it was four times this. In theory, a king had no wergild since the slaying of a king could not be atoned for with money: even to attack a king was punishable by death and forfeiture of all possessions, whether the attack was actual, or 'intended' by harbouring the king's enemies. For practical legal purposes, where it was necessary to have a notional wergild so that compensations to the king could be paid (these were sometimes expressed as multiples or fractions of the injured party's wergild) a king's price was set at fifteen times that of a thane, making it a very costly business to trespass against the king.

the freemen

The class of freemen comprised the lower ranks of English society, above the 'unfree' or slaves. It was subdivided into a number of different grades or ranks, which varied across the nation and during the course of the period. Broadly speaking, the highest grade of freeman, who could be every bit as wealthy as his superior the thane, was the *geneat*, otherwise known in Danelaw areas as the *dreng*. (*Dreng* was to the Norse what 'knight' was to the medieval English mind, and 'chivalry' was rendered by *drengskapr*, *dreng*-ship or 'knighthood'.) The *eald geneat* ('old retainer') Byrhtwōld at Maldon showed considerable loyalty to his lord, proper (to the medieval mind) to a certain social position and high birth. Such a man was probably an independently wealthy landowner with considerable estates, which he would have inherited from his family and would pass on in turn to his children. Such men held their lands outright, paid rent and rendered service to the king, though their service was usually not connected so much with food-production as providing a watch over the highways and escorts for the king, his envoys and guests; from this comes their Midlands title of *rādcnihtas* (riding-knights). Their wergild is usually given as six hundred shillings.

Below the *geneat* was the so-called *gafolgelda*, or rent-payer, a tenant farmer, whose landholding was based on some kind of lease, though the details are obscure. Similar in kind was the *gebūr*, with a wergild of two hundred shillings. He rendered service to his lord, usually two day's work a week, and three at harvest-time and sowing-time, a rent of tenpence at Michaelmas, twenty-three measures of barley and two hens at Martinmas, followed by a lamb at Easter, and also had to share in the shepherding of his lord's flock and the ploughing of his lord's fields. For this undertaking, the lord (that is, the legal owner of the

Englishmen at work: the ploughman with his team of oxen (centre); the harper and smith (top); a householder in discussion with his family. From a manuscript c. AD 1000.

land) provided the farmer with a quarter of a hide of land, two oxen, a cow, six sheep, his farm tools, his domestic implements, and seven acres of land already sown with seed. The tenant was thus equipped to go about his business on the land, and the demands of food-rent and money-rent were a kind of 'interest' payment on the initial outlay. Ordinarily, the land and equipment remained the lord's property and reverted to him on the tenant's death, though a farmer who prospered to the extent that he accumulated sufficient wealth could presumably buy the freehold of the land from the lord if both agreed the price. Though this sounds a heavy burden on the farmer, it was not impossibly severe since the numbers of *gebūras* were great. It should not be forgotten that even a *gebūr* might have a slave or two to help him.

Cotsetlan were a grade lower than *gebūras* in the hierarchy, and held so little land – five acres – that they paid no rent, but did service instead. This rank may have consisted of manumitted slaves who could find no other livelihood.

The name for the class of freemen as a whole was *ceorlas*, and aside from the main landowning and agricultural types there were also free merchants, free smiths, free carpenters, indeed many of the artisan class were churls. In his *Colloquy on the Occupations*, Ælfric, the noted grammarian, puts forward the following conversation between a *mangere* or merchant and an inquirer into the nature of various occupations men follow:

> 'What do you say, merchant?' [concerning his way of life]
> 'I say that I am most useful to the king, and to the ealdormen, and to the wealthy and to all men.'
> 'How?'
> 'I go out on my ship with my freight, and travel across the sea, and sell goods, and buy costly things such as are not to be found in this country; and I bring them to you here over the sea with great peril; and sometimes I suffer shipwreck, so that all my goods are lost to me, and I myself hardly come out of it alive.'
> 'What sorts of thing do you bring here across the sea?'
> 'Purple cloaks, silk, rare garments, herbs and spices, wine, oil, ivory, costly jewels, gold, tin, brass, copper, silver, glass, and many other things besides.'

Some of these imports, such as the metals and wine,

An Irish iron-bound bucket found at the Oseberg ship burial. The Viking kingdom in Dublin was a great centre of commerce. Trade as well as war took place between the Vikings, England and Ireland.

A panel showing Sigurd roasting slices of dragon's heart. Myth played an important role in Anglo-Saxon and Viking life; and gave many people examples of how the various classes were expected to live.

oil and glass, were familiar in England though still part of a luxury-goods trade in and out of the country. The merchant does not specify what goods he takes from England to sell, but other evidence suggests that wool and woollen goods had always been a mainstay of the export trade. By selling his English woollen cloaks on the Continent for a profit and then making a shrewd investment in some

precious and unusual commodity to bring back with him, a merchant could make a good return on a sea-voyage, though he would have to pay a toll or customs-dues to the king in the foreign port, and his English home would be assessed by the king for taxes in the same way as any other freeman's possessions; he would not be able to avoid liability simply by being absent, since the king could seize his property if he failed to render his dues.

An apparent anomaly in the Anglo-Saxon class system is the existence of the *wealas* (Welshmen) in independent settlements, who sometimes appear to have the status of slaves, yet whose position in regard to the law seems to have differed from that of slaves proper. They probably represent the last vestiges of a subject British population, ruled by Anglo-Saxons and lower in status in the eyes of the law, yet not actually legal slaves owned by a master. In Alfred's time and beyond there existed men known as *wealh-stodas* (interpreters) who acted as go-betweens and representatives of the Welsh-speaking communities.

Minstrels, poets and entertainers were also usually of churl status, as were many clerics and monks. For some of these men, the church offered an escape from the rigours of farmwork, as well as spiritual advancement. The decision to become a monk could theoretically not be taken by anyone lower than a freeman, since he would not be legally at liberty to determine his own future: he would be arrogating his master's authority in entering the church without first having obtained his lord's permission.

In all, the lot of the freeman class was not as dire as may sometimes be thought. Great store was set by communal entertainments to relieve the grinding monotony from the everyday agricultural round. Riddles, some translated from Latin but most native, were popular, as well as the composition of poetry to the accompaniment of the harp. As we know from the story of Caedmon, even the cowherds and farm-workers would gather together in the evening to drink beer and pass around the harp; there can be no clearer indication that these men of the *ceorl* class had some leisure hours after the day's work was done, and that

Noah's Ark from the Anglo-Saxon illustrated Hexateuch, *second quarter of the eleventh century. This is a translation from the Latin into Old English of early chapters of the Old Testament. It is unique, an illustrated copy in the vernacular, although it may originally have been just one of a number of translations produced for lay patrons.*

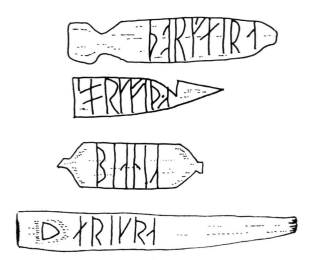

Viking runic 'name-tags' from Bergen. These were used by merchants to identify their cargoes, perhaps by attaching the tags to bales and sacks, or to the strapping which secured them.

they had the raw materials to brew their own beer. The fact that they were expected to be able to construct verses while strumming or plucking at the harp-strings also betokens a fairly sophisticated group of individuals, who could appreciate a well-wrought piece of verse and a skilfully-played air; they were certainly not the barbarous rustics of popular imagination.

the unfree

This group, known in Old English as *theow* ('servant'), probably constituted the major part of the workforce in earlier times, when war-captives could be cheaply bought. The group divided into two categories: those who were born unfree (in deference to the principal that the son of a slave is also a slave), and those who were 'penal slaves'. The first category was composed of captives and other men bought specifically for the purpose of serving the purchaser. In times of desperate famine, men with no hope of saving themselves would sometimes sell themselves into servitude in order to have a better chance of regular meals.

The penal slaves were freemen who had committed some crime for which the penalty was loss of freeman status; such crimes included working on Sundays (except at one's lord's command) and stealing. A man's relatives could buy him out of slavery by offering the owner his wergild as a freeman, for as a slave he had no wergild at all. Thus if a freeman killed

a slave he needed only pay the owner the nominal value of the slave as a possession, usually one pound, the equivalent of eight oxen. Slaves could be bought and sold in the same way that other livestock was exchanged – equally, without legal status and a wergild, slaves could not be fined for their misdeeds. They were usually punished either by flogging or by mutilation; the death penalty was used sparingly, since it was bad policy to destroy one's stock except where unavoidable.

If the master chose to pay the fine for the crime the slave would be spared any public, legal punishment; if the master chose to mistreat or kill the slave the law would not prevent him, though the church frowned on this as unchristian behaviour. Indeed, the church seems to have been in some doubt about slavery in general, and did not feel at all comfortable about allowing fellow Christian men to be held like chattels, which was strictly counter to the notion of man created in God's image. It was soon felt to be unrighteous to sell one's countrymen abroad into the hands of foreigners (for example, the Frisians) and this practice was made illegal in the late 600s, although it undoubtedly continued into the Viking Age. Stories of saints' lives often contain scenes where the holy man intervenes to protect a servant from unjust or unduly severe punishment. Some churchmen even took positive steps to affect the lot of slaves, by setting aside money for the purchase of worthy bondsmen from their owners.

Harvesting the corn with sickles: two men carry the mown stems to the cart where another lifts them with a pitchfork; the overseer has an early English equivalent of a factory hooter!

What were the slave's duties? It seems probable that the most menial and distasteful tasks were reserved for the unfree, since freemen might be expected to decline the worst sorts of work, while bondsmen and women had no choice. Thus the ditch-digging, muck-spreading, tree-cutting and similar tasks would be left to those in no position to rebel against doing them. In his *Colloquy on the Occupations*, Ælfric has this conversation between his inquirer and a ploughman:

> 'What have you to say, ploughman? How do you go about your craft?'
> 'See, lord, how hard I toil! Each day I have to go out at dawn. Then I have to drive the oxen up to the ploughland, and yoke them to the plough. No winter is so severe that I should dare to rest at home – I dare not for fear of my lord. And when I have got the oxen yoked up, and have fastened the ploughshare and the coulter on the plough, I have to till a full acre or more.'
> 'Do you have any assistant?'
> 'Yes, I have a boy, who must drive the oxen on with a goad. He is hoarse now, because of

the cold and his shouting.'
'What more do you do? Do you have still more to do?'
'Yes, lord, I have a great deal more to do! I have to fill up the bins with hay for the oxen, and give them water, and clean out their stalls.'
'Alas, that is a great hardship!'
'Yes, lord, it is indeed a great hardship, because I am not free.'

In return for this life of servitude, the bondsman was rewarded customarily by small gifts: for example, a swineherd received a pig with its offspring to keep; a slave-woman got a yearly allowance of corn, a sheep or three pennies in the winter, a measure of beans at Lent, and a measure of whey or one penny in the summer. Food-gifts were also traditionally given at Christmas and Easter, and a share in the harvest. Slaves must also have had some time to call their own, since it was possible for some to buy their freedom with money from the profits of work done in their own time on their own land – perhaps donated to them as a gift by the lord.

Slave-ownership was probably never very profitable among the Anglo-Saxons, because they had no great public undertakings that would require the continued toil of vast armies of labourers. It was often better in any case to allow the servant to buy his freedom, for even then he was not a free-man, but a 'freedman', probably without free relatives to support him. Such a man would find the enforcement of his legal rights almost impossible without backing, which was usually provided by his former owner. Thus, though no longer a slave he remained a servant. The freedman had taken the first step on the road to full legal status, which might be attained by his sons or grandsons.

There are indications that some royal bondsmen were not men of this sort but skilled technicians – smiths, carpenters, and the like. These were then kept in bondage in order to satisfy the vast appetite that kings and nobles had for fine and costly things. These may even have been Welshmen, native craftsmen maintained at the king's expense to ensure a steady supply of *hord-maðmas*, treasures which could be used in the traditional extravagant exchanges of gifts at the feast. This may be the origin of some of the supposed Celtic characteristics of early English art.

As the Anglo-Saxon period progressed there was a steady decline in the numbers of bondsmen in society, and a similarly steady decline in the rights of the churls. As Wulfstān's *Address* points out, the oppression of the poor by the wealthy in his day caused many freemen to surrender their freedom in exchange for security, and led to the blurring of the distinction between unfree men and the lowest grades of churls. Even as the thanes moved towards the position of a military élite, the churls – those who were not exceptionally wealthy – were being reduced to a one-class, 'half-free' state in which they were dependent on their social superiors for security, legal standing, and the means of existence. For their part, the thanes and nobles tended to amass larger and larger estates into the possession of fewer and fewer families, so that already England was moving towards the later medieval situation in which the peasantry were ruled by a handful of baronial families supported by a military cadre of knights. The Norman Conquest probably halted this process for a while (rather than introducing it, as is usually thought) since most of the more powerful English families lost their leading male members at Stamford Bridge or Hastings, and William's Norman henchmen were too numerous and too selfish to take over the old system intact.

chapter 8

saints, scholars and holy places

Religion in early England, especially pre-Christian belief, is a subject about which certain knowledge is difficult to acquire. The probability is that the English, even as late as the tenth century, retained certain customs and attitudes inherited from their pagan forebears. To what extent these practices were simply a matter of superstition and things done 'for good luck' is difficult to define, since references are mainly incidental or accidental. The advent of Christianity altered forever the society of the early English. On the simplest level, it introduced a new and powerful social group – the priesthood and monks, with their hierarchy of abbots, bishops, archbishops and papal legates. But Christianity struck deeper into the old ways than the mere addition of a professional and wealthy class only partly subject to royal authority. In order to understand the changes that the doctrine of salvation brought, it is worthwhile first examining the former beliefs of the heathen English.

the high gods

A heathen, it is said, is an ignorant person who persists in worshipping something that he can see and feel. English heathens were no exception. They venerated their gods at shrines, often in woodland glades, where they set up idols of the deities. The names of a few of these gods have survived, though their worship was outlawed by successive law codes in an effort to eradicate it. Yet the gods would not be forgotten while their names remained on the lips of the people, as they still are, in the names of the days of the week. 'Sunday' needs no explanation: the veneration of the sun as the bringer of all kinds of bounty probably goes further back in human history than we can guess.

'Monday' is, not surprisingly, the day of the moon. Among all the Germanic tribes, strangely, the sun was regarded as feminine and the moon masculine; this belief is almost unparalleled elsewhere, and betokens great antiquity for the worship of the sun among the linguistic ancestors of the northern European peoples.

'Tuesday' is the day special to the god Tīw, who was at one time the supreme Heavenly Father of the Germans; his name is related to that of the Greek Zeus and the Latin Jupiter. In later times he declined to being a mere war-god as his cult faded, but his memory lives on in a few English places named after him (Tuesley in Surrey, for example). 'Wednesday' was named after Wōden, who was originally a god of the dead and of magic; his cult was particularly associated with the warrior-chieftains who carved out their own small kingdoms and held them by force of arms. Wōden's worship informed the culture of the aristocracy, and helped shape the 'warrior ethic' of Anglo-Saxon society. Wednesbury in Staffordshire is one of the places which commemorates him.

'Thursday' was sacred to Thunor, more familiar under his Norse name of Thor. As the mighty god of thunder, he had specific attributes connected with the weather, and was regarded as the bringer of rain to swell the crops, and fine weather to harvest them.

St John the Evangelist from the Grimbald Gospels. Early eleventh century. Latin. The decoration of the Gospels is distinctive in styles, although the overall iconographic scheme of this illustration is reminiscent of miniatures in the Athelstān Psalter and the Benedictional of St Æthelwold.

Bronze helmet crest from the sixth or seventh century; such boar emblems were placed atop the helmets' crowns where they were thought to watch over the wearers.

Thundersley and Thunderley, both in Essex, recall his name. 'Friday' was named after the goddess Frig, the wife of the All-father. She was particularly associated with fertility in men, beasts and crops; Froyle in Hampshire is one of the few places still containing her name.

'Saturday' was not so named until much later, in honour of Saturn, the Roman god. There were other heathen gods of whom record survives, however. For example, the genealogies of English kings were all traced back to the divine ancestor, Wōden, the god of the kings who founded the dynasties and whom the kings may have regarded in some way as their spiritual progenitor, as well as wanting to enhance their claim to the thrones they occupied. But the kings of the East Saxons did not look back to Wōden, preferring to take their descent from the ancestral god of the Saxons, Seaxneat, the Sword Companion. Whether this god was different in kind from Wōden, or just a more nationalistic version of the same deity, is unclear, since no myths concerning him survive into modern times.

When we compare Old English records with Norse material, which both derive from a common religious tradition, we may detect faint echoes of gods or god-like heroes who have all but faded away completely. Thus, we sometimes find Christ called *Frēa*, meaning 'lord': the same name as the Norse god Frey bears. In fact, the cult of the Lord and Lady (in Norse, Frey and his sister Freyja) occurs widely in Europe, having spread from the Near East where it originated. It is worth remembering that for centuries Christ has been called Our Lord. To complicate matters further, another word meaning 'lord' occurs as a god's name in Norse: this is Baldur, whose story concerns how he was unwittingly slain by one of the other gods while engaging in the sport of throwing weapons at him, since he was supposedly invulnerable to harm. Echoes of this story have been discerned in an Anglo-Saxon poem, *The Dream of the Rood*, which describes the suffering of the Cross which bears Christ at his death; the poem contains obscure details which do not accord with biblical tradition but may belong to some early version of the story of Baldur. Elsewhere, the name Baldaeg occurs, as the son of Wōden.

The Norsemen also told of a magical smith who forged the keenest weapons in the world, since he was of divine origin. They called him Volund, and he figures in a late Norse poem *Volundarkviða*. By chance, an early English poem also deals with this story (though it differs from the Norse one in some ways) and there are other traces of him in Old English literature. Though probably not a god in the narrowest sense, his tale formed part of the body of myth common to Anglo-Saxons and Scandinavians. His English name, Weland, is preserved in the name of the prehistoric barrow Wayland's Smithy.

So few are the literary allusions to heathen practice, and so unhelpful in general, that it is impossible to do more than guess at the form that worship took before Christianity was accepted by the English.

The most important aspect of heathen worship seems to have been the sacrifice of an animal to the god, followed by a ritual meal at the shrine. This was later forbidden by the codes of law designed to suppress pagan practices, though the church did allow men to slaughter animals as before in order to prepare a communal meal for the celebration of the Christian festival. The churchmen were also advised not to destroy well-built pagan temples, but to smash the idols within and purify the building so that it could afterwards serve as a church. This willingness to adopt and adapt heathen practices and shrines to Christian purposes probably allowed the survival into later times of certain aspects of pre-Christian behaviour with the church's blessing – or without its outright

Viking amulet incorporating elements of the new faith Christianity and the World Serpent of pagan mythology.

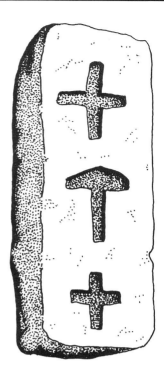

Danish soapstone mould from which the smith could cast amulets to suit any client: either Christian cross or pagan Thor's hammer.

condemnation – so easing the transition from the old ways to the new.

Nothing can more clearly illustrate this than the fact that the central mystery of the Christian faith, the Passion, Death and the Resurrection of the Lord, is named in England 'Easter', from the pagan 'Eostre', a goddess (according to Bede) whose name appears to be linked with the word 'east' and the Latin *aurora* (dawn). Her name suggests some cult of spring renewal personified by a goddess whose title recalls the return of the sun at daybreak, and whose special festival was at the time of the vernal equinox when the sun appears to triumph over the darkness.

Christmas is now probably the most widely-observed festival of the religious calendar; it owes its popularity to having replaced the earlier *Geola* (our 'Yule') which was the midwinter celebration. Yule seems to have played an important part in the pagan year, probably due to a certain amount of food having to be consumed because it could not be preserved, coupled with a period when there was little oppor-tunity to carry out work on the land due to the short days and poor weather.

It is never explicitly stated that human sacrifice took place among the heathen of this country, though we do know that Saxon raiders sometimes sacrificed some of their captives by drowning them. Odd references in later texts, such as the verses concerning the hanged man in *Beowulf*, do not point specifically to sacrifice so much as the hanging of an outlaw. From the continental districts where the Angles originated there is evidence of the drowning of men in marshpools – their preserved corpses have lasted into modern times to startle peatcutters working in the soil where they lie. But here again, it is not clear that these men and women were actually sacrificed to a god, and contemporary Roman authority has it that drowning was the punishment for cowardice, sodomy and adultery.

An important part of heathen religion was sortilege, the casting of lots. The reasons for this are not certain but probably faintly recall a time when the man who 'drew the short straw' was considered to have been chosen for death by the god who presided over the affair. The practice was closely connected with the Wōden cult and with the runes. As mentioned above, Wōden had first been a god of death and the magic arts associated with the raising of ghosts in order to learn secret wisdom believed to be known to departed spirits. Later Norse sources explicitly recount that the chosen victim was to be killed by being hanged while being stabbed with a spear, Wōden's traditional weapon. This had been the god's fate in order to acquire knowledge of the runes and their uses, and it was considered appropriate to follow his example. The runes themselves were an ancient alphabetic script common to the Germanic nations, and used for a variety of purposes. In the minds of the pagans, runes were a powerful force which could be tapped for man's benefit, and so all runic inscriptions were in the nature of charms. Though this may represent only one narrow aspect of the characters, which were otherwise used for quite prosaic inscriptions such as records of ownership, there are so many runic texts in existence for which no plausible explanation can be given that spells and charms seem the only answer. These include repetitions of the same character, and meaningless jumbles of letters in unpronounceable sequences. The possibility remains that these are perfectly straightforward texts written in some sort of code, but if so we are no closer to understanding what the runes meant.

Each runic character had a name which was also some significant word from the language beginning with the sound the letter represented: thus the s-rune was called *sigel* (sun); the m-rune *man* (human being), the d-rune *dæg* (day) and so on. Most significant are the names of gods which are included: the o-rune was named ōs (god, later taken to mean 'estuary' due to the occurrence of a similar word), the ng-rune was named 'Ing' (a god of fertility, identified with Frey), and the t-rune 'Tīw' (the god Tīw). Runes did not die out when the country was christianised, but the overtly pagan elements were bowdlerised to make them an acceptable tool for righteous men. Thus, ōs lost the meaning 'heathen god' and was assumed to represent the word 'estuary'; *thurs* (giant) was amended to *dorn* (thorn tree); and eventually the script fell into the hands of the Church, who did not shrink from using it for its own ends (as it had the temples and festivals). Soon Christian crosses began sporting inscriptions in runic scripts, suitably expanded to allow the spelling of unfamiliar words with runes for 'x' and 'q', which did not figure in the original series of signs.

The purposes to which the script could be put varied with the skill of the user. Some texts record just a personal name, presumably of the owner, giver or maker of the object on which the runes occur. The Ruthwell cross in Dumfries bears an inscription which has been identified as a substantial part of the poem *The Dream of the Rood*, in a Northumbrian dialect. Here the runes add to the splendour and impressiveness of the monument, which also has carvings showing biblical scenes and some very accomplished scrollwork on its other faces.

A more unorthodox use of runes is recorded in Bede's story of a thane who was captured after a battle and bound in fetters. Meanwhile, a Christian cleric who happened to be a relative of his was saying prayers and singing masses for the release of the thane, and so effective were these appeals to God that whenever the prayers were being said the thane's fetters fell away from him. His captors were understandably disturbed by this and asked him whether he knew spells of unbinding and had the runes written down on him. This indicates not merely a belief in the power of runes to work charms, but a more significant belief in the popular imagination that they had the power to release bindings. The power of binding and unbinding is particularly associated with the god Wōden, who uses it as a means of rendering his enemies harmless – he imposes what the Vikings called the *herfjottur* (army-fetter), which paralyses the warriors by sapping their will and control over their bodies. The English thane was evidently credited with a similar ability which he was able to utilise through a secret runic text hidden on him. In fact, short runic writings often appear in places which would not have

been obvious when the object was in use – on the back of a scabbard mount from Chessell Down, for example, where it would have been seen only by the owner – which tends to confirm that some people felt it prudent or preferable to keep their runes hidden.

Other types of article have runes set on them in the boldest and most ostentatious manner, as on the ninth-century Thames scramasax, where they may have been included as much for decoration as for practical purposes. Tastes and fashions change, and as the more objectionable pagan associations of the script were forgotten they became a more strictly practical means of writing which was widely recognised and used in England. Ciphers and codes based on the traditional arrangement of the characters into groups became popular, especially in closed communities of monks who seem to have used such secret writings for quite mundane purposes. Even the most famous rune-bearing object, the Franks Casket, has one of its texts encoded: all the vowels are substituted for unfamiliar runes and rune-like signs.

Central to the Wōden cult was the vision of heroism and the warrior's values implicit in this. The popularity of the god with the chiefs of war-bands was due to the military success which his favour could confer. In fact his cult sustained the system of martial rivalry between chiefs, and between warriors within these groups. The chiefs were in ceaseless competition with their peers to secure maximum advantage from whatever opportunities presented themselves, and to attract into their service the strongest and bravest young men. The chiefs were competing for prestige and for wealth, particularly treasure. The warriors themselves were competing for their leader's favour and for the choicest items of plunder, which were the badges of martial success. The lord was duty bound to share out the riches among the men (this kept them brave in battle and happy at the feast), while the men in turn had to forgo the credit for the successes they achieved (this kept the lord in high repute and more willing to hand out costly things).

The problem with the martial system was that sooner or later the interminable strife it caused would wipe out all the less successful war-bands and chiefs,

Line drawing of the crucifixion from the Ramsey Psalter. Late tenth century. The script and decoration to the Psalter suggest that it was made at Winchester, even though it may have been for use at Ramsey Abbey. The line drawing of the crucifixion is considered one of the masterpieces of late Anglo-Saxon art.

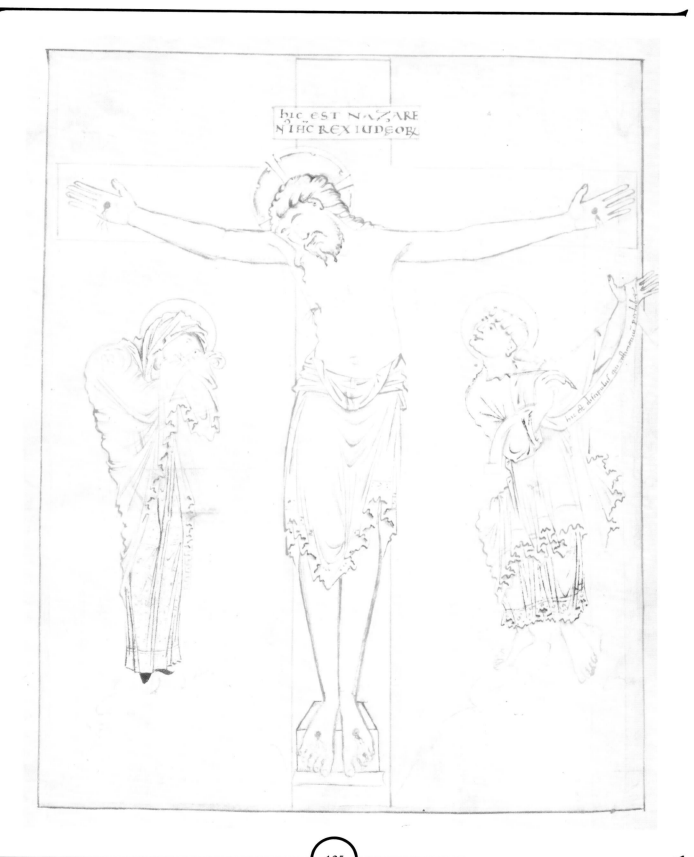

and leave one final victor who would no longer need his war-band to compete with his now-defunct rivals. The system could only function while there was a good supply of treasure to take from weaker neighbours and hand out as rewards. Once the craftsmen who made the gems, arm-rings, and costly weapons, were too few, due to the incessant warfare, to supply the demand for their products, the social system would have to collapse or evolve a new relationship between its chieftains and warriors. This stage was never reached however; partly because no single chief or king ever managed to acquire such total and absolute power that no rival dared stand against him, and partly because the coming of Christianity created new stresses within the social system, and a new and more rewarding kind of heroism – that of the missionary and the martyr.

Of more immediate importance to the bulk of the people than the aristocratic cult of Wōden and his heroes was the belief in a power called *Wyrd.* This was not a goddess as such, but rather a natural force which encompassed everything. The notion that some men are 'doomed to die' has been with us for a long time: it is mentioned in *The Battle of Maldon*, where such men are described as *fæg* (fated, fey) and was current among soldiers (and Londoners) in World War II in a saying referring to enemy shells and bombs that 'if it's got your name on it, there's nothing you can do'. The idea is that death is inescapable in the appointed hour, but otherwise need not cause one to worry. Those who are destined to die on the day of the battle, therefore, will do so even if they flee, and those who are not so doomed are safe from mortal harm, although they may suffer lesser injuries.

The matter of men being 'doomed' leads into the area of the attitude to life in general, and death in particular. The beliefs among the warriors of Byrhtnōth's day were not so very different from much earlier times. Heathen men had believed in an all-powerful god who had created the world and everything in it, who had made men and given them intelligence; this god was, it is believed, called Ealfæder (the father of all). Yet he, and the lesser gods such as Wōden, Thunor and Frey were in turn subject to a greater power, the impersonal force known as *Wyrd.* The word is related to the verb 'become' in Old English (*weordan*), and its meaning is difficult to pin down with modern words. Among possible meanings are: 'that which comes about or happens; the course of events; the passage of time; fate; the way of the world'. The central idea behind all these phrases is one of 'happening' or 'changing', and events unfolding according to a pattern or overall scheme. *Wyrd* was outside the hierarchy of supernatural beings, which ranged from elves and goblins to the gods themselves, with saints and angels slotted in at later times. No one worshipped *Wyrd* or made shrines or offerings to it: it was entirely impersonal and could only be perceived in the coming about of events in a manner and sequence which suggested a pattern; in that sense it was possible to regard it as a sort of predestination. Sacrifices to the gods could bring good luck or help in this or that difficulty, but could do nothing to alter the overall pattern of existence which was inexorable and immutable. *Wyrd* did not create the pattern, it was the pattern.

The coming of Christianity inevitably challenged the concept of *Wyrd*, for it was irreconcilable with the orthodox Christian teaching that God is all-powerful and therefore subject to no higher authority. No religion, indeed no social system, can tolerate the presence of two omnipotent beings: it simply comes down to the old conundrum of the irresistible force and the immovable object, played out on a grand scale. The early Christian missionaries and teachers were content to foster the notion that their God was essentially a more powerful version of the old Ealfæder; that is to say, the greatest of the gods but still firmly within the power of *Wyrd*. As more orthodox beliefs were disseminated by ever stricter church dignitaries, *Wyrd* was inevitably demoted to a mere aspect of the Christian God – his divine Providence. But, though the church managed to account for *Wyrd* within the framework of their own doctrines, they could not prevent the old ideas from persisting among the ordinary laymen, who continued to assign coincidence and the inexplicable alike to the ancient power. Thus we read in *Beowulf* that: *Wyrd oft nereð unfægne eorl ðonne his ellen deah* ('*Wyrd* often spares a man who is not doomed when his courage is good') where *Wyrd* could be rendered 'the course of events' or 'the way things happen in the world'. This proverbial wisdom could be used, as here, simply to remind people that no one knows in advance whether they will be overtaken at last by *adl oððe yldo oððe ecghete*, 'sickness or old-age or the foeman's sword', and so all should bear themselves with courage in the face of apparent disaster.

It seems that this attitude went very deep into the minds of warriors, and even the ordinary men. They

St Peter-at-Gowts Church, Lincoln; its round-headed arched windows are a typical feature, as are the alternate broad and narrow cornerstones.

accepted that life was, if not actually unfair, at least totally indifferent to the suffering of men and women. No amount of weapons and no amount of prayer could solve their problems; destruction and death awaited them, and they had no means of escape. Yet they continued to live according to their customs, fighting back against the forces of darkness that must overwhelm at the last, and this naked resistance was the more courageous because it was without hope of rescue or salvation, or even the comfort of knowing that their deeds would be remembered. *Wyrd* was immutable, and it stood against them; yet they would fight on and never bow to it while they still had breath.

For the fortunate few, noble lives and gallant deaths would mean the only immortality they could aspire to: their names would be recalled and their actions retold over countless years. The idea of living a heroic life full of brave deeds thus came to be considered a mere means to achieving fame and praise among one's peers, although this had not been its purpose, for it had been widely recognised that personal immortality was unlikely and unproven, and only fame could be relied on as a means of ensuring continued praise from fellow warriors.

The arrival of Christianity changed the picture completely, for under the new religion a man could live well in this life and be rewarded, both here on earth and afterwards in heaven. The sheer desperation of the old ideas was recognised and rejected, in favour of a system where hope of eternal salvation was open to all who believed sincerely and acted according to conscience rather than the dictates of the heroic code. Even the humblest and weakest could share in this new heroism, although previously they had been excluded from the more martial kind. The time was not far off when men could come to regard the moral struggle against iniquity and vice as altogether more important than the physical warfare of kings.

The process of conversion of the English spread from two directions: while the north came under the influence of the Celtic church, centred on Iona, the southern kingdoms were visited by a mission from Rome under Augustine. The Roman method of winning converts was to first enlist the support of the kings and nobles who had power to encourage the spread of the faith. Since the king was a central figure in the old religion, and had something of the aura of high priest about him, his conversion to Christianity immediately removed one of the main props of the heathen faith.

The missionaries seem to have stressed the success

The ornate and beautiful pectoral cross taken from St Cuthbert's coffin. Executed in gold and cloisonné, *garnet inlays. It is of seventh-century Northumbrian work.*

Anglo-Saxon crucifix reliquary. Cross, sheet gold, walrus ivory and enamels on a cedar-wood core: Christ; walrus ivory. AD 1000. It seems likely that the wood might have been regarded as a piece of the true cross. The reliquary was also found to contain a human finger. The cross that Knut presented to New Minister, Winchester, also contained relics, as did that given by King Edgar to Ely.

The Christ is Anglo-Saxon in style and is markedly similar to the line drawing of Christ in the Ramsey Psalter. Opinion is divided as to whether the metalwork is English or German.

of Christians, and to have presented the new God as one who could bestow victories and prosperity on those whom he favoured, and there were many Bible stories to support this claim. Even the most introspective Saxon kingdom had received news from the Continent of the incredible fortune and prestige of the Roman emperors and their successors, who were known to have won seemingly impossible victories over peoples such as the Huns (who were obviously not Christian). Thus the new faith became identified with the splendour of Rome, and those who accepted it became gallant religious warriors struggling against the pagan. This in turn legitimised the perennial strife of kingdom against kingdom, which could now

become a holy war against the infidel. The kings may have seen the new religion in such terms, or they may simply have found it flattering to identify themselves with the legendary emperors, and to be included in the social circles of the Christian world.

Part of the missionaries' strategy was to ridicule the old beliefs as futile and simple-minded. If we can trust Bede's account of the conversion of King Edwin of Northumbria, the priests of the heathen religion were also beginning to find them so: Paulinus, having made some headway with the king, is asked to await the decision of the witan before the new faith can be promulgated throughout the land; Cefi, an *ealdor-bisceop* (heathen high priest), makes this speech before the king:

> See, O King, what kind of learning is now preached to us. I truly confess to you what I have clearly perceived: that the religion which we held and practised till now is entirely without power or usefulness, because none of your thanes has more diligently or more heartily devoted himself to the worship of our gods than I have, but nonetheless there are many who received greater gifts and benefits from you than I have, and they have had greater prosperity. Well, I know that if our gods had any power they would have helped me more because I served and obeyed them more willingly. Because of that it seems prudent to me that we should accept those things which have recently been preached to us, if you think them better and mightier.

The priest then seized a weapon and mounted a stallion (both of which were forbidden to heathen priests) and rode out to the temple, which he burnt down after first hurling his spear at it – both acts of destruction associated with Wōden, who may have been the god Cefi had previously served.

Even here, in the reported speech of a heathen priest, the accent is firmly on the practical and worldly benefits to be gained from Christianity. The idea of Christ as a young hero doomed to be overcome by his foes, yet able to undo the worst evil that they could do to him, also appealed greatly to the Anglo-Saxon mind, possibly because stories of a similar kind were already known concerning gods such as Baldur. The death and rebirth cycle must have been familiar, since it turns up all over Europe and the Near East, connected with the growth of crops and their harvesting, and the mystery of the sowing and return in the next year.

The spread of the new faith did not at first overturn the old ways, which remained dear to people's hearts and continued to resurface intermittently. Many early kings accepted Christianity for themselves, only to be succeeded by confirmed pagans who would not tolerate it. Most kingdoms had become at least nominally Christian by the mid-600s, but the new religion was not firmly established throughout the land until the end of the century. That was far from the end of the story, however. The Roman church could not tolerate any challenge to the authority of the Pope, no matter how innocuous. Any deviation from the official line was regarded as at best ignorant folly, at worst foul heresy. For its part, the Celtic church firmly maintained its own ways, many of which had developed during the period when contact with the rest of Christian Europe had been slight. The Celtic brand of Christianity was humbler, more personal, altogether more self-reliant than the Roman; it lacked the organisational expertise acquired by the Roman clerics in the management of their often vast estates. These administrative skills were among the attractions of the church for southern English kings, who were able to harness them for their own purposes, so far as these were not directly counter to Christian teaching. Equally, the Roman pattern of organisation within the church endowed the office of bishop with considerable importance and extensive holdings of land. Some unease was felt among churchmen about the splendour and wealth of these bishops, who were frequently members of noble families. Indeed, some bishops surrounded themselves with an entourage of dashing young men in exactly the same way a warlord would do, and spent their time feasting and making merry with their friends rather than tending to the spiritual needs of their sees.

Matters finally came to a head in the 660s over the calculation of the date of the Easter festival. Celtic and Roman methods differed to such an extent that it is recorded of one king and his wife, who belonged to different churches, that one was enduring the Lenten fast while the other was enjoying the Easter feast. Obviously the tensions caused by such differences within what should have been a single church had to be resolved. The point about setting the date for Easter was that its celebration must coincide with the equinox, with the first month of the lunar year, and

St Dunstan seated at his writing table with quill, penknife and inkpot; he wears a bishop's mitre and is seated in a 'Cathedra' or Episocopal throne.

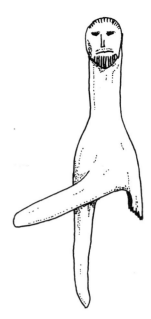

The cult god found in a Danish bog, in the region from which the ancestors of the English emigrated. A suitably-shaped piece of a tree has been given crudely carved features.

with the moon about to wane. All these had symbolic significance representing rebirth, regrowth and a new beginning. At the Synod of Whitby in 664, the two sides confronted each other. Needless to say, the Roman church emerged victorious, due to its intellectual and doctrinal resources and its tradition of esoteric and abstract learning, with which the simpler faith of the Celtic church could not compete.

Christianity brought with it monasteries, which had been an entirely alien concept to the early kingdoms, except those where the Christian faith persisted among the native population, who would have been familiar with the idea of a monastic or eremitic existence. As houses of God, and centres for craftsmen and clerics, the monastic establishments flourished under successive kings. By the late ninth century the feeling seems to have grown among laymen that the monasteries' considerable landownership, and the favourable terms on which they held their land, posed a threat to the status of men outside the church. This, coupled with the reported avarice of the church and the setting up of bogus monasteries by wealthy families to gain more agreeable terms of land-tenure, brought about a movement to completely overhaul the law relating to monks and their holdings. At about this time on the Continent, the Benedictine Reform was begun, a movement within the church to

establish a more ascetic and selfless kind of existence for those who truly felt drawn to the service of God through self-denial. Implicitly, the movement was also designed to discourage the kinds of abuse of monastic status which caused so much resentment among secular landowners.

the old ways

If the arrival of Augustine did not immediately drive out the worship of the gods of the heathen English, much less did the church he brought with him succeed in eradicating the age-old practices of the country-folk. In fact, as we saw earlier, the church strove wherever possible not to antagonise those they wished to convert, and chose to take over, with suitable amendment, as much as possible of familiar custom. The observances of the high gods were often stripped of their overt pagan elements and reused; the simple beliefs and traditions of the humbler folk were allowed to continue as long as there was no obvious sacrilegious intention.

In taking over these traditions, the church had often to excise the memory of some pagan god or spirit, and this was neatly achieved by canonisation: thus, the holy light of British folklore, called Sinclair, became St Clair; Brigita became St Brigit or St Bride. Holy wells, to which therapeutic or restorative powers were attributed, became linked with stories of saints who caused waters to gush forth from the bare earth. The list of such miracle stories is almost endless, and tends to confirm the ubiquitous nature of these earlier cults, which almost always extend far back into prehistory. The beliefs, which formed no real system of religious doctrine, occur all over Europe in basically similar forms. The Celts who dwelt in Britain before the Romans came are known to have venerated holy wells and springs; to this day, people travel to Lourdes in search of miracle cures for disease. The name of the deity to be invoked in the cure changes according to the formal religion of the people, but the place itself and the basic notion of thaumaturgical powers at work in the spring water is remarkably persistent.

The country-folk placed their trust in the stones

Ornately-bordered illuminated miniature from the Bene-dictional of St Æthelwold, c. 970 – 980. A poem at the beginning of the manuscript states that Æthelwold 'commanded also to be made many frames well adorned and fitted with various figures decorated with numerous beautiful colours and with gold'.

Runic futhorc from the Thames scramasax (above): although of magical use, the intention behind the inclusion of these inlaid runes on the weapon seems also to have been decorative.

The Norman crypt of Canterbury Cathedral; the Norman building programme eventually replaced nearly every trace of important Anglo-Saxon architecture, yet many of the builders of these Norman buildings were undoubtedly English.

and trees, elves and spirits, as their ancestors had done since time out of mind, rather than in this or that god. These powers were more approachable than the mighty powers of the sky, and were more sympathetic to the needs of the humble. Their services could often be bought by small offerings of food left out for them at night, or by binding them to service through charms. Characteristic of these goblins is their love of mischief and their readiness to take offence. They are often thought of as turning milk sour or hiding small belongings – the antics of a naughty child rather than of a demon. It is usual to refer to them as the fair folk or the good people, for fear of offending them so that they will no longer help the household. Brownies and similar sprites of this kind are common elements in folklore throughout Europe and beyond, and seem to persist in the popular imagination regardless of the religious climate of the times. Thus, children in our own period grow up with the idea of Jack Frost (perhaps a frost giant), the sandman (who brings sleep), Father Christmas (who brings the cheer of the Yule), and so on. Whatever the origins of these concepts, they are deeply ingrained in our tradition and show no sign of being forgotten.

Less benign were the *scinnan* and *scuccan*, the corresponding creatures who represented forces of adversity. These probably correspond to the bogey-men with which young children are frightened in order to make them stay away from dangerous places. These creatures inhabited the more unwholesome areas such as swamps, and may be remembered as the Jack o'Lantern who lures unwary travellers to a watery end. They are usually creatures of the night, or at least of darkness, and are afraid of the daylight which is harmful to them. Such stories may have been suggested by visits from nocturnal creatures – that they were not seen during the day may have suggested that light was in some way inimical to them. The snufflings of small night-feeding animals could easily populate the surrounding dark with terrifying spectres in people's minds.

Just what these wights and elves were supposed to look like is not certain. Some Anglo-Saxon references to elves places them on a par with the gods, suggesting that they were creatures of some stature. Elsewhere, a manuscript illustration shows a traveller attacked by small winged men with bows. The word 'elf' is associated with an ancient source meaning 'white, shining' from which the Anglo-Saxon word for 'swan' was also derived: presumably, elves were characterised by a shining, otherworldly appearance. *Scinna* also appears to be a derivative of the word 'shine'. Archery seems to have been a forte of theirs – finds of prehistoric flint arrowheads were described as 'elf-shot', while a sudden stitch or pain could be attributed to the attack of elves, gods, or witches.

If elves were beautiful and perilous, there were other beings who were hideous and deadly. One such is the monster Grendel in the poem *Beowulf*, a hideous travesty of the human form inhabiting a cave beneath a pool in a wild and desolate area. Of similar kind may be the *grima*, the 'hooded one', if this is not simply a name for Wōden. The seas and rivers were haunted by *nicoras* possibly conceived of as some kind of sea-serpent or eel, while beneath old grave-mounds lurked dragons, guarding their hoarded wealth against the avarice of unwelcome guests. Some or all of these may have been imported with the Anglo-Saxon immigrants, yet they are not so different in kind from the sorts of supernatural beings already thought to inhabit Britain.

A class of creatures which is not easily classified is that of the war-spirits known from Norse sources as *Valkyrja* (Valkyries). These are essentially female beings who serve the battle-god and hand out victory according to his will. Something similar is believed to have been known among the English, where a swarm of bees in the sky is called a *sigewīf* (victory-woman), and the word *wælcyrge* (the same as *Valkyrja*) is used to translate *Erinyes*, the Greek Furies, blood-thirsty and vengeful female spirits. The origin of these ideas may lie ultimately in war-priestesses who dedicated themselves to the god of battle and acted as his servants and advocates on earth. Confusion between these and supernatural battle-spirits caused fusion of the two concepts into Boudicca-like figures in popular imagination.

An even simpler kind of faith among the lower orders of society connected good luck, and especially good health, with certain trees, stones, or springs. Standing stones, whether single megaliths or imposing alignments such as Stonehenge, were held in a kind of reverential awe. Those with holes in were often believed to be able to cure diseases of children, if they were passed through the hole, or to restore injured limbs which were thrust through. The stones acted as a kind of focusing point for the mystic curative powers of the earth, and the holes functioned as sockets into which human bodies could be plugged for a charge of restorative energy. Such rudimentary beliefs recommended themselves to concerned parents and desperate sufferers from, for example, arthritis in the absence of any better solutions.

The ancient English were not, however, in any way 'backward' or primitive in their medical practices. Great care was taken to acquire and collate medical treatises from all over Europe, and the Saxon 'leech' was as skilled a healer as could be found anywhere at that time. Herbal lore and rune-lore went hand-in-hand to effect cures for a variety of complaints. How much of this was faith-healing and how much biochemistry is not clear, but the church regarded the relief of suffering as one of its special duties and trained men in the arts of medicine.

Veneration of sacred spots such as wells, cairns and mounds, was still known in the time of King Knut, who passed strict laws to prohibit it. A number of these traditional holy sites were taken over by the Church in an effort to bring men into contact with Christ at their accustomed meeting-places. It is therefore likely that many churches in our own day stand on ground that has been hallowed for tens of centuries. Once Christianity became firmly established in daily life the sacred plot lost its former significance – especially in those cases where some 'saint' was brought in to explain away any memory of earlier pagan legends of the place – and became special only through its connection with the Church and with the dead ancestors in its graveyard.

chapter 9

the warrior's way

nglo-Saxon society, in common with most societies of the time, was more overtly violent than today. War was virtually a continuous condition; both the organised warfare of Vikings and Englishmen, and the *ad hoc* raiding of adventurers and rebels. The wasting and despoiling of recalcitrant areas, moreover, was a tool of government which kings were willing to use to assert their authority. Violent death, such as public execution of criminals and war-captives, was commonplace in normal life. It is probably untrue to suggest that life was cheap then, since there were severe penalties for murderers; it would be closer to the truth to say that life was precarious, for rich and poor alike, due to hostilities, disease and an unreliable food supply. Neither king nor servant enjoyed any real security in life, except that which they could derive from religion.

The status of the warrior within this society was generally high. Martial values had been accorded high honour among the Germanic tribes from before Christ's birth, and the right of the freeman to bear arms (and to use them in self-defence) was considered a fundamental symbol of his legal status. Only slaves could not bear arms, because it was thought unwise to have men with possible grievances bearing weapons; and because slaves were, in any case, property, and the killing of a slave was not strictly murder but wilful damage to the master's chattel.

From the time of the great migrations of tribes at the close of the Roman period, there had existed a symbiotic relationship between warlords and their followers, organised into war-bands, known by a variety of names in English, the commonest of which is *werod* ('protective force'). The *werod* constituted the lord's bodyguard and his strike-force. It consisted, normally, of a core of experienced and hardy men – the *dugud* – supplemented by a number of younger warriors – the *geogod* – who were learning the art of warfare; those who survived would one day become the *dugud* in turn. In addition, the constant warfare and political strife caused a steady stream of exiles and wanderers, some with their own followers, who also bolstered the forces of any lord who would accept the risk of becoming their patron, and taking on their feuds and enemies as his own.

The giving and acceptance of gifts, the feasting of the *werod* in the hall, and the boasting of deeds to be done were all important symbolic acts within the warrior culture. Treasure had a significance beyond its value as material wealth: warriors were expected to surrender to the lord all the booty taken in war, and the lord, in turn, was supposed to hand out costly gifts to his followers on ceremonial occasions.

No ceremony was more important than the initiation of a new member of the band, the ceremony for which has been reconstructed as follows: first the prospective retainer knelt before the lord, who was seated on his 'gift-stool' or chair; he rested his hand on the hilt of the lord's sword which was unsheathed, lying across his knees; he kissed the lord's hand, and rose to take the oath of loyalty; kneeling again, he placed his hands together between those of his new leader, and rested his head on the lord's knee; then rose and kissed him. On completion of the rite, a symbolic gift was given to welcome the newcomer, usually a weapon or piece of battle-gear. Periodically, further gifts were made by the lord in honour of the warriors, to increase their prestige among their peers. A man's worth was commonly judged by the spendour of the clothes and adornments he wore. Like many

peoples before and since, they tended to wear their wealth on their bodies in the form of fine clothing and rich jewellery and weapons. An Anglo-Saxon warlord needed no 'plastic money' to show his status: he wore it in the gold chain round his neck!

The warriors' feast in the lord's hall played an important part in the social lives of the professional fighters, for it was at the feast that they had the chance to demonstrate their prestige, receive further gifts and escape the tedium of their way of life. Conspicuous consumption of costly feasts by the élite helped to reinforce the distinctions between professional warriors and the farmers who relied on them for protection. Personal honour was regarded as of paramount importance, and some men would go to any lengths to protect their good names. Indeed, some became obsessed with their reputation and would avenge any slight, real or imagined. This preoccupation with *lof*, a good name and the approval of one's fellows, led more than one man to his downfall.

Strong drink played a part in Anglo-Saxon society which is difficult for us to understand: drunkenness was regarded as an admirable quality. While we may sometimes feel a kind of boyish admiration for the man who can hold his drink, in modern times it tends to be thought that the habitual drunkard acts out of weakness and an inability to cope with life. Yet drunkenness was apparently regarded as a kind of blessing, and a lack of strong drink was considered a cause for grave distress. Intoxication through beer-drinking meant a degree of escape from the savage reality of their world, and also released people's inhibitions so that, as the drink flowed, their hearts opened and the bonds of friendship and companionship grew. Unless human nature has changed beyond recognition in the last thousand years, however, the beer-swilling warriors must often have felt their good sense desert them and their anger spill over into violence as the feast became a drunken brawl.

Alcohol must also have played a part when the warriors came to make their promises to their lord. These were freely-given speeches declaring before the assembled company that the speaker would do great deeds in his lord's name. In making such a boast, the warrior was putting his reputation on the line before his friends and family. Failure to live up to his words

'Luxuria' personified; Anglo-Saxon warriors throw down their weapons (above) and take to merrymaking (below); the shields are convex and the spears have lugs below the blades, while the men in the lower panel are holding pennants or banners.

would bring the ignominy of the oath-breaker, or cheap fraud who takes the leader's bounty and deserts him when he sees no further profit to be gained from the association.

The feasters were entertained by *scopas*, poets who composed verses to the accompaniment of the harp. When a warrior carried out his promise, his words were translated into deeds; equally, once the vow was fulfilled the poet might sing of his prowess and gallantry, so that his deeds were translated back into words. Wandering minstrels and story-tellers travelled widely throughout the land, and even on the Continent, singing the praises of the man whose hospitality they were enjoying, and retailing tales of their experiences. Religious pilgrims also formed an important link in the communication network, as well as the waifs and itinerants who clung to the edges of society. These were the poor men, some crippled through disease, others the wretched survivors of famine or raiding, who relied on the munificence and generosity of the wealthy for their very existence. Bible stories, legends and heroic tales formed part of their repertoire, as well as *risqué* riddles and historical narratives.

When not sitting at the mead-bench, nor actually fighting, the warriors must have spent some of their time hunting, or at least accompanying their lord on the hunt. The older men of the *dugud* may have had specific duties assigned to them individually, such as the care of the bowers or the running of the household. What the more restless and more aggressive young men did is not clear, but contests of strength and skill, board-games, and horse-races seem to have been popular. Icelandic sources also mention horse-fights, with attendant betting, and bear-baiting as diversions for the wealthy.

The conduct of war, as we have seen from *The Battle of Maldon*, was by no means a matter of orderly formations or carefully-executed manoeuvres. Essentially it was more personal, and more haphazard, than conflict today. Elementary precautions against avoidable disaster were taken, such as the driving away of the horses and the adoption of a defensive or offensive position, were taken before the first blows were exchanged. The Vikings had a battle-formation known as the *svinfylking* (gathering of pigs) which involved a mass of infantry drawn up in a wedge. This had been associated with the battle cult of their god Ōdin, and was known to the English also: therefore in *The Battle of Maldon* the phrases occur *East-seaxena ord* (point of the East Saxons) and later *on*

orde stōd (he stood at the point), with reference to the apex of the v-shaped line of men. From this idea of 'point, forefront' comes the use of the word to denote 'keenest, bravest men', and the rendering of the first phrase above by 'flower of the East Saxons', and the second by 'he stood among the best men there'.

In the poem the line itself is called *bordweall* (shieldwall), *scyldburh* (shield-stronghold), and *wīhaga* (war-enclosure, or war-hedge). The idea expressed in these terms is of a line of shield-carrying foot-soldiers stretched continuously across the enemy's front. Whether the meaning of *wīhaga* can be taken to show that they held their spears out before them like a hedge is debatable, though such an obvious means of deterring an enemy's rushed attack is perfectly likely on a priori grounds.

Once the decision to fight had been taken, the initial hostile act was the sending of a hail of missile weapons on to the enemy lines; this was known as the *beaduscūr* (battle-shower). In heathen and early Christian times it had been customary for a single

The Abingdon Sword. Iron with silver mounts inlaid with neillo, Anglo-Saxon. Late ninth, early tenth century. The most renowned of a group of Anglo-Saxon swords with elaborately decorated hilts.

warrior to cast his spear over the entire force of the enemy indicating that the fighting should begin. This was a symbolic act: the dedication of the entire host to the battle-god. Although there is little evidence for this tradition surviving so late among the English as to have happened at Maldon, it is perfectly possible that the Vikings could have enacted it, as it was still common practice among them, and survived well into the medieval period as something men might do for good luck.

The theory was that the battle-shower might create thinly-manned areas in the battle-line, which could then be exploited in the next phase of the conflict, the *beadurās* (battle-rush). On the evidence of the poem, a great shout went up from both armies as the advance troops rushed forwards to clash with

The Abingdon Sword. The human figure and the bird on the upperguard may well be symbols of St Matthew and St John. The Bull of St Luke and Lion of St Mark feature on the other side of the upperguard.

the foe. This phase was often a critical point in the struggle, since the first onslaught was the fiercest, while the warriors were fresh and eager for glory. A successful attack which managed to penetrate the gaps in the enemy line could sweep the shieldwall aside and fragment it into small groups, to be dealt with piecemeal. Equally, an effective defence which succeeded in absorbing the brunt of the first attack could inflict heavy casualties at little cost, and form the starting-point for a purposeful counter-attack. Most usually, however, the battle-rush made headway at certain points and was rebuffed at others, and the fighting broke up into small skirmishes as the business of hand-to-hand hacking and slaying got underway.

At Maldon the English force was breached in parts but was evidently not overwhelmed, and began to rally. Face-to-face conflict, with sword and axe, spear and shield, was a strenuous business in those days, and there must have been lulls in the mêlée during which both armies caught their breath, rested and searched for replacements for damaged equipment. It must have been during these pauses that the warriors made their famous speeches of encouragement, if these are historical. In the poem the English consistently speak of going 'forwards' to the Danes, which suggests that the Viking troops were bunched together behind their own shieldwall, maybe at some distance from the defenders. The fighting must then have taken place in a series of short and bloody encounters in the 'killing ground' between the two sides.

The *Chronicle* and other Old English records refer to victory in such terms as *wælstowe geweald habban* (to have control of the place of slaughter), meaning that the opposition has been driven from the field, or wiped out, or taken captive and unable to offer further resistance. This obviously gave the victors the opportunity to first loot the dead, then tend to their wounded comrades. Captives were not infrequently sold off as slaves: the Danes had an agreement with the Norman state that they could take all their plunder and prisoners there for sale. Not infrequently, royal or noble prisoners who fell into enemy hands were slain outright, often in sickeningly cruel ways. Thanes and reasonably wealthy men could be ransomed by their relatives if they could establish contact with the foe. Vikings who fell into English hands were usually regarded as having the same status as native robbers, and met the same fate: they were summarily hanged. Sometimes a particular Dane might escape this fate, if he had some powerful relative to send an entreaty to his captor; sometimes, also, solitary Vikings who fell into the hands of the freemen and bondsmen they had harried met a gruesome end, such as being flayed alive.

Christians had a duty to pray for the souls of their dead warriors, and to recover their bodies for burial with full honour. The heathen Vikings usually followed the tradition of burning their dead on the battlefield on which they died, on a funeral pyre decked out with the weapons of both sides' dead, so that they could take these tokens of their glorious death with them into the afterlife. This custom had the practical advantage of preventing the enemy digging up and abusing the dead Vikings.

War-gear varied according to the wealth of the individual who purchased it, both in quality of manufacture of separate items, and in the range of goods available. For the yeoman (*ceorl*), war-gear may have meant no more than a leather jerkin, a leather cap, a spear and shield, and perhaps a knife and cudgel, or a bow, thrust through the belt for emergency use only. In fact, the foot-soldier armed with spear and shield had been the backbone of English (and Viking) armies since long before their conquest of Britain. The bow was widely used for hunting, but was used in war mainly by the yeoman classes. The Northumbrian nobleman's use of it in *The Battle of Maldon* is remarkable. However, the Norwegians seem to have had less prejudice (or more common sense) about the weapon, and it may be that in areas of heavy Viking settlement, the bow was not considered unacceptable for a nobleman's use in war.

The thane, on the whole better able to provide himself with good quality equipment, would almost certainly have worn a mail-coat and helmet of some kind, as well as carrying a large wooden shield and a sword worn on a baldric. He would have used a stout thrusting-spear and probably a number of slender throwing-spears. The ealdorman is represented in the poem as clad in a war-coat, either of mail or possibly of lamellar plates. His sword and spear and other equipment were costly items in themselves, and excited the greed of his foes, suggesting that the 'golden-hilted sword' was real and not mere poetic fancy.

In the main the Danes would have been similarly equipped to the English. They may, as a professional army, have been slightly better equipped than their foes, many of whom were only part-time warriors. They might have worn thicker and warmer clothing, including furs, as a protection against the cold life at sea – though probably not for fighting on an August day. Viking soldiers made much greater use of the two-handed axe than did the English at this time, though Knut's bodyguard popularised it with the native troops. From the axe's characteristic shape it was known as the 'bearded axe' (*skeggöx*), because of the drooping lower edge of the blade, which was mounted on a shaft perhaps a yard (a metre) long; there was a smaller kind of axe called *half-dynna* with a square lower edge used for fighting aboard ships where it doubled as a grappling-iron.

If, as the *Chronicle* suggests, Óláf Tryggvason was present at the battle, his contingent of Baltic seamen would have added an exotic air, probably wearing high-necked shirts and the outlandishly voluminous trousers favoured by Rus warriors, made from yards of cloth gathered at the waist and knees. His men might have worn the typical Viking helmet: a small, conical type beaten out of a single sheet of metal. They might also have carried the Viking weapon known as a *hoggspjöt*, a kind of pole-axe with a spearhead mounted on top, resembling other weapons, such as halberds, used in the later medieval period.

One striking difference between the Danish armies of the late tenth and early eleventh centuries, when contrasted with their predecessors, was their background organisation. It had always been a problem for Viking leaders to hold their forces together: there had often been a conflict of interests as the older men wished to take their allotted share and use it to buy land, while the youngsters wanted to carry on fighting and acquire ever greater wealth. The existence of the great circular military forts throughout Denmark, established at this time and abandoned soon after, shows that these camps were purpose-built to house the armies being enlisted by the Danish royal family, with which to conquer England and Norway. The levels of organisation, executive control and planning necessary to bring these forts into existence and to maintain the armies garrisoned there exceeds anything previously seen in those parts – in fact, there is little evidence for any large public defensive works undertaken by the Danes at all, except for the Danevirke, a rampart-and-ditch earthwork stretching across most of the base of the Jutland peninsula.

The resources needed to undertake the construction and manning of these camps must have been out of the reach of all save the king – in this case Harald Bluetooth or Sven Forkbeard. The men who were billeted in them were no longer opportunist thugs, but hired soldiers or foreign mercenaries who were subject to some sort of discipline. This allowed them to co-operate in comparatively large numbers and in a professional manner. Harald Gormsson is credited with the foundation of the partly-mythical Viking fort of Jomsberg on the Baltic coast of Prussia, inhabited by warriors aged between eighteen and fifty who submitted to a rigorous code of conduct. Jomsberg may be a memory of such places as Trelleborg, Fyrkat and Aggersborg where the military forces were mustered before the attacks on Britain began.

If the Vikings of Jomsberg were a military élite of warriors who lived and died in an exclusively martial society, their religious or spiritual counterparts were the *berserkar* and *ulfheðnir*. Both these groups were regarded with no less fear and awe by their companions than by their foes. They were religious zealots of a peculiar kind, fanatical devotees of the cult of Óðin, who knew only one virtue – naked ferocity – and one goal – death in battle. They fought largely naked except for their animal skins (*berserkar* means 'bear-shirts' and *ulfheðnir* means 'wolf-coats') under the protection of their god, to whom they turned for inspiration and their particular kind of battle-fervour. Before a fight, they entered a kind of fit or trance in which they were seized with blood-lust and, heedless of friend or foe and without the least regard for personal safety, they rushed forward with a weapon in each hand carving a bloody swathe through the ranks. Their objective was never to win battles or to gain personal honour; it was simply to achieve a gory and glorious death in fighting (*vapndauðr*, 'weapon-death') and to be allowed entry to Óðin's heavenly hall, which was reserved for men of unrestrained courage who died in this way.

The demoralising effect just a few such men could have on the ranks of yeomen and local government officials ranged against them must have been total. Yet the berserks were not favoured by far-sighted leaders,

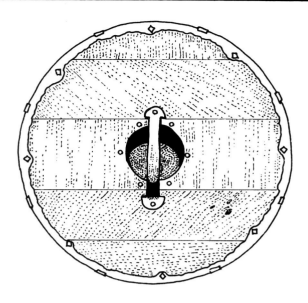

Flat, round shield of simple design. Wooden shields of this type were, probably common to both English and Viking armies.

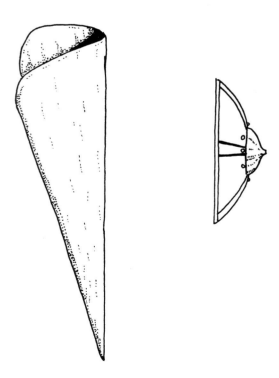

Long curved Viking shield of the very end of the Viking Age (above, left). Profile of convex English shield showing a prominent boss and a metal rim, faced with protective bands, perhaps also of metal (above, right).

for such men belonged to a bloodier, wilder and more reckless age, when leaders looked no further than the next battle and the next feast; the berserks just did not fit into the prototype medieval armies of the tenth and eleventh centuries. Furthermore, if no opportunity for fighting was provided by their patrons, they would soon tire of peace and begin challenging their fellows, stirring up enmity in order to bring about bloodshed. Even the most unprincipled heathen Norsemen now shunned such wanton, callous and belligerent fighters.

Turning to a consideration of English weapons, we may begin with the spear, the commonest offensive weapon. From evidence found in graves we know that it consisted commonly of a wooden shaft (usually long-since perished, though detectable by a dark streak in the earth) some two yards (two metres) in length. The foot may have been tipped with an iron shoe, while the head was usually long and leaf-shaped with a pronounced central ridge tapering towards the tip; in section it is lozenge-shaped. The head itself was most often of beaten iron (though more costly examples are pattern-welded) and had a socket into which the shaft was driven by force of manual pressure, and secured with a small spike resembling a nail punched through the metal and the wooden shaft inside. The head ranged in size from four to twenty-four inches (ten to sixty cm) long. Often there is evidence of shallow, semicircular grooves running either side of the central rib, which serve to lighten the tip without foregoing structural strength. Another common English feature, seen in manuscript illustrations and on surviving examples, is the small pair of 'wings' protruding from the shoulders of the weapon, preventing it piercing an opponent's armour so deeply that it could not be withdrawn. Indeed, the manuscripts sometimes show the wings attached directly to the shaft, immediately below the spearhead itself. If these were made of wood, as is perfectly possible, they may simply have perished in the ground and have escaped the notice of excavators. Decoration on the flat of the blade was common also, and it is perfectly possible that the wooden spear-shaft was painted.

Akin to the spear, yet distinct from it, was the *darod* or dart, an inferior weapon which could be

Ornamented English iron spearhead, secured by a silver-headed rivet.

The axehead for a two-handed battle-axe of the kind used by Saxon infantry.

produced in large quantities. It may have been no more than a metal-tipped wand, and the *ceorl* could carry two or three of them to hurl at the foe before the hand-to-hand fighting began. No doubt some of the articles now classified as 'spearheads' were once attached to these rudimentary javelins.

The shield was virtually ubiquitous among English warriors, judging by manuscript sources. It is fairly well known to today's archaeologists due to the presence of metal fittings which frequently survive in graves, though the wood itself has rotted away. Typically the shield was a round wooden board of laminated construction, with an iron boss (called the

rand) in the centre. This boss fitted over a hole in the centre of the board, and was usually conical or globular. The shield was provided with a straight metal bar on its inside which served as a grip, the knuckles of the fist protruding into the hollow.

The wooden board, known as the 'orb', was rivetted to the boss through holes in the outer, splayed edge of the rim of the boss. The orb itself was covered in leather or cowhide, though King Athelstān issued an edict against the covering of the shield in sheepskin. It was sometimes furnished with decorative metal fittings on its face, as on the famous example from the Sutton Hoo burial. Sizes of excavated shields vary from 30 to 76 cm (12 to 30 in) in diameter, and the wooden lathes which made up the orb were evidently quite thin – one example was no more than 12 mm (½ in) thick – which must have made the shield light and manoeuvrable. Though the richest ornamentation took the form of metal plates and fittings, painting of the shield's surface was quite likely, and manuscripts show swirling patterns of lines and dots. Some bosses were likewise engraved, or tipped with a small, flat metal disc plated with enamel decoration. Manuscripts consistently show shields which are curved into a 'watchglass' shape, and archaeological finds confirm that some bosses and other fittings were fashioned to accommodate this design. The lathes themselves seem often to have built up in layers at right-angles to their neighbours – like modern plywood – for added strength without any increase in weight. In *The Battle of Maldon*, there is a reference to *bordes lærig* ('shield's ?rim') which seems to refer to some sort of band or binding running round the perimeter of the shield's face: such features are clearly shown in some contemporary illustrations.

It is perfectly possible that the very lowest social orders, those who were not normally called upon to fight, did not possess shields with metal fittings, but a cruder wooden or wicker substitute which may have been only roughly circular. The Bayeau Tapestry shows English warriors using shields which are almost square, but with rounded corners. The long, nose-to-knee kite shield favoured by Norman cavalry is shown being used by some Englishmen, though it cannot have been very practical for foot-soldiers.

A weapon dating from Anglo-Saxon times but abandoned thereafter is the *seax*, a kind of single-edged sword, though sometimes no more than an up-market dagger. Originally the ancestral, native weapon of the Saxons, who derive their name (*Seaxe*) from it, it varied between 35 and 75 cm (14 and 30 in) in length. It was seldom a cheap substitute for a sword, rather an alternative type of hand-weapon: if we substitute the word 'cutlass' when we meet the word *seax*, this may give some idea of the status it enjoyed. These weapons were often richly decorated with inlays of precious metal in geometrical patterns, while some carried inscriptions recording ownership. One, recovered from the River Thames, is inlaid with the entire runic futhorc. The *seax* was apparently worn in a sheath at the hip, secured to the belt by a series of metal rings along the top edge, holding the weapon horizontally. Characteristic of the *seax*, though not of the sword, was the small cross-guard which barely projected beyond the width of the blade. The pommel often followed contemporary sword styles, and was commonly decorated. The very smallest examples were doubtless never intended as weapons in the strictest sense, more as domestic personal knives similar to those used by fishermen and woodworkers today.

One type of weapon for which there is little evidence is the sling. There is a reference to a *stæflidere* which may be a staff-sling – a kind of catapult, more powerful than the smaller hand-sling – but there is no evidence at this period for the manufacture of shot. Few spots in England could not provide a ready supply of stones of a suitable size, which would have been just as effective as the purpose-made clay pellets found in southern Europe.

The weapons described above may be considered to have been ubiquitous for the mass of troops, such as fyrd-warriors and farm-hands conscripted into military service. There were, of course, costlier and nobler items available for those with the disposable wealth to purchase them, and of these the most highly prized and the richest in symbolism, was the sword. Such was the importance accorded to this weapon that examples are hardly ever found in graves: they were too precious to be interred with the dead, and were handed on from father to son, or from lord to follower. Aside from their material worth as costly treasures, their symbolic worth lay in their associations within warrior groups. Only in exceptional circumstances, we may assume, were they actually buried and allowed to pass out of use.

The sword's blade was usually around 75 cm (30 in) long, relatively thin and straight-sided, tapering to a shallow point. The best blades were produced by a lengthy process known as pattern-welding, in which strands of iron rod were twisted together to form a metal plait which was then beaten flat and fitted with an edge of tempered steel. This mode of manufacture produced blades which were both pliant and able to retain their cutting edge in use. However, they were expensive and slow to produce, and were replaced generally by beaten iron types, under Carolingian influence, in the eighth century. The disadvantages of the poorer quality were compensated by the larger numbers, and, presumably, cheapness.

The hilt has been subjected to typological study, since there is evidence for changing tastes in the details of pommel and cross-guard, which may help to

date excavated finds. Often, the cross-guard consisted of no more than a block of bone through which the tang projected to form the core of the grip, itself often of bone. On later weapons, under Viking influence, the quillons of the cross-guard tend to droop towards the blade; earlier examples are usually straight and flat. The grip was often bound with leather strapping, or wound about with wires, for a better grasp. Pommels varied in shape: they were most often of roughly triangular form, but particular types are discernable, known as 'lobed', 'walnut' and 'cocked-hat'. Viking design was also responsible for the blades becoming thicker and heavier. Owners' and makers' marks were not uncommon, and extensive use was made of decoration and precious metals. Apart from 'personalising' the weapon – a precaution against theft – this served to make it a precious thing in itself, adding to the prestige of the owner.

The discovery in graves of swords which have corroded into a solid mass along with their coverings allows us to ascertain the nature of sheaths and scabbards. Most often, the body of the scabbard is made up of two lathes of wood, held apart by edgings and bound with leather. The top was protected from the sword's cross-guard by a metal mouthpiece known as a 'frog', while the end was reinforced by a 'chape' which prevented the scabbard being split and damaged. Some scabbards appear to have been lined with sheepskin, whose grease would protect the iron blade against rust as well as easing the blade in and out. Metal plaques and studs were often used to decorate and protect the outer face. Normally the sword hung from a baldric over the right shoulder at the left hip.

There is little evidence that the English used the axe in war, though this is not at all improbable in itself. The early English used the *francisca*, a kind of throwing-axe, but no late examples of this weapon are known to have survived. The Sutton Hoo ship-burial also provided a find of a battle-axe of all-metal construction. In later years, Viking styles predominated, and though axeheads are not uncommon finds from the later Saxon period, they are usually described as 'Viking' on account of their shape. Under Knut, the two-handed axe became the favoured weapon of the king's bodyguard, the house-carls. Throwing-axes are small, tomahawk-like weapons with sharply upward-curving blades. The curvature of the blade may well have served some purpose when

Sword decorated with inlay from the River Witham, of classical Scandinavian type.

the weapon was thrown, perhaps underarm.

Unusual as it was for a nobleman to use the bow in war, proficiency with it was expected from an accomplished 'gentleman'. From literary accounts, it seems that the bow was little used by the fyrdmen either, but there are a good many contemporary illustrations of archers. The Normans commented on the bad quality of English bowmen. Archaeological finds connected with archery are quite rare apart from small arrowheads which are not specifically military, since the bow was a hunting weapon. Bows illustrated consistently represent staves of about half the height of a man, though it is impossible to be certain how accurate these illustrations are meant to be. Actual bows found in graves usually consist of a muddy brown line, where the wood has rotted and discoloured the earth. Arrowheads are no real indication of the bow's use in battle.

One find of arrows from Germany consisted of wooden rods which had been hardened by holding the tips in a fire; they had no fitted point at all. Such arrows would have been adequate for dealing with 'soft' targets such as unarmoured fyrdmen, allowing the metal-headed shafts to be retained for the armoured warriors. The bows used were staves of yew, cut as sections along the outer face of a suitable length of timber. This enabled the weapon to benefit from a composition of stiff outer wood and the more elastic heartwood. Bows often seem to have been capped with horn 'shoes' which served as a protection for the thin, tapered ends of the shaft, and as a means of attaching the string. This was most often of twine, or of animal sinew, though a Norse source mentions the use of human hair. Arrows were carried in a quiver worn over the shoulder, or at the waist on a belt.

We know that thanes were required to equip their retinues, and that fyrd-warriors were required to arm themselves; it is not clear whether the general fyrd, consisting of all the able-bodied men of the district, was supplied with equipment from a public armoury, or whether they simply brought along whatever armour and weapons they had. One would expect that such men would take the precaution of wearing stout clothing, such as a leather jerkin – no match for a sword, but good enough against fire-hardened arrows. For those who were regularly called upon, a metal-studded jerkin would be an affordable piece of armour, and for those with ample means, a mail-coat offered the best protection.

Though little survives of Anglo-Saxon mail, the evidence suggests that it was made by native smiths. It consisted of metal rings, each linked to its four neighbours; the ends of the rings were hammered together in a butt-joint, or rivetted. The mail-coat from Sutton Hoo, once believed to be of butt-jointed construction, has now been shown to be made up of rivetted links. Butt-joints are much more likely to bend apart when subjected to the stress of combat.

It has been suggested that the Bayeux Tapestry represents metal rings or plaques fixed on to an undershirt and while this is far from proven, it is quite certain that some sort of garment must have been worn beneath the mail to prevent the rings being driven into the wearer's flesh when the coat was struck or pierced. This undershirt may have been a leather jerkin, or a padded or quilted jacket. It has been shown that mail is most effective at stopping arrows if some substantial clothing is worn on top of it – this slows down the arrow so that the mail can withstand it. The relative scarcity of mail on warriors in Anglo-Saxon illustrations may support the theory of this having been their custom. Yet a mail-coat was a costly thing, and few warriors would have been content to hide such a prestigious garment: when mail is shown in drawings of the period it is as the topmost piece of clothing, probably a sign of rank and wealth. Early depictions show a coat which reaches from the shoulder to the hips, with elbow-length sleeves, often with vandyked edges; later we find the more familiar knee-length, long-sleeved coat, split fore and aft to the crotch to allow the wearer to ride a horse. This is probably the kind of mail-coat the Bayeux Tapestry is meant to show, though the effect here is of a pair of metal long johns (needless to say, even the hardiest warrior would not choose to ride in such a garment!).

Armour made up from scales or plates was used in Eastern Europe at this time, and is believed to have been worn by Vikings around the Baltic. Normally, it consisted of metal plates riveted to a sturdy (probably leather) jacket so that they presented an unbroken metal surface. A variation was that of metal plates linked together by metal rings so that the armour hung under its own weight from the attachment points at the shoulders. Such kinds of protection must have formed an alternative to mail, though they would have been less flexible. It has not been proven that the English used such plate-armour, though it is by no means improbable. The English were quick to adopt Viking equipment suitably adapted to their own needs, when it proved superior: thus the Anglo-

A Norman helmet, complete with nose guard. In the Bayeux Tapestry Harold's Anglo-Saxon housecarls are shown wearing very similar helmets.

Saxon warrior came to use a mail hood later known as a 'coif'. They called it *healsbeorg* (neck-protector) which developed into the word 'hauberk' and came to mean the mail-coat as a whole.

The mention of the mail hood brings us to the question of protective headgear among the English. Manuscripts frequently show warriors wearing some sort of hat or helmet, yet only three helmets of Anglo-Saxon date are known to survive from the period: those from Benty Grange, Sutton Hoo, and Copper-gate (York). All are comparatively early – the Coppergate is latest, and belongs to the ninth century. Both it and the earlier Benty Grange example have evidence of a mail 'curtain' hanging from the lower rim and extending over the neck, while the Sutton Hoo helmet features metal plate extensions covering the cheeks and neck, as well as a fixed face-plate. These surviving examples were all doubtless the property of wealthy men, who could afford the best protection that money could buy. There is little doubt that Sutton Hoo was a king's tomb, and that the treasures found there represent a royal hoard, perhaps the accumulated wealth of an entire dynasty used in fitting out the grave.

From archaeology we know almost nothing of the headgear of the ordinary foot-soldier. From manuscripts, however, we can see that the spear-carrying infantry were equipped with a small, crested cap and the very fact that these have not survived suggests that they were made from perishable material – most probably leather. A leather helmet could be easily, cheaply and quickly made in comparison with a metal equivalent. If it were made from boiled hide stretched over a mould (*cuir bouilli*) it would be tough and stiff enough to serve against all but the sharpest weapons.

Manuscripts often show a style of helmet consisting of a circular rim, to which are attached two metal bands which intersect at the crown to form the outline of the bowl. This 'skeleton' helmet must have been filled in with horn or metal plates, or perhaps a leather skull cap worn beneath the frame. The Benty Grange helmet was of this type, but had small triangular horn plates attached outside the frame, like roofing shingles. The advantages of this method of construction were lightness and cheapness, in combination with a good measure of protection. It is perfectly possible that substantial numbers were produced to equip those freemen who regularly engaged in military service.

Helmets of the 'Norman' type, with the whole bowl beaten out of a single piece of metal were favoured by their Viking forebears in a much earlier period. Examples of this type occur throughout Europe, some with a projecting nose-piece (a nasal) but many without. A characteristic Viking refinement was the addition of two metal straps extending from a broad band round the brow to meet the nasal, and so enclose the eyes and nose in armoured protection. The 'beaten-out helmet' or *Spangenhelm* was most often roughly conical or nut-shaped, sometimes reinforced with metal straps and a rim. Scandinavian examples of pre-Viking date often have elaborate cheek-pieces and metal plates to protect the face and neck. Similarly, English helmets, though not of *Spangenhelm* type, often appear to have imitated these designs. The Coppergate example has extended cheek-pieces and an exaggerated nasal; that from Sutton Hoo has a full face panel which, with the cheek-piece drawn tight around, would have offered complete protection to the head.

The paucity of surviving examples hampers study of Anglo-Saxon headgear, and this scarcity may be assumed to show that helmets were not regularly buried with their owners. As war-gear, they were made to last longer than just one lifetime, and as with the sword and mail-coat, they were usually passed on to the succeeding generation. Professional warriors were given military equipment on entering a lord's service; if they died or moved on, the equipment would be passed back to the lord; in this sense, except for those thanes and noblemen who bought their own, all such items were notionally loaned rather than given to the lord's followers.

Written sources mention a kind of wind-instrument, perhaps a modified bull's horn such as was otherwise used for drinking which was used for military purposes. It may have been purpose-made, however, as some drawings show various types in use. No example is known to survive, which suggests that it was probably woodwind rather than brass. Viking armies are known to have used horns, which may have helped fleets stay together in mist at sea, and it is possible that some sort of signalling system might have been used – horns and trumpets in conjunction with flags and standards. However, although they undoubtedly had the technological resources, it is doubtful that either English or Viking armies would have evolved such systems since both armies preferred to fight in the time-honoured ways and did not bother overmuch about obeying orders which tended to stifle personal initiative.

Flags or standards were carried into battle by designated men; *Beowulf* describes one such *cumbles hyrde* (banner's keeper). The standard was used to mark the position of leader. At Hastings, King

A central-European helmet, made of triangular pieces riveted together. It is described by its museum as a 'Spangenhelm'.

Harold had two banners: his personal one, and a national one alongside it. Probably the most famous banner of the period, however, is the Danish one seized by English forces from a defeated foe in Devon in 878 according to the *Chronicle: Ðār wæs se gūðfana genumen ðe hī raefen hēton* ('there that banner was taken which they call "Raven" '). The Danes apparently attributed magical properties to it, and regarded its capture with dismay. Military thinking of the time set great store by the seizing of the enemies standard. A flag was the symbol of an army's pride and self-esteem, its strength and success. The loss of the flag was therefore a symbol of failure and defeat, and caused panic even if the day was not actually lost. In effect the standard represented the army's spirit and soul, and the foe who took the soul took with it the will to fight and the belief that victory

was possible. It is quite likely that English armies would have had colourful embroidered banners, since English needlework (*opus anglicum*) was famed throughout Europe. The standard itself was a large textile square or triangle, with dagged edges or decorative streamers. Carolingian armies used the 'dragon-banners', an ingenious adaptation of the wind-sock principle. A fabric tube, closed at the far end, was mounted behind a carved or moulded facsimile dragon's head, the mouth of which was open and hollow. As the head moved forward, the air passing through the hollow mouth caused the bag to inflate, and so the dragon appeared to flutter overhead.

On the whole, warriors' equipment was designed with two objectives: to work efficiently and to impress. The ornamental inlay on a sword's blade was as important a feature of the weapon as its hard edge. Warriors from all ages and periods have always sought to impress and intimidate others by a fine show, whether through the tawdry, colourful uniforms of the Napoleonic period or the stark, functional dress of modern times. The need to decorate and personalise is one of mankind's oldest and most basic impulses. The warriors of northern Europe held the view that an object should be ornamented in order to give it character; the finer the decoration, the worthier and more valuable the object. Thus ornamental motifs were applied to even the simplest items of everyday use: a bone comb had ring-and-dot patterns scratched on its sides; a small metal buckle sports a sun-wheel design; a wooden bucket has criss-cross lines over its surface. The design is usually abstract, either pure geometric pattern or repetitive interlacing or stylised creatures. Naturalism was not tolerated until much later and the craftsmen went to great lengths to turn apparently intractable shapes, such as animal and human forms, into mere elements in a design. Unfortunately, relatively little survives of the more accomplished work and the fraction we possess merely serves to remind us of the great deal we have lost.

Viking tastes and styles merged with native English traditions to produce new and vigorous styles in English art, particularly in metalwork and jewellery. Their influence was also responsible for the introduction of new types, such as the Celtic penannular brooch, which were not previously in use among the English, but which soon caught on and became very popular. Scandinavian motifs such as the curious gripping beasts, were adapted into English art, which benefited from the infusion of new ideas. Religious art was heavily influenced by Carolingian traditions, particularly in the field of pen drawings in manuscripts. This influence increased with the greater influx of French monastics when the Benedictine reform of the monasteries got under way in England. The result was a greater naturalism in English drawing, although medieval artists had problems with perspective, which makes their work seem childishly inaccurate to our modern eyes.

If the purpose of the applied ornamentation was to excite greed and awaken the desire in the beholder to own the object, then it may fairly be stated that the art was successful. Few people can see the fine and delicate workmanship on the Sutton Hoo treasures without feeling the urge to handle the items and to take them home for further study!

Whether military buildings were severely functional or magnificently ornamented cannot be ascertained. Their function was not so much to impress as to provide strongholds to act as bases for the English defence forces.

In so far as the *burh* (fort or stronghold) was also the dwelling of the thane, it must have been at least moderately comfortable. The later *burh*s, from after the time of Alfred, were purpose-built, based on the dwellings of leading men. Aside from these, the Anglo-Saxons generally used ditches as their only form of earthwork – though Offa's Dyke, to take one example, was an impressive and co-ordinated enterprise requiring planning and construction skills that we can hardly guess at, given the lack of written communication then. Roman and earlier fortifications still standing were also taken over as bases to use against the Danes.

The *burh*s played an important part in English military planning – and in the regeneration of town life in the later period. They were manned, according to Alfred's statutes, at the ratio of four men to a pole 5.5 m (5½ yd) of wall; thus each man was responsible for 1.25 m (4 ft 1½ in) of wall, probably representing the amount of room he occupied when armed with spear and shield, giving him enough room to wield them. Obviously no *burh* could accommodate enough men to stand round the length of its walls at 1.3 m (4 ft) intervals; the fort itself was held by the thane and his followers who constituted a permanent garrison, while the others were to be drawn from the surrounding countryside when the call to arms came.

We shall look in the next chapter at the economic impact of these *burh*s, many of which lie beneath our modern towns.

CHAPTER 10

town and country

the word 'town' derives from the Saxon *tūn*, an enclosure. The modern concept of a town simply did not exist a thousand or more years ago – the nearest the Anglo-Saxons came to evolving towns of a modern kind was the series of *burh*s, military strongholds acting as centres of administration and local government. Each *burh* was manned, as previously mentioned, at the rate of one soldier to every 1.25 m (4 ft 1½ in) of rampart. Each soldier was, in turn, drawn from the surrounding countryside in the ratio of one from every hide of land. A hide is the notional amount of land required to support a freeman, meaning enough land to feed not just the freeman, but also his wife and children, and perhaps his own parents, plus enough workmen to farm the land. A hide was not an exact measure of land (such as a hectare, for example); it differed according to the quality of the soil, its accessibility to the plough, and many other factors.

It would be virtually impossible to administer a system based on so nebulous a concept as the hide, and so it would have proved had each district not been assessed at some point and a number of hides allocated or calculated for each part. This number was then fixed and all assessments for tax or public duty were made on the values assigned. The result of the allocation of hides, region by region, were gathered together in a document known as the *Burghal Hidage*. Despite its rather unprepossessing title, this document is of great importance for the study of the *burh* system. The network of fortifications across Wessex, later extended into the Danish areas, required elaborate supply and support systems which were calculated for each area through its 'official' assessment of hides. The records preserved in the document have

been tested for accuracy: for example, Wareham's *burh* was allocated 1600 hides: thus it had 1600 men manning its walls; at 5 m (5½ yd) for every four men, Wareham should have 2012 m (2200 yd) of wall; in fact the surviving banks there total some 1993 m (2180 yd).

The *burh* fortresses were used as a means of protecting the English from foreign attack. As English power extended into the Danish areas, from the beginning of the tenth century, the *burh* became more than a stronghold: in the Midland areas, the Danes had established their own five boroughs: Lincoln, Stamford, Nottingham, Derby and Leicester. These had been centres for the Danish settlement, which was still organised into 'armies' a full generation after the original freebooters had arrived. The boroughs were more than simple chieftains' settlements, however; they represented Viking domination, and were a source of great pride to the Danes. When Wessex began the long process of re-conquest, the model of the Viking centres was followed, and when the boroughs eventually fell to the English they kept some of their former stature.

During the next century and more, *burh*s were established wherever there was need, on the principle that no habitation should be more than twenty miles from one. This not only increased the protection offered by ensuring that no village was too exposed, it also made the gathering of the defending soldiers a simpler and more manageable task. Where local conditions proved inconvenient, families were 'invited' to relocate nearer the stronghold; if they resisted, they were forced to move either into a *burh* or its immediate area. Whilst this simplified many aspects of administration, it also meant some people losing their

livelihood; accordingly, incentives such as low tax assessments were probably offered to allow the newcomers to adjust to their new lives.

The concentration of population in and around these strategic sites led to an increased awareness of the possibilities of trade and commerce. The assessments for tax became more accurate at the same time, as kings took an even greater than usual interest in the sums due to them, and backed up their rights with a more effective administration. As the towns became centres of manufacture and trade, so the surrounding countryside must have been reorganised to allow for

From the Bayeux Tapestry: (above) a nobleman's house and armed retinue. He is seated on an ornamented bench, with his sword drawn. Below, he indulges in his outdoor pastime, hunting with hawk and dogs.

the shift in population. And as Alfred had devised, or rather extended, the *burh* system until it became a tool of English government, so he reformed the army, dividing in two the total force of men liable to serve; while the first division was out on campaign, the agricultural work was carried out by the second and vice versa. The men in the garrisons, being thanes' permanent bodyguards, were exempted from this. Alfred and his successors clearly saw the maintenance of food production as a key means of ensuring that the military measures did not founder.

If *burh*s served initially as military strongholds, and subsequently as administrative centres, as the threat of Danish incursion abated, it was inevitable that they would become focal points for the establishment and exercise of royal control over the surrounding district. Royal residences were necessary for early Anglo-Saxon kings, who were constantly on the move to avoid their entourage exhausting the food supplies in any one area. Following the expansion of the *burh*s, urban life grew in importance, and with urban life went direct royal control and a heavy tax burden which extended across the whole social structure, but which could only be sustained and regulated from local centres of royal power.

Many *burh*s acquired mints, producing coinage under royal licence, and with the licence-holder subject to severe penalties if he abused his position. The profession of moneyer could be extremely lucrative while the king benefited from the striking of coins: the moneyer had to purchase the dies from which coins were to be minted from the royal treasury, at no small cost. He could vary the method of assessment of tax payment accepting renderings either by weight (the bullion value of the coins) or by tale (their face value). It is probable that many dues (such as heriot) could be commuted to money payments, which may have been preferable, since kings must usually have preferred to receive cash (on which they had already made some profit) rather than odd pieces of metalwork which would have to be melted down to realise their value.

The Anglo-Saxon farms and villages, *burh*s and towns are mostly still with us. By far most of the place-names in England are derived from names given by Anglo-Saxons. Some are very old and belong to the early period of English settlement – these are the 'tribal' names usually found in the early English gains: names such as Hastings (Hæsta's people), Reading (Reada's people) and Barking (Berica's people). They are named after local leaders, in many cases probably the chief who brought the tribe over from the Continent. While these are obvious names given to tribes, which were later loosely used for the region where the tribes settled, and evidently given before the small local groups were absorbed into larger kingdoms, most English place-names are less helpful, since they refer to geographical or topographical features which could have received their designations

A page from an English work on the medicinal properties of plants; those illustrated are the Teazle (called Wolf's Comb) and Yellow Bugle (Henep). Such works, combining the herblore of the classical world with native tradition, were invaluable aids to early doctors.

at almost any time before the Norman Conquest.

A few English towns still have names which they bore before the English came, though usually in a modified form. Among this group would be, for example, York: the earliest mention of this name is believed to be in 150 BC, when it had the form Eborakon (the yew-tree place); to the Romans it was known as Eboracum. When the Northumbrian English took over the site, they established a *wīc* (trading centre) and the place was called Eoforwīc – *eofor* was their attempted pronounciation of the British name, but *eofor* was also their own word for the boar, and a common personal name. When Northumbria fell to the Danes, the name passed into

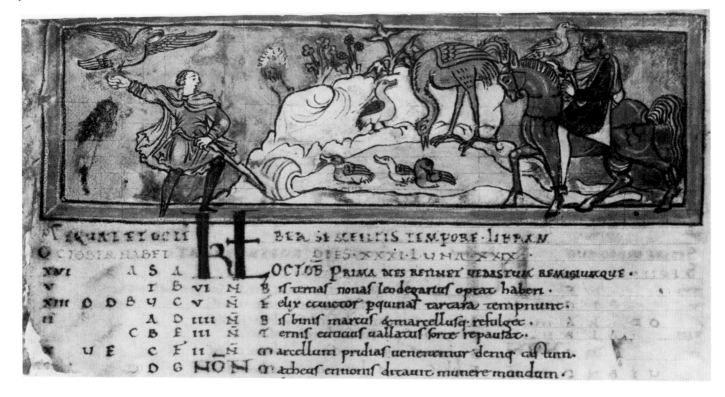

Another hawking scene: here the fowler is armed with a club. The month of October from a Saxon calendar.

Scandinavian speech, though the nearest they could get to it was Jorvík, now made famous as the name of the historical exhibition of the Viking Age. Local pronunciation of the word is still Yorik, commemorating the Danish form.

Many places established or developed under Roman occupation were fortified, the word for such a place being *castra* (fort, castle). Though the early English were usually excluded from these places, they often took over the name, which in the course of time developed into the element 'chester' which is found in many town-names, with variants such as '-cester' and '-xeter'. Examples are: Colchester ('*castra* on the River Colne'), Leicester ('*castra* of the tribe called Ligore'), Wroxeter ('*castra* called Viroconion').

In the far western counties, a higher proportion of place-names are actually Welsh, and in Cornwall they are nearly all Cornish, because the English had much less impact, and much later, in these regions. An example is Creech in Dorset, from the Welsh *crug* (a hill). Stray Welsh survivals also occur much further east, as in Crayke in Yorkshire, and Creake in Norfolk, from the Welsh *craig* (a rock). Very common throughout the country is the survival of British names for rivers; we have seen this already in the poem *The Battle of Maldon*, where the river is called Panta, derived from the word *pant*, a valley.

The majority of English place-names are formed from a quite small number of elements denoting common landscape features, whether natural or man-made. These may be combined with each other, or with words for animals or (most commonly) personal names. Such elements are:

bearu (wood, grove)
beorg (hill, burial-mound)
bæce (stream)
bold (homestead)
brycg (bridge)
brōc (stream)
burh (fort)
burna (stream)
cirice (church)
clif (cliff, ravine)
clōh (valley)
cot (hut)
croft (small field)
cumb (valley)
dæl (dale, valley)

denn (swine pasture)
denu (valley)
dic (ditch, rampart, dyke)
dūn (hill)
ea (river, land by a river, island)
eg (island)
ecg (ridge)
fenn (marshland, swamp)
feld (open land)
flēot (stream)
ford (ford, river-crossing)
fyrhð (wood)
geat (gate, road)
grāf (grove)
græf (pit, trench)

halh (water-meadow, narrow valley)
hām (homestead, village)
hamm (enclosed land, field)
hangra (slope)
haga (enclosure)
heafod (headland)
hǣð (heath)
hyll (hill)
hol (hollow)
holt (wood)
hop (dry land in a swamp)
hōh (spur of a hill)
hrycg (ridge)
hūs (house)
hyrst (copse, hillock)
hyð (hythe, haven)
lacu (stream)
land (land, estate)
lēah (grove, wood)
lǣs (pasture)
hlið (slope)
hlaw (grave-mound)
mǣre (boundary)
mere (pool, lake)
mersc (marsh)
mǣd (meadow)
myln (mill)
mynster (minister, mother church)
mōr (wasteland, moor)
muða (river-mouth)

nǣss (ness, headland)
ōfer (river-bank)
pæð (path, track)
port (port, town)
rið (stream)
sǣ (sea, lake)
scaga (shaw, copse)
scelf (ledge)
sīde (hillside)
slæd (slade, valley)
stān (boulder, stone)
stall (place)
stede (religious place)
stoc (outlying settlement)
stōw (place, meeting place)
strēt (Roman road, street)
stīg (pathway)
ðorp (outlying farm, dairy farm)
tūn (enclosure, farm)
trēow (tree)
wæd (ford)
weald (woodland)
worðign (enclosure)
wæsse (marsh, fen)
wæter (lake, river)
welle (spring)
wīc (trading post, village, dairy farm, salter's workshop)
wudu (wood)
worð (enclosure)

Forging the sword of Sigurd of the Volsung. 'By fire were its outer edges forged, by venom drops was it tinged within'. A change in Viking sword construction took place around AD 900 when pattern-welded blades began to be replaced by new blades that were lighter and tougher. Blades were often traded by merchants, and were sometimes marked with the symbol of the maker.

From these common elements come a great many English town-names, often in slightly altered forms. A few examples will suffice: Appleton (Berkshire) is *apple+tūn* meaning 'orchard'; Bolton (in many counties) is often *bold+tūn* meaning 'homestead enclosure, fenced-off land near the dwelling'; Combwich (Somerset) is *cumb+wic*, village in a valley.

Examples of personal names, presumably of erstwhile owners, include: Colton (Norfolk), 'Cola's *tūn*'; Snettisham (Norfolk) 'Snæt's *hām*' Molescroft (Yorkshire), "Mūl's croft".

Animal names occur in such examples as: Ely (Cambridgeshire), 'eel island', where eels were caught in the fens; Enford (Wiltshire), 'duck ford'; and Ilmer (Berkshire), 'hedgehog pool'.

Occasional oddities occur, such as places named after supernatural beings, such as Shincliffe (spectre

Viking brooch illustrating a Norse horseman using his spear two-handed.

cliff), or Hascombe (witch's valley), or dedicated to heathen gods (Thundersley, Wednesfield, Tysoe) – or simply called 'heathen temple' (Harrow, Weedon). Some names throw light on aspects of early English social conditions and physical environment: Stratford and Stretton, denoting Roman roadways; the 'chester/cester' group discussed above; Eccles, a British word for 'church' which occurs widely; Berechurch and Bradkirk, denoting churches made from planks; Thatcham, 'the thatched farm', rather than roofed with shingles; numerous names containing the elements 'ford' and 'bridge'; Wardlow commemorating the look-out posts; and numerous Kingstons, denoting royal ownership at some stage.

When the Norsemen came to settle, rather than plunder, they took over existing estates in many cases, and renamed them according to their own custom. Chief among the distinctive Scandinavian elements is the ending -by, as in Whitby, Hemsby, and Grimsby. Names of this sort are common in the old Danelaw areas, and hardly found at all outside it. The English name was often simply forgotten, so that unless it happened to be recorded in a charter, for example, there may be no trace of it. However, many Danish settlers of later generations either could not afford such lands, or perhaps preferred the soil conditions they were used to in their homeland, and consequently established new settlements, outliers from the main farms set up by the English, frequently along streams

Wild boars in woodland being hunted on foot: the centre figure has a spear and grips the hilt of a sheathed sword, while his companion has hunting dogs and a horn. The month of September from a Saxon calendar.

and small tributaries of main rivers. These were on virgin soil, and in all probability had never had an English designation, so the Viking settler who gave his name to his farm was effectively naming the area he had cleared as well.

Sometimes the incomers simply could not cope with the English sounds they heard – we saw earlier that Eoforwic was renamed as Jorvík. Similarly, they replaced English words such as *shelf* and *ship* with their own forms *skelf* and *skip*. *Shaw* became *skaw*, *ridge* became *rigg*, *church* became *kirk*, and the pattern of northern English place-names that we know today was laid down. Peculiarly Scandinavian elements include: *bank* (a ridge) perhaps replacing English *bench* and *bekkr* (stream) for the English *bæce*. Other Scandinavian elements are as follows:

bigging (building)	*gata* (road)
bōd (shelter)	*holm* (islet)
brekka (hillside, slope)	*haugr* (mound, hillock)
kjarr (brush, scrubland, marsh)	*hulm* (land by water)
	eng (meadow)
erg (hill-pasture)	*kelda* (spring)

lundr (grove, copse)
skali (hut, booth)
skogr (wood)
sætr (hill-pasture)
slakki (shallow valley)
steinn (boulder, stone)

dorp (outlying farm)
dveit (clearing)
toft (homestead)
vað (ford)
viðr (wood)

Even from this short list, it is evident that there is greater emphasis on farming hilly land: *-erg, brekka* and *sætr* all refer to the Scandinavian practice of driving livestock into the upper dales during the summer months to take advantage of the grassland there, a tradition observed in Norway and Iceland. Also significant are the words *dorp* and *dveit* referring to satellite settlements on newly-cultivated land, though *dorp* had the same form in English and cannot

always be distinguished from it by spelling alone.

Later names are surprisingly few: straight imports such as Richmond and Belvoir were rare, or at least have not stood the test of time by ousting the rival English names. Sometimes the Norman French noble chose to use the Latin equivalent of the English name: thus Pontefract for Pontfreit, though this is much closer to the spoken form 'Pomfrit'. Even the French names show normal development of English sounds, so they must have been adopted and absorbed quite quickly after their introduction. Thus Belvoir is reduced to 'Beaver' and Beaulieu to 'Byoolee', though in both cases, the Norman French pronunciation was very different from standard modern French, and the last example was probably pronounced something like 'Byo-lyoo' when it was named.

chapter 11

transport – wheels and keels

Britain in the tenth century was radically different in appearance from today. Comparatively little land had been cleared for agriculture, and the whole landscape was divided by natural barriers such as dense woodland, streams, rivers, marshland, hills, rough and broken ground, upland ranges and moorland. Communication was possible in this inhospitable environment only by the maintenance of the road network. Roman roads, some still traceable today, cut their rectilinear paths across the country, seemingly regardless of the natural obstacles. Their metalled surfaces were almost certainly in a state of terminal neglect by the tenth century, but they may still have proved the quickest, because most direct, route between major towns. More important were the great prehistoric trackways which marked out the trade-routes used in the dim past, and which were still heavily used in Saxon times – many lie below modern roads, or have been superceded within living memory by the motorways. These ancient tracks, and other lesser paths, came into being to serve the needs of villages and farmsteads in the New Stone Age; the network was expanded with the arrival of the Celts who brought more advanced means of transport – their light, two-wheeled chariots – and who brought new land into cultivation. As succeeding generations grew up, extended the field system, and pushed back the boundaries of the wilderness, so new paths and tracks were created to serve the new areas.

With the arrival of the Anglo-Saxons, heavy traffic abated for a while, as political and economic conditions did not favour large-scale mobility. The road network certainly played an important part in the settlement pattern of these early immigrants by favouring some locations over others. The system left by the Roman administration seems to have remained largely undisturbed, while the roads themselves fell into disrepair through lack of an efficient support system to maintain them. Saxon settlements linked themselves to each other by bridle-paths and riding-tracks; inevitably, they also linked themselves by similar pathways to the nearest section of main road. Once kingdoms with defined central authority arose in the seventh century, the advantages to the administration of the land afforded by good roads reaching throughout the territories became apparent. Never was this truer than when Alfred had to contend with the Danes, and he had to coerce his local reeves and thanes to maintain the roads for which they were responsible. As West Saxon authority extended over southern England, so the movement of English armies was facilitated by the absolute obligation on all freemen to repair the thoroughfares in their district.

In seventh-century Northumbria, the pious kings ordered posts to be set up at roadside springs, and drinking-vessels to be hung there for the convenience of thirsty wayfarers. It is quite likely that similar measures were undertaken elsewhere on behalf of public-spirited landowners. Hut-like shelters for travellers caught on the road at night or in bad weather are also known to have been set up. Under the laws of an early king, the main roads were the only legal routes for travellers, unless they were prepared to shout or blow horns to advertise their presence. This was to prevent outlaws skulking in

Felling timber with axes: wood was a vital resource on which men relied for housing, for simple tools, for transport, and of course as a source of heat and light. The month of July from a Saxon calendar.

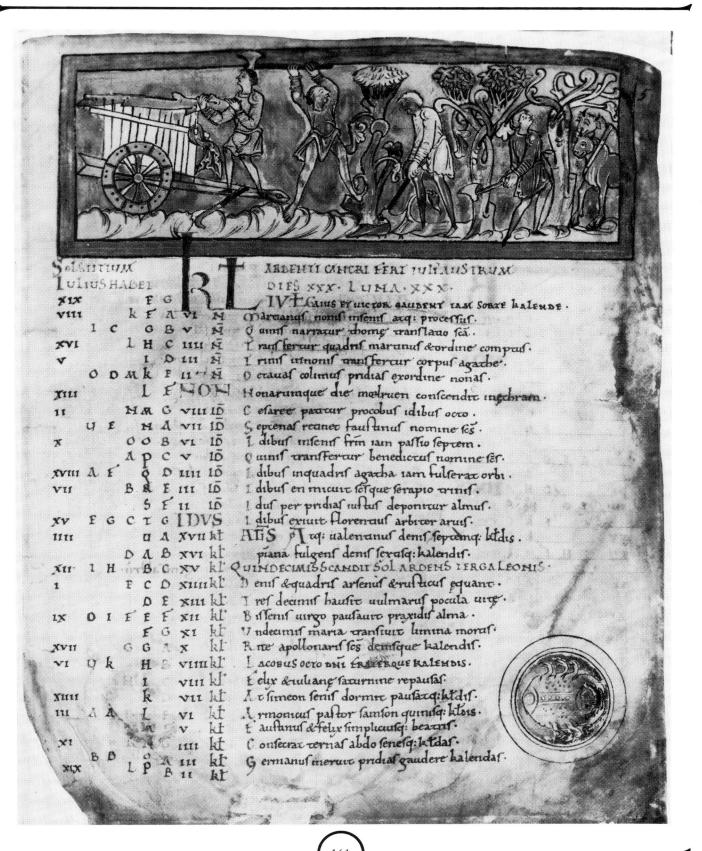

Solstitium
IuLIUS HABET

ARDENTI CANCRI FERAT IULIA USTRUM
DIES XXX · LUNA XXX ·

XIX		F G		KL	IUL Gaius et uictor gaudent iam sorte kalende ·
VIII		k F A VI	N		Marcianas nonis insenis atq; processus.
I	C	G B V	N		Quinis narratur thome translatio sca ·
XVI		L H C IIII	N		Transfertur quadris marinus & ordine compus.
V		I D III	N		Trinis uinonis transfertur corpus agathe·
	O D M k	F II	N		O ctauas colimus pridias exordine nonas.
XIII		L E	NON		Honarumque die moelruen conscendit ingebram·
II		H M G VIII	ID		C esaree pascur procobus idibus octo ·
U	E	H A VII	ID		S eptenas renes faustinus nomine scs
X		O O B VI	ID		L dibus insenis frm iam passio septem ·
	A	P C V	ID		Q uinis transfercur benedictus nomine ser ·
XVIII	A F	Q D IIII	ID		L dibus inquadris agatha iam fulserat orbi ·
VII		B R E III	ID		L dibus en micuit scrque serapio trinis.
		S F II	ID		L dus per pridias iustus deponitur almus.
XV	F	G C T G	IDVS		L dibus exiuit florencius arbicor aruis ·
IIII		U A XVII	kt		ATIS P tq; ualeuanus denis septenq; ketdis ·
		D A B XVI	kt		piana fulgens denis sexasq; kalendis ·
XII	I H	B C XV	kt		QUINDECIMIS SCANDIT SOL ARDENS TERGA LEONIS ·
I		T C D XIIII	kt		D enis & quadris arsenus & rusticus equant ·
		D E XIII	kt		T res decimis hausit uulmarus pocula uirg ·
IX	O I	F E F XII	kt		B issenis uirgo pausauit praxidis alma ·
		F G XI	kt		U ndecimis maria transiuit limina morus ·
XVII		G G A X	kt		R ite apollonaris scs denisque kalendis ·
VI	U k	H S VIIII	kt		LACOBUS OCTO DNI FRATERQUE KALENDIS ·
		I VIII	kt		F elix & iuliane saturnine repausas ·
XIIII		R VII	kt		A t simeon senis dormit pausatq; kltdis ·
III	A A	L VI	kt		A rmonicus pastor samson quinesq; kltbis ·
		M V	kt		F austinus & felix simplicausq; beatus ·
XI		N IIII	kt		C onsecrat ternas abdo senesq; kltdas ·
	B B	O A III	kt		G ermanus meruit pridias gaudere kalendas ·
XIX		L P B II	kt		

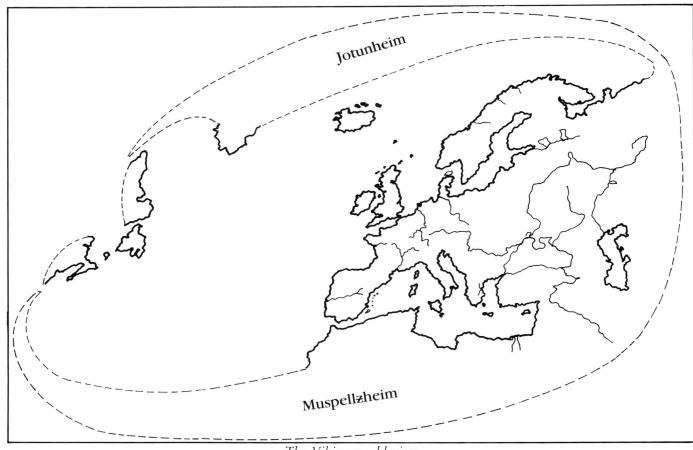

The Viking world view.

lonely places from pretending to be voyagers who had become lost. It also kept strangers on the highways, where they could be observed by the king's servants.

In a land such as Britain then was, with abundant natural barriers to communication and the highways still dangerous and difficult, the movement of goods by water must have been an attractive alternative. With shallow-draught vessels it was perfectly possible to navigate along even quite minor waterways deep inland. Ships and smaller craft must have been, on balance, safer, faster and more efficient than road haulage, which presumably relied on draught horses or handcarts – though these vehicles would have been used to transfer goods from the smithy or the barn to the hythe, and vice versa. Royal centres seem generally to have had access by water, and kings derived part of their revenue from import taxes paid by merchants bringing their goods ashore in ports where official royal agents oversaw their trade.

The Vikings were instrumental in this sea-trade, and the rapid growth and economic development of places such as Dublin and York may be directly attributable to their position on Viking trade-routes. They became nodes in a network which extended beyond Europe, deep into the heart of Asia through Russia, and out over the wide sea to North America. Icelanders with a certain amount of wealth and a yen to see the world could set off to Norway, and thence to Britain, Ireland, northern France, Sweden, Denmark, or the southern Baltic coast, and be sure to find expatriate countrymen wherever they went. In those days, the sea around Britain's coasts was not a defensive moat but a broad highway leading men back and forth across its expanse. Only the Frisians of the northern nations could rival the Scandinavians for seafaring expertise; aware of this, the Danes harried their coasts and plundered their trading centres until their power was broken.

Physical evidence for all this traffic is not difficult to discover, though the craft themselves have disappeared. Exotic items turn up in the least expected places: Indian cowrie shells, Arabic silver coins, Oriental silks, and even a small statue of Buddha, have been found in northern European graves. The Rus (eastern European Vikings) had close trading links with Byzantium and its empire, known to them as Miklagarth, the Great Enclosure. Links were also forged with the Muslim Arab world, principally in connection with the slave trade, in which the Rus played an important part by raiding Slavic settlements and enslaving anyone unlucky enough to fall into their hands. The Moorish appetite for slaves, particularly fair-skinned women, was almost insatiable, though the Rus spared no effort to meet the demand.

Humble vehicles such as farm-carts are not known to survive from Anglo-Saxon times, though no one knows what the archaeologist's trowel may one day bring to light. Contemporary illustrations show heavy, wooden, four-wheeled waggons drawn by oxen or horses. They appear to be of a type found throughout Europe, in which the shafts were connected to the leading axle, which was in turn joined to the rear axle by a beam. Upon this 'running gear' rested the bed of the waggon and the driver's seat, which was raised above the level of the cargo area. The wheel were spoked and had a thick wooden outer rim which may have been replaced periodically. There is no evidence for the presence or absence of metal felloes in manuscript drawings; though technically well within contemporary capability to construct, on unmetalled roads they would probably have been superfluous.

    The best surviving example of a cart from the period is the one interred in the Oseberg ship-grave. This was a highly decorative waggon, clearly made for some wealthy client to impress those not so fortunate. It was sturdily made and had evidently seen some use before being buried, though its function while in service is still unclear. It may have been a processional waggon, perhaps linked with the cult of the fertility gods, as other evidence in the grave suggests.

    The handcart was probably commonly used for carrying goods over short distances, as horses were expensive and oxen slow, and both too useful to be wasted on errands that could be carried out by an unaccompanied farm-hand. Sometimes, however,

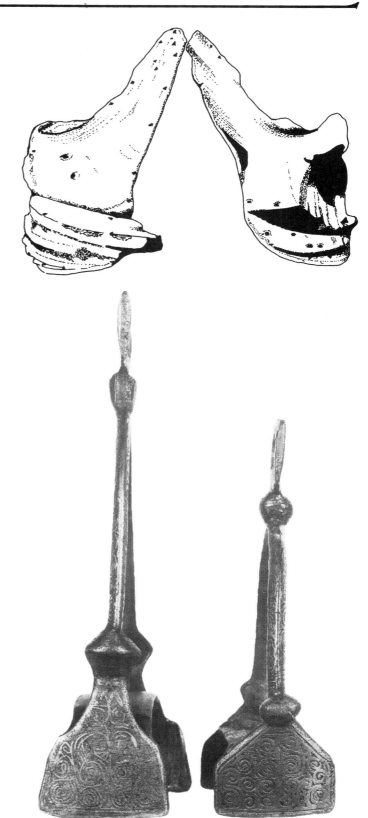

Oseberg saddle-frame, made from two carefully-shaped wooden plates which would have been padded with horsehair and covered with leather or sheepskin when in use.

Two iron stirrups, from the River Witham, Lincolnshire (left) and the Thames Battersea (right); both are heavily ornamented with an interlocking scroll motif.

The Seagry Stirrup Iron, inlaid with copper and brass. Anglo-Scandinavian (above). First half of the eleventh century. Stirrups were prestigious possessions and an important part of a mounted warrior's equipment. The Seagry Stirrup is probably of English manufacture although strongly influenced by Scandinavian design.

there was probably no real alternative to the use of pack-animals to carry merchandise, or tax-payments rendered in food, over marshy, steep or rough terrain which carts and waggons could not negotiate. When thanes rode out on campaign they had to take a supply of provisions for themselves and their dependants; in order to keep up with the mounted men, horses and mules were loaded with goods to provide a solution to the problem of maintaining adequate stores.

In general, when the wealthy travelled they rode on horseback, while the poor had to walk. An early bishop was noted for his humility because whenever the king gave him a horse to help him tour his see, he gave it straight away to some poor man whose need was greater. It was clearly regarded as humiliating, or at least a little undignified, for a man of such high rank to have to walk.

Gilt-copper alloy jug. Anglo-Saxon, second quarter of tenth century. The handle is in the form of a twisted snake, while the spout is in the form of an animal head. It is possible that the jug is a cruit, the vessel from which wine and water is poured into the chalice: if this were so, it would make the jug one of a very few liturgical vessels to survive from the Anglo-Saxon period.

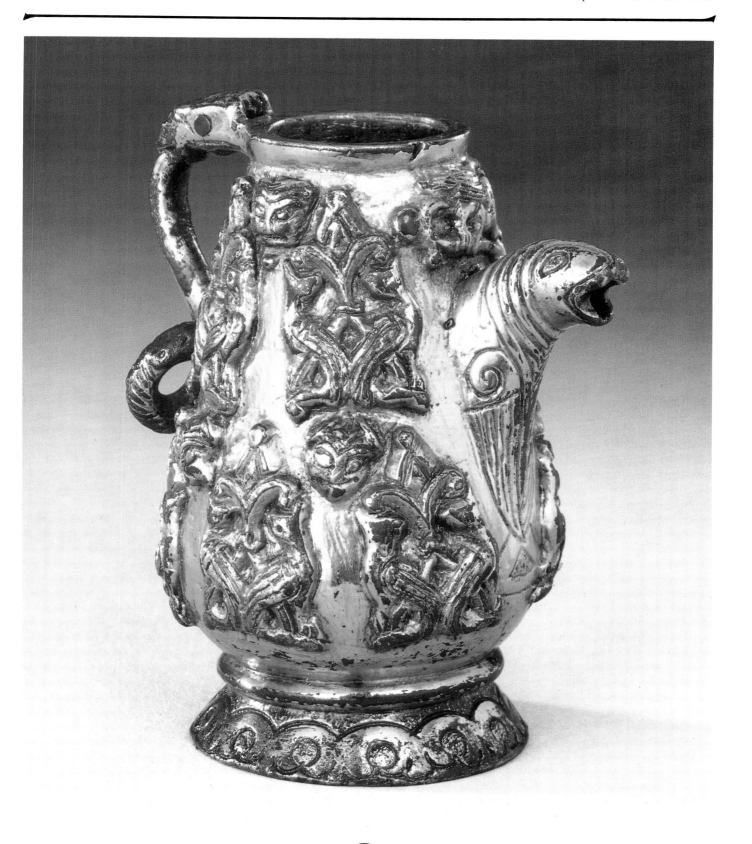

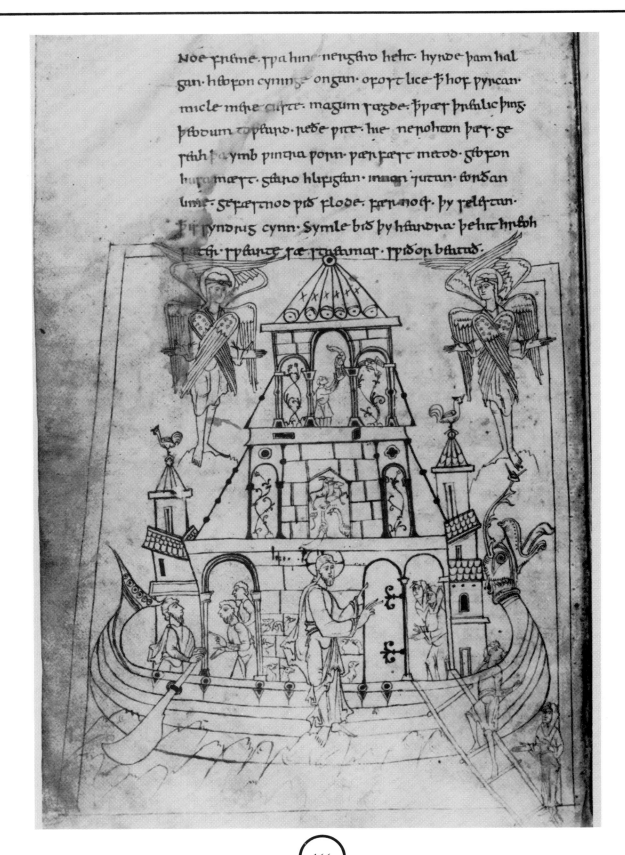

In winter things were easier. Sledges were used to move goods around, and this must have been a welcome relief for the menials who had to push the handcarts in summer. Though no English example survives, the Oseberg find again provides evidence, this time in the form of a complete Viking-age sledge with characteristic upturned runners. Cruder kinds have come to light elsewhere in Scandinavia, showing the origin of the vehicle as a simple hollowed tree-trunk with a slight point at one end, where a hole is provided to accept the rope by which it is dragged. The Oseberg sledge, like a similar example from Gokstad, consisted of runners attached to a flat bed, onto which a separate box-like cargo hold could be mounted, perhaps allowing the goods to be stored and transferred from vehicle to vehicle without unpacking them each time. With the superstructure in place and loaded, it would have been too heavy for a man to pull, and may even have been attached to a team of dogs.

Skis were an important means of getting around in Scandinavia, and were presumably introduced by the Vikings if they had not been in use earlier. In form, they were evidently shaped much like their modern equivalents, with an upturned front, a design that is shown on Swedish rock-carvings dating back to the Bronze Age, that is to say about a thousand years before the Vikings. Traditionally they were associated with the goddess Skaði, the deity who gave her name to Scandinavia, who hunted in the great northern forests and snow-fields wearing skis and armed with a bow. Skates were also known – in their simplest form just lengths of bone with a smoothed surface and holes at either end, through which thongs passed to secure them to the feet. One of the northern gods (the Æsir) was believed to own a magic bone with which he could walk over lakes – this seems to be an oblique reference to skates.

When considering the movement of goods and people in the Viking age, one inevitably has to consider the ships of the period. These were often prized possessions and it is not hard to understand why: with a ship the entire world became accessible and the furthest places could be reached. More importantly, with a ship one could travel beyond the confines of the known world out on to the vast encircling sea that separated the lands of men from the regions where giants and dwarfs dwelt. The ship had a place in contemporary society and culture similar to that of the spacecraft in modern society – a cunningly-designed, beautifully-made machine which made possible the infinite expansion of the known world and might lead to confrontation with strange, alien beings. The more practically-minded, however, probably regarded their vessels as people of the

An English conception of Noah's Ark: the dragon-headed prow and steering paddle at the rear are features of contemporary ship-building, while the superstructure appears to be a three-storied house with turrets.

A motif from the tapestry recovered from the Oseberg ship burial – probably a processional wagon.

Norman ship from the Bayeux Tapestry, used here to transport horses and their riders, with kite-shields at the bow. The Viking ancestry of such vessels is obvious.

twentieth century might very fast or very luxurious cars – as a means of moving around, but in a conspicuous style; part of the status-reinforcing equipment of the rich and powerful.

A few Viking ships have survived, some impressive luxury vessels, others cargo-carriers. The best-preserved is the ninth-century Gokstad ship, excavated from a huge grave-mound in southern Norway. At nearly 18 m (60 ft) long, and with an unladen weight of about nine tons, she was built mainly of oak with pine fittings. The hull was clinker-built, the individual boards (strakes) being first nailed together then lashed to an internal framework. This construction allowed the hull to retain some elasticity, so that the ship could bend and stretch in heavy seas. A keel ran the length of the underside, while the third strake from the top is pierced by a row of holes which accommodate the oars. The whole outer hull was caulked with hair and tar.

Provision was made for the crew, which may have numbered seventy, to fasten their shields along the topmost strake (the gunwale) which must have been an impressive sight. The mast was tied into the rib framework by means of a block bound with iron, seated on the deck; this allowed the propulsion of the whole vessel by sail power without the mast being torn out of its mounting. When not required, the mast could be taken down and stowed on raised wooden brackets. The mast was raised and lowered by strong ropes running from the prow to the top of the mast and then down to the stern. Further ropes fastened the mast to the sides of the vessel, but full details of the rigging are not known.

Steering was by means of a huge oar, called in English the *steorbord* (steering-plank); this was fixed to the right-hand aft section of the hull with bindings of plaited osiers, and for this reason the right-hand side of a ship is still called the 'starboard' side. In use, the steering-board extended below the keel, but its flexible mounting enabled it to be swung up out of the way when necessary. Spars were used to stretch the sail so the vessel could carry out tacking manoeuvres, but rowing would have been the only means of propulsion when entirely unfavourable winds were met with. The oarsmen probably sat on some form of benching, judging by the low position of the oar-holes, and may even have had sea-chests, made specifically for this purpose. In the stern there was a raised section of decking to help the helmsman steer, and this may have been where the skipper stood. Although not a Viking warship (*drakkar*), the Gokstad ship was well-made and sleek, and must have been used by a Viking chief for transporting himself and a band of followers, perhaps across vast distances – a replica of the craft was sailed across the Atlantic at the end of the last century, and the captain commented on her excellent sea-going properties.

One warship, the example found at Ladby, does survive. Though of similar structure to the Gokstad vessel, she was about 1.8 m (6 ft) shorter, and was only half as wide (about 2.1 m (7 ft) as opposed to over 4 m (13 ft) at Gokstad); she was also much lower, at about 50 cm (20 in) from gunwale to keel, as compared with over 127 cm (50 in). The shallow draught must have made sailing a hazardous business, but the slender hull would have been correspondingly easier to row.

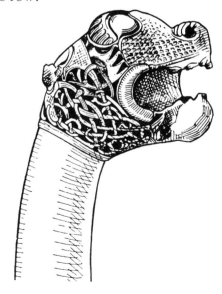

The prow of the Oseberg ship.

Carving on the prow from the Oseberg ship. Bands of elaborate carving outline the edges of both sides of the prow. The carving shown is from a panel on the prow facing in towards the deck.

The ship in the grave-mound at Oseberg appears to have been of the type called *karfi*, a scaled-down longship. Elaborately carved and lavishly equipped, this was a small, coast-hugging vessel for the private use of a local chieftain. Craft of this type must once have been common in the waters round Scandinavia, and we should probably think of the early raiders arriving in such craft having sailed along the Danish and Frisian coast as far as the straits of Dover, then quickly crossed to British coastal waters.

English vessels are scarce, but not unknown. The most famous is the 'ghost' ship of Sutton Hoo, long since rotted but its presence betrayed by the rusted iron clinch-nails under the mound. There appeared to be no facility for a mast on this example, nor on the Nydam ship, which is believed to be the kind of vessel the early Saxons used in order to cross over from the Continent. Yet contemporary literature and manuscript illustrations refute this. In the renowned poem *Beowulf*, which some think may have been partly inspired by the Sutton Hoo burial, the dead hero Scyld is laid *on bearm scipes . . . be mæste* ('in the ship's hull by the mast' (lines 35 and 36)). The Sutton Hoo vessel may not have been typical of contemporary craft, since it was chosen for the burial of a dead king, and could in any case have been ritually prepared to carry its cargo to the otherworld. In Bede's *Ecclesiastical History*, however, we read of sailors borne to

safety by following wind, at about the time when *Beowulf* was composed and a full century before the first Viking raids.

In the face of Viking sea-power, the English ships were outclassed. Accordingly we read in the *Chronicle* for the year 896:

> Then King Alfred ordered long ships to be constructed in answer to the *æscas* [Viking ships]; these were nearly twice as long as the others; some had 60 oars, some had more; they were both faster and steadier, and also higher, than the others; nor were they built on the Frisian pattern, nor on the Danish, but rather how it seemed to [the king] himself that they would be of best service.

Although this home-made fleet never did really rival the Vikings in their own element it must have been a welcome sight to the English to see their seas patrolled by skilfully-made friendly craft. Alfred was a talented engineer – it might be nearer the truth to say that he was clever at finding solutions to practical problems – but the new ships evidently suffered from too great a draught, which made it impossible for them to follow the enemy as close to the shore as was necessary, without risking running aground.

After the large-scale settlements of the late ninth century English ship-building traditions were reformed to take advantage of the experience of the newcomers, and later vessels may have been indistinguishable at a glance from Scandinavian types. The arrival of Viking mercenaries must also have brought new ideas and designs to the native shipwrights. Equipped with

Elaborate Thor's Hammer in silver. Christians were known to call on Thor for specific favours, or in matters of great difficulty. The sagas record a Viking who, though a Christian, always called on Thor at sea.

great square sails and manned by teams of sailors operating in shifts, such ships may have been capable of speeds in excess of six knots, and of covering up to a hundred miles in twenty-four hours. Yet merchant shipping continued to rely on using foreign vessels, particularly Frisian, and the ownership of sea-going vessels was strictly controlled. This was especially true under Ethelred, who made a serious but abortive attempt to build an effective fleet by levying ship-taxes and stipulating the provision of sailors and their equipment as part of the overall system of dues incumbent on freemen.

Alfred is remembered as the father of the English navy (although this should not be confused with the achievement of Samuel Pepys, who may justly be called the founder of the British navy). Alfred's fleet, no less than Ethelred's, acted as part of the king's military defence force, although his men were sea-going coastguards and mobile war-bands, rather than sailors of the Royal Navy.

The tiller of the Gokstad ship. The Gokstad ship is functional and strong, with decorative carving kept to a minimum. The far more ornate Oseberg ship was probably not meant for open water but served either a religious function or was reserved for use in the fjord.

Chapter 12

Coinage and taxation – the king commands

According to the old adage, there are only two certainties in life – death and taxation. Ignoring the first of these for the moment, it is well to remember that the Old English taxation system was extremely efficient, chiefly because the administration was well-run and carried on undisturbed despite changes of reign; kings came and went, fought their way to the throne, or were thrust upon it, fled the country or were brutally murdered, or passed away in old age. It mattered little to the royal officials. When Harold fell at Hastings and England fell into the hands of William and his followers, the Normans set about slicing up territory among themselves, and dismantling every worthwhile thing which belonged to the native regime. But the Conqueror recognised the administrative system as a great asset for a king who was reluctant to be defrauded of any part of what was due to him. He left the monetary system in relative peace while he turned his attention elsewhere.

An English king could raise income by levying taxes on his subjects, but the payment of these taxes was something of a problem. Farmers might prefer to render tax in foodstuffs of various kinds, each of which would have to be rated for tax purposes individually. Since the tax would have been expressed as a requirement for 'x' pounds of silver, smiths and merchants could opt to pay in bullion: a dozen silver bracelets, say, to the weight required. The problem with this was that there was no easy method of ascertaining the purity of the metal, nor of relating this to the king's behest. Even in the ninth century the need was felt for a standard coinage which could be used to avoid the suspicion that the tax-payers were deliberately obstructing the authorities, or that the tax-collectors were over-harsh in their requests. Various coins had been in use, first as conveniently-sized pieces of bullion, and later as expressions of royal power, in the form of imitations, often quite crude, of Roman coins.

Offa of Mercia tried to impose coinage during his lifetime, but it fell to Alfred of Wessex to institute a worthwhile system based on the West Saxon penny. The pennies were minted at London, notably, and bore an extremely unflattering portrait on the obverse. The Danelaw was not to be outdone, and soon began producing copies from its own mints in the five boroughs; the Viking kingdom of York also had its own coinage for a while. The value was principally for the prestige of the kings of York, since the Vikings accepted coins only as bullion in Scandinavia.

Athelstān took the final step of introducing a single coinage to be used throughout the country, and made this possible by establishing mints at numerous important centres, many of them places integrated into the *burh* system. Foreign coins were not acceptable as payment under his legislation, which must have made overseas trade a matter of barter or the

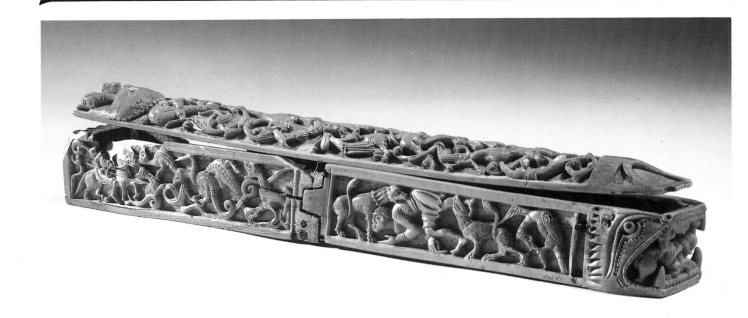

Walrus ivory pen case with glass inlay. Anglo-Saxon. Mid eleventh century. This has been identified as a case for quill-pens. The elaborate carving varies on the faces of the case and is in a range of styles, from Anglo-Saxon to proto-Romanesque.

acceptance of foreign money only by weight. In 973, King Edgār decided to get to grips with the monetary system to use it for his own advantage. He had all existing coin-types demonetised and taken out of circulation. The coins were returned to the centres of coin production – the mints, operated on his behalf – where they were melted down and restruck as Edgār's own penny. Furthermore, the new pennies had a strictly limited period of usage before they were recalled and reminted. Moneyers had to buy their dies from the king, so he benefited from periodically updating the coins in use. But the great advantage of the system was that forgeries and underweight coins could be quickly detected at the recall, and any offending moneyers punished. It was a legal require-ment for the moneyer to show his name and town on the coins he struck, which pointed out just who was responsible when discrepancies were found.

Upon Ethelred's abdication and Knut's accession, the mints must have been working flat out to keep up with the demand for money with which to pay the Danegeld and the other taxes levied to support the English army. As the situation eased under Knut's rule, and the Viking threat subsided, demand must have dropped and emergency mints set up to meet the sudden upturn in demand were soon idle. This may be the case with the site at Cadbury: an Iron-Age hillfort was refortified in the early 1000s, and a mint established there. Coins bearing the legend *CADANBYRIG* are known, and the site has been excavated. Archaeology revealed that it was abandoned

about 1020, after around ten years of occupation, spanning the period of crisis at the end of Ethelred's reign, and the relaxation under Knut afterwards.

Athelstān had fuelled the demand for money by a series of measures which affected commerce. He made it illegal to do business above the value of twenty pence, which was then the price of a cow, except in a *burh* where the deal could be witnessed. This allowed both buyer and seller some measure of security in the event of dishonest dealing; it also helped to centralise commerce within the *burh*s. In combination with the other administrative measures, the king was putting himself in a position to affect the economic lives of his subjects, and to raise large sums of money for himself. By Ethelred's time, there were sixty mints producing coins around the country: their services were required to manufacture the Danegeld payments which began at ten thousand pounds after Byrhtnōth's defeat in 991, and had risen to forty-eight thousand pounds in 1012. Aside from the economic effects of making these payments, the sheer bulk of coins handed over must have created problems within the domestic commercial world. It has been calculated that the Danegelds and the huge pay-off to Knut's army drained twenty million pennies out of circulation in

England – each of which had been hand-made by a professional. The sense of squandered wealth and fruitless effort is overwhelming.

Although many dues were commuted to coin payments over the years, people – even kings – still needed to eat. Many rents and customary dues continued to be settled by gifts of food. The following rents were due to Christ Church, Canterbury, each year from the estate at a place called Burna in Kent, according to a charter held there recording an agreement between the owners of the estate, named as Ealhburg and Eadweald:

> 40 ambers of malt and 240 loaves; 1 weight of cheese; 1 weight of lard; 1 adult heiffer; 4 wethers; 10 geese; 20 hens; 4 loads of wood . . . and each Sunday 20 loaves provided with savouries.
> ('Amber' is the Latin word *amphora* meaning a jug for wine; in English, it probably denoted a pot of some specific type.)

Gifts such as these covenants to provide food to the church were undertaken voluntarily by landowners for the good of their souls. The charters which record the gifts often call on those who come after not to discontinue the practice through wantonness or greed, for fear that their souls might suffer for it. The Church itself must often have distributed the food to the poor and needy, and to pilgrims and cripples visiting the church's shrines. At this time there was considerable interest in miracles, especially miraculous cures of chronic diseases. Minsters and churches which housed particularly obliging relics had to cater for substantial crowds of hopeful travellers and their relatives.

To what extent the early kings of the small Anglo-Saxon states were law-givers is unclear. By the time Alfred came to draw up his law-code for Wessex in the late 880s, there was at least one native model available to him, the *Laws* of King Ine who died in 726. This code was appended to Alfred's laws and numbered sequentially with it. Other codes existed, such as one associated with Offa of Mercia, though they were not necessarily all known to Alfred and his advisers. The king introduced his code with an exposition of how the laws of Moses were subsequently adapted from their Jewish application so as to be suitable for Christian men, and how various councils of wise and holy men had since worked hard to incorporate the basic principles of Christian faith into

A lead die for the production of silver coins for King Alfred's London mint.

a system of legal instructions.

The main purpose of the law-codes was to make certain types of antisocial behaviour illegal, and therefore punishable. Foremost among the objectives the law-makers set themselves was the reduction of feuding among the English. In former times, protection for the individual rested on his being a member of a large family, including uncles and cousins of varying degrees. To attack any member of the family ('clan' might be a better term) was to attack the family as a whole. Thus, a man who unwisely slew another could expect a visit from every able-bodied male member of the dead man's family, each of whom was bent on vengeance. The slayer of the first instance would be summarily slain, and the family to which he belonged would gather to visit his slayer; this tradition of raid and counter-raid could go on for generations, and must have cost many innocent men their lives. It was also an unwelcome drain on the kingdom's resources for it took a heavy toll of brave, loyal and militarily able young men – just the men who should have been the backbone of the kingdom's army. Nonetheless, the feuds persisted, especially in more out-of-the-way regions such as Essex, and were even exported to the New World where they continued among the back-woodsmen.

Clearly, something had to be done to provide an acceptable alternative to further bloodshed. As the

RESPICIS APLIS

ARIES IN VES IT.

DIES·XXX· LUNA·XXIX·

APREI· POSSIDET APRILIS UALERICUM IURE ILIDIS.

XI			M	N	N IIII	N	Nonis inquadris coepit pausare nicocras.
	E	B	F	O	B III	N	Irruas casta capit nonas teodosia uirgo.
XIX			P	C	II N	N	pridie lactatur ambrosius archus & auctor.
VIII		G	P	D	NON		ultima paschalis nonis incensio splendet.
XVI	I	C	R		VIII ID		Idibus octauis theodorus sidera sensit.
N		H	S		VII ID		Septenis meruit eufemia scandere arcos.
		I	G		VI ID		Macharius miris profulsit sidere senis.
III	O	D	I	U	A V	ID	Quadratus quinis pausat septemq; puelle.
		A	B		IIII ID		Demetrius quas tus marcellus &idibus aequant.

honour of the family was at stake, there could be no question of asking everybody to simply forget about the matter. The practice of appeasing the offended party by presenting gifts grew up; this was formalised into the payment of wergild which represented the sum payable by the slayer and his family to the kin of the dead man in settlement of the dispute. Any further action on the part of the aggrieved kinsmen was not considered mere revenge but a separate act of hostility. Wergilds for different grades of freemen were laid down in law, so that no one need feel that they had been cheated out of adequate recompense. (These sums are discussed on p. 113.) Sometimes the dead man was deemed to have put himself outside the law by having acted illegally; such 'outlaws' could be legally slain without any wergild having to be paid. Such a case would be, for example, when a man was caught red-handed in the act of stealing – he could be summarily slain, or he could be handed over to the king's power, from which he might be able to buy his freedom by paying his wergild to the king. If the king so chose, the thief would die on the gallows.

The devisers of the wergild system had some difficulty in dealing with accidental deaths; a price having been established for each freeman, the relatives of those who met death through bad luck or natural occurrence must have felt disappointed that there was no one from whom they could claim a wergild. This is illustrated in *Beowulf* where a king's favourite son is accidentally killed by a younger brother. No wergild was payable since the kin who should pay and the kin who should receive were the same people. The king is said to feel as an old man does who sees his son hanged on the gallows. In this case, if we are right in assuming that the poet refers to the death by hanging of a convicted criminal, the old man would have no son and no wergild to soothe his feelings. (It is possible, however, that the reference is actually to a man chosen by lot to hang as a human sacrifice, though it is not possible to prove this, and it would not affect the father's feelings, in any case.)

Once the notion of wergild was widely accepted,

Noblemen feasting: three noblemen are seated on a couch drinking from goblets, flanked by armed retainers; at left a reclining reveller pours wine from a pitcher, while at right an entertainer plays. The month of April from a Saxon calendar.

The ideal of kingship: an English king with crown, sword and sceptre, surrounded by his aldormen, while at right a felon is hanged from the gallows.

Silver penny from York showing Viking emblems of the sword and Thor's hammer; c.910.

Silver penny from York showing bow and arrow motif. The flights of the arrow are crudely represented; c.920.

Silver penny from York showing Viking raven motif, and bearing the legend ANLAF CUNUNC, *'King Óláf (Guthfrithsson)'; dated c.940.*

which it presumably was by the time of the English settlement of Britain, it could be extended from its original purpose into other areas. Thus, Ine's law (number 50 in Alfred's series) stipulates that if anyone fought in the king's house he shall forfeit all that he has inherited and it shall be at the king's discretion as to whether he live or die. If anyone fought in a minster, he should pay 120 shillings; in the house of an ealdorman or of another king's councillor 60 shillings as a fine (to the king) and 60 shillings to the victim; if in the house of a *gebūr* or a *gafolgelda*, he

Silver penny from York showing a Viking war-banner, minted by King Óláf Sihtricsson; c.942.

London penny struck by King Alfred with a very unflattering portrait of the king in imitation of Roman originals; c.871-99.

London penny struck by King Ethelred before 1016.

should pay 120 shillings as a fine and 6 shillings to the victim. If a fight broke out in open country, the fine of 120 shillings remained. The amounts payable to the 'plaintifs' are graded according to social status, like the wergilds. Anyone shown to have sold his country-men (whether free or unfree) out of the country had to atone with the value of his wergild. Wergilds were graded not according to status, but according to land held: those with a whole hide had a wergild of 120

shillings, those with half a hide 80 shillings; those with no land were valued at 60 shillings.

Occasionally the law was content to let events take their own course: Ine's law 'Concerning when a British servant slays a free man' determines that:

If a British servant shall slay an English man, then he who owns him shall deliver him to the lord and kinsmen, or pay 60 shillings in exchange for his life.

If he then does not wish to buy the slave off, the lord may free him. His kinsmen shall then pay the wergild, if he has any kindred among freemen. If he has none, the contenders are to settle the matter themselves.

It would have been impossible to legislate for every case, and the councillors who drew up the code did not try. They laid down general principles which judges had to interpret and apply to the cases before them. Accidental killings, such as when a man was carrying a spear over his shoulder and another injured himself on it, were later brought into the legal framework as negligence rather than murder.

It was not unlawful for a man to kill when ordered to do so by his lord. Even the church did not condemn this: Christian men were obliged to honour the commandment 'Thou shalt not kill', but the kingdom had to be defended. Anything done on the instructions of one's superior was regarded as morally the responsibility of the man issuing the orders.

Loyalty to the lord was promoted at every opportunity. Even the duty of avenging a slain kinsman was not allowed to come between lord and follower. 'There is no kinsman dearer to us than our lord', as one troop of warriors stated when relatives offered them safe conduct away from a besieged fort. They chose to fight on though their lord was dead and prospects of survival slim. This was at a place called Merantun in Wessex in the year 755. The sentiment was echoed over two centuries later on the flat marshland outside the small Essex *burh* at Maldon. The words of the old retainer Byrhtwōld ring out:

'Mind shall be the harder, heart the keener,
courage the greater as our strength dwindles.
Here lies our leader, cut down,
the good man in the dirt. May he ever grieve,
who now thinks to turn from this war-play.
I am old in life: I do not wish to leave,
but rather beside my lord
– beside so dear a man – do I think to lie.

920 Norse kingdom of York reconquered by Wessex; King Edward is recognised as the foremost monarch in Britain.

924 Athelstān becomes king.

c. 930 Byrhtnōth, son of Byrhtelm, is born.

932 Athelstān Half-King becomes ealdorman of East Anglia.

937 The Battle of Brunanburh: Wessex defeats an alliance of Danish, Welsh and Hiberno-Norse somewhere in northern England.

940 King Athelstān dies; Edmund becomes king.

c. 944 Ælfgār's daughters marry, one to the king, the other to Byrhtnōth.

c. 945 Ælfgār is elevated to the position of ealdorman.

946 Prince Edgār is fostered by Athelstān Half-King; King Edmund dies, and is succeeded by Eadred.

c. 950 Ealdorman Ælfgār makes his will.

c. 951 Ealdorman Ælfgār makes his last witness to a document.

955 Byrhthferth attests charters as ealdorman (? of Essex); King Eadred dies; Edwig becomes king.

956 Byrhthferth ceases to attest charters; Athelstān Half-King also ceases to attest charters; late in the year Byrhtnōth attests a charter as ealdorman of Essex.

959 King Edwig dies and Edgār succeeds him; Wessex, Mercia and Northumbria are united under his rule into the kingdom of England.

962 Athelwine, son of Athelstān Half-King, becomes ealdorman of East Anglia; Northumbria loses its possessions in Midlothian to the kingdom of Alban.

968 Prince Ethelred is born; Óláf Tryggvason is born; Ramsey Abbey is founded.

970 Ely Abbey is founded.

973 Northumbria cedes its lowland Scottish territory to Alban.

975 King Edgār dies; Edward becomes king.

977 Óláf Tryggvason becomes a member of the Rus court at Kiev.

978 King Edward is assassinated at Corfe Castle; Ethelred becomes king.

979 Thōred is appointed jarl of Northumbria. Viking attacks on Britain resume.

983 Ealdorman Ælfhere of Mercia dies.

987 Óláf Tryggvason marries Queen Geyra of the Wends (according to his saga).

990 Geyra dies; Óláf raises a fleet and sails west.

991 Ealdorman Athelwine is taken ill; Æthelflæd (Edmund's widow) dies; ealdorman Byrhtnōth dies at Maldon; King Ethelred arranges a treaty of assistance with Normandy; the Danegeld is paid for the first time.

992 Ealdorman Athelwine dies; jarl Thōred is last mentioned in documents.

994 Óláf Tryggvason becomes Christian and settles down with his new wife.

996 Óláf returns to Norway where he is accepted as king.

1000 Óláf is killed in battle on the Baltic.

1012 Largest payment of Danegeld is made; forty-eight thousand pounds.

1013 King Ethelred flees to Normandy; Sven of Denmark seizes the throne.

1014 Norse power in Ireland is diminished by the defeat of the Hiberno-Norse at the Battle of Clontarf, outside Dublin. King Sven dies; Knut Svensson assumes his father's claim to the throne; Ethelred returns and drives Knut from the country; Thorkel the Tall, a Viking leader, defects to the English following the murder of St. Ælfheah.

1016 On the death of Harold Ironside, Ethelred's son, Knut assumes the kingship of England as well as Denmark and Norway.

appendix 1

the poem of the battle of maldon

What was the character of Old English poetry as a whole? And how does the text concerning the events at Maldon fit into the corpus of Anglo-Saxon verse? A modern reader approaching Old English verse in translation will often formulate an impression of a very difficult and unnecessarily obscure medium. This is a not wholly inaccurate picture; there is a great deal of difference between the Anglo-Saxon world and ours, and the differences are not always obvious to us. Their language, as it has survived in written texts, had an extensive vocabulary capable of expressing complicated ideas and abstract concepts, as the translation of much theological and philosophical material into the vernacular testifies. The language used its own resources to find names for new ideas far more than English does: for example, 'trinity' was rendered as *drines* (threeness).

Anyone scanning a page of Anglo-Saxon will be surprised at how foreign-looking it is, even when transliterated into modern script. There are few recognisable words and quite a few unfamiliar combinations of letters (hn-, hw-, cs-, hr-, hh-). Yet the fact remains that Anglo-Saxon is the acorn, so to speak, from which our modern language has grown, and it contains hardly any features which are not present to some degree in modern English. The spelling system, though its appears outlandish, was at any rate a closer rendition of the sounds of the words in speech than modern English is, mainly because modern English has had a thousand years of outside influence on its orthography, mainly from French, Latin and Greek. Attempts to harmonise French and English pronunciation have simply left a jumble of exceptional forms; this has even separated words which were once closely connected: for example, the chance differing spellings have severed the verbs 'deign' and 'disdain', probably for ever.

The comparatively straightforward system in use before the Norman Conquest was doomed once it got into the hands of bookish scribes and philologists who itched to show off their (often spurious) learning by inserting a 'p' into words like 'receipt' (though not in 'deceit') and a 'b' into 'debt' and 'doubt', where it had never been pronounced since the words came into the English language.

Anglo-Saxon spelling may be summarised thus:

J, q, v, and *w* were not used. *K* and *z* were rarely used, the latter mostly for biblical names.

B, d, l, m, n, p, r, t, and *x* had approximately their modern values.

There was also the now-obsolete letter Ð (eth) denoting the sounds we now spell *th*, and þ (wen) which is transcribed by *w*. The shapes of many of the letters were quite different from their modern forms – they were similar to the rounded letters used to write modern Irish.

C had its modern pronunciation (as in 'call' not 'cell'); before '*e*' and '*i*' it had the sound 'ch' ('*cinn* is our word 'chin'); *sc* represented the sound we spell 'sh' (*scip* is 'ship'). *G* had the pronunciation of the modern letter (as in 'gall' not 'gel') except before '*e*' or '*i*' where it was pronounced 'y' as in 'yell' (*giet* is our word 'yet'). *H* was pronounced like the modern consonant, even before others such as *hn-, hr-, hl-, hw-.* Sometimes it occurs between vowels, where it represents the sound heard in Scots 'loch'; next to '*e*' or '*i*' it had the sound sometimes made at the beginning of the word 'huge' (between 'h' and 'sh'). *F, s,* and *đ* had their voiceless pronunciations ('fee', 'see', 'theme') normally, except between vowels or in the middle of a word where they were 'voiced' ('eve', 'ease', 'them').

There were seven vowels in Anglo-Saxon, each of which had both long and short pronunciations. Although ancient scribes rarely marked the difference, in modern editions of the texts a macron (–) is placed over the long forms. *A* was pronounced long as in 'cart'; shortening this gives a sound rather like the southern English pronunciation of 'cut'. *Æ* was pronounced as in 'cat' when short, while when long it had a quality like the vowel of 'has' spoken with full stress. *E* was as in 'get' (short) and somewhat like 'gate' (long). *I* had the sound in 'pit' when short, and in 'peat' when long. *O* was pronounced as in 'cot' (short) and 'caught' (long), and *u* was as in 'pull' (short) and 'pool' (long). Finally, the vowel spelt *y* was that which occurs in the French words *tu* and *pur*; these sounds can be reproduced by pronouncing the corresponding *i* sound with rounded lips.

There were three common diphthongs: *ea* as in 'hair' (short) and 'player' (long); eo was e+o pronounced in quick succession; io was as in 'ear' when short and 'seer' when long.

Scribes wrote -*cg*- for the sound heard twice in 'judge' ('bridge' is spelt *brycg*); and -*ng*- always had the combination heard in 'finger', never as in 'singer' or 'ginger'.

It is often stated that Old English verse is alliterative verse, meaning that it consists of lines held together by the repetition of a particular sound beginning several words in the line. Such statements seem to imply that Old English verse is *merely* alliterative, and that it has no other art or skill than the bringing together of words sharing a common sound. This is very far from the truth. The basis of the verse is not really the alliteration at all, but the rhythms of stressed syllables. Each line will normally consist of four loud or stressed syllables, split into two groups of two by a mid-line pause.

The distribution of soft or unstressed syllables around the stressed ones gives variety to the rhythms; since the work of the German scholar Sievers into the permissible patterns, the classification is called the Sievers Five Type System – though there are actually more than five types. If we represent full stress by F, minor stress by M and unstressed syllables by O we may draw up the following list:

Sievers Type A: F O F O *as in* Winston Churchill

B: O F O F *as in* a piece of cake

C: O F F O *as in* a small fortune

D: F F M O *as in* sleep fitfully

E: F M O F *as in* buying a house

In addition, extra syllables are sometimes tacked on to the line or inserted within it – these are always unstressed.

Alliteration is used only in the initial sound of each stressed syllable; conventionally, all vowels alliterate with each other, and *sc*, being a different sound from *S*, does not alliterate with it. Normally one or both stressed syllables in the first half-line will alliterate with the first stressed syllable in the second. We may represent this thus:

AB:AC or BA:AC or AA:AC.

For variety of poetic effect the alliteration may be crossed: AB:AB; or it may be transverse: AB:BA. Rarely, all four syllables alliterate, or the third one fails to; in such cases corruption of the text must be suspected, though the verse of the high Middle Ages did have these features.

The would-be poet had quite a lot to learn before he could compose verses. Moreover, he did not have formal instruction in the technicalities of versification; to begin with, his major task must have been to memorise a good selection of set phrases describing familiar themes for poets: lord, hall, treasure, follower, warrior, hero, battle, various types of weapons, war-gear, horse, ship, tribe, leader, enemy, courage, loyalty, hatred, strength, and so on. In committing the conventional terms for such concepts to his memory, he unconsciously absorbed the rhythms of the half-lines so that when he came to compose he was already working to the patterns.

If the aspiring poet/singer knew a few old songs he would already have laid the foundation of a stock of phrases which would have been added to every time he met a new and pleasing way of expressing an idea. Once he had a good store of these half-lines he was in a position to begin combining them with each other, and with new ones of his own devising, to make a narrative sequence. Here he came up against the alliteration factor: an expression for an old warrior is *hār hilderinc* (hoary battle-man) which can only be used for the first half of a line because its two stressed syllables both begin with 'h' (that is, they alliterate). As the first half of a line, it can only combine with a second half-line whose first stressed syllable also begins with 'h', to preserve the alliteration. In *The Battle of Maldon* this phrase occurs with *hyssas bylde* (emboldened the young warriors).

Had the poet chosen to describe Byrhtnōth as, say, *Byrhtelmes bearn* (son of Byrhtelm) as he did elsewhere, he could not have combined this phrase with *hyssas bylde* since firstly, the *last* syllable would alliterate (on 'b') and secondly, the third syllable would fail to alliterate. In such a case he would have had to find another expression for 'encouraged the warriors' with 'b' at the head of its first stressed syllable; he could, for example, have said *beornas trymede*, which has the same meaning (gave strength to the warriors).

From the above we may deduce that a poet needed a good range of words and phrases referring to favourite themes, beginning with a variety of different sounds. This he had in the poetic vocabulary of his verse tradition. Words occur in poetry which must have been lost from ordinary speech long previously, probably being retained because they continued to turn up in poems handed down and memorised by successive generations of poets. Some words have a poetic meaning which differs markedly from their common usage: for example, *beorn* has a prose meaning 'bear' and poetic meaning 'warrior'; *bord* has a prose meaning 'plank, table' and a poetic meaning 'shield'. Some words occur in poetry which are unknown in prose texts, though we cannot be sure how much this depends on the accident of survival of one text rather than another. Particularly characteristic of Anglo-Saxon verse is the formation and use of compound words: for example *æsc* (spear) + *wīga* (fighter) gives *æscwīga*, a warrior who fights with a spear. Compounds must have been especially useful for the purpose of providing conveniently alliterating phrases to fit into given contexts. A notable class of compounds are the so-called 'kennings', small riddles or puns describing some familiar subject. An example is the sea, which is variously described as the 'gannet's bath', the 'swan-road' and the 'whale-path'. The use of these little jokes earned the minstrel the name of *hleahtor-smið*, 'the maker of laughter'.

A successful composition depended very much on the poet's ability to come up with an apt, alliterating, rhythmic term to describe his thought. As verse seems to have been delivered to the accompaniment of the harp, it may be that the poet was able to fill in with musical passages while he gave thought to his next verse.

The poem *The Battle of Maldon* comes at the very end of the Old English verse tradition when the compactness and austerity of phrase which characterises the earlier poetry was already giving way to a looser, more natural style of presentation in which there are more unstressed syllables to the line. This was a result of linguistic changes which made the older verse seem archaic and unnecessarily terse; the larger number of soft syllables of later poetry represent the inclusion of words like 'the', 'and', and 'then' which were normally omitted in the more rigidly conservative tradition. There are in *The Battle of Maldon* many lines where one or more small words could be excised without unduly altering the meaning; their inclusion reflects the poet's preference for intelligible poetic language.

The poet evidently had some skill in the handling of alliteration since it is present in every line save one (183) which is considered, on quite separate grounds, to have been corrupted or miscopied. He managed to include crossed and transverse types of alliteration, and a few examples of near-rhyme which add to the rich overall effect of the poem. A feature which has attracted much adverse comment is his limited number of rhythms – he favours types A, B and C, and where he used D or E types it is in set phrases which are found commonly in other poems. While this is undoubtedly true, it is only fair to point out that type A accounts for more than half of all the lines of Anglo-Saxon poetry because simple phrases, of the type noun + noun, tend to follow this pattern.

The very strong narrative quality of the poem marks it out from the bulk of contemporary verse. Admittedly little comparable poetry survives; *The Battle of Maldon* may have been one small example of a whole genre of occasional verse which, due to its temporary nature, was not considered worth recording. The fact that this verse deals with the death of a famous man, on whose patronage a group of monks was capitalising, allowed this single example to avoid the fate of the others.

In order to give a just appraisal of the work, we require something with which to compare it; unfortunately, very little 'battle poetry' has come down to us. The two other poems which offer reasons for comparison and study are those commemorating the battles of Finnesburh and Brunanburh. The poem of Finnesburh is old, even by Anglo-Saxon standards; it is fragmentary and poorly transcribed, like that of Maldon; it is 'heroic' and conservative, also like that of Maldon. The poem of Brunanburh, on the other hand, is a propaganda piece extolling the virtues of the English kings, set in verse. It is perhaps not surprising that the poem of Maldon resembles that of Finnesburh to a greater extent than it does that of Brunanburh; in *The Battle of Maldon* the poet deliberately set out to bring back to life the ancient virtues of the English tradition.

The language of the poem is interesting. Some of the words used are characteristic in form of the late tenth century: for example, the reduction of three consecutive consonants (Byrhtelm, from Byrhthelm; Dunnere, from Dunnhere; the form of the ealdorman's name Byrhtnōth, which earlier has the first element spelt *beorht*, and in the eleventh century is often changed to *bryht-* or *briht-*, the origin of our word 'bright'). Some textual spellings show Anglian influence (*hals* for West Saxon *heals*) though this is probably due to the prestige that Anglian forms had in poetry. Many purely poetic words are thought to be Anglian in origin, so it seems that the style of poetry in the tenth century was heavily biased towards the language of the Midlands.

Most of the text is consistent with the Winchester standard, showing that the scribe who wrote down the text was competent in the orthography of classical Old English. It is unlikely that the spelling was 'tidied up' by Elphinstone when he made his transcript, since in many places he evidently did not understand what he was copying: for example, he wrote *hem to* in error for *he mid*, which mistake he would not have been likely to make if he had known enough Anglo-Saxon to interpret the letters on the manuscript.

Little of the poet's grammar or vocabulary can definitely be ascribed to Essex, though two points stand out: the spelling *dē* for *dȳ* shows a known Essex pronunciation of this vowel; and the word for 'tribute' in Byrhtnōth's speech to the Vikings is in the form *gofol*, which occurs elsewhere in the south-east, as distinct from the standard form *gafol*. On balance, it is quite possible, and perhaps likely, that the poet was from the south-east, that he knew something of the area where the battle was fought, and of the men who participated, and furthermore that he thought it worthwhile praising the men of Essex and the surrounding area, as well as 'aliens' such as Æscferth, who remained loyal to their lord. It is equally possible that he was present on that day and saw the events that brought an end to Byrhtnōth and to his followers. In any event, he had some very clear and definite information about what happened and how it came about, so he must at least have got the story from eye-witnesses. The reason for the crisp, uncluttered narrative, then, becomes clear: he wanted to set out intelligibly the sequence of events 'for the record', to accuse the guilty and to praise the worthy.

The military vocabulary of the poem is largely the standard poetic stock of words denoting warrior, leader, and so on. It may be summarised thus (the number after each word refers to the occurrences of the word in the text):

Armour	*byrne* (3); *heregeatu* (1); *rēaf* (1)
Army	*folc* (8); *werod* (4); *æschere* (1); *fyrd* (1); *heorðwerod* (1); *here* (1); *prass* (1); *geðrang* (1).
Arrow	*flān* (2)
Battle	*gūð* (8); *hild* (8); *wīg* (7); *gewinn* (3); *wīgplega* (2); *beadu* (1); *beadurǣs* (1); *gecamp* (1); *fǣhðo* (1); *gefeoht* (1); *feohte* (1); *gārrǣs* (1); *gūðplega* (1); *getoht* (1)
Bow	*boga* (1)
Fortress	*burh* (1); *fæsten* (1)
Herald	*ār* (1); *boda* (1)
Lord	*eorl* (10); *ealdor* (5); *frēa* (5); *hlāford* (5); *ðeoden* (5); *winedrihten* (2); *bēahgifa* (1); *heorra* (1); *hlēo* (1); *sincgyfa* (1)
Shield	*bord* (12); *lind* (2); *scyld* (2); *rand* (1)
Shieldwall	*bordweall* (1); *scyldburh* (1); *wīhaga* (1)
Spear	*gār* (10); *ord* (10); *æsc* (2); *darod* (2); *franca* (2); *spere* (2); *æscholt* (1); *sceaft* (1); *wælspere* (1)
Sword	*swurd* (6); *bill* (2); *mēce* (2); *ecg* (1); *īren* (1)
Viking	*wīcing* (6); *sǣman* (3); *brimman* (2); *flota* (2); *lidman* (2); *sǣlida* (2); *brimlīðend* (1); *fǣrsceaða* (1); *sǣrinc* (1); *wælwulf* (1)
Warrior	*man* (9); *hyse* (7); *wīga* (7); *ðegen* (4); *ceorl* (3); *gefēra* (3); *hæleð* (3); *cniht* (2); *bana* (1); *cempa* (1); *dreng* (1); *feða* (1); *fyrdrinc* (1); *gārberend* (1); *guma* (1); *gūðrinc* (1); *heorðgenēat* (1); *hilderinc* (1); *hīredman* (1); *genēat* (1); *rinc* (1); *scealc* (1); *secg* (2); *wīgend* (1)

It will be obvious from the above that the poet had a favourite word for each concept: for example, he used *bord* for 'shield' twelve times, the other words hardly at all. He also made use of compounds with elements he had already used as discrete words: *gūðrinc* for 'warrior' from *gūð* (battle) and *rinc* (man).

The word *heorra* may be significant in defining the dialect of the poet, as it is not a normal Old English word for 'lord'. It is probably the same word as the German *Herr* (master), and may betray a Saxon (rather than Anglian) origin for the poet, with a dialect which retained some specifically Saxon words and pronunciations.

Strangely our poet nowhere mentions any form of helmet, nor even indicates that any kind of headgear was worn. There are no words for 'helmet' in the list given above, though Old English poetry had a number of terms to describe various types. We must assume from the facts of the narrative that both Byrhtnōth and Gōdric wore some head-covering in the battle, since otherwise the ealdorman with white hair (called *hār* meaning 'hoary, grey-haired) would have been easily distinguished from the (presumably more youthful) thane when he seized the horse.

A helmet was specified as part of the war-gear that a thane had to provide for military service, under contemporary law. If one of the thanes brought his helmet and wore it in the fight, there is little reason to suppose that the others did not. It may be accident that has destroyed all references to helmets if they occurred in the parts of the text which are lost. Possibly, though, it could be that the poet was deliberately avoiding mention of helmets for some reason. We might then suggest that the poet felt that helmets were not part of the traditional 'lord and war-band' image he was trying to create, and that to mention them would be likely to spoil the effect he was trying to produce. In any event, it is very unlikely that the Englishmen had dispensed with their head-gear, even in the heat of an August day.

appendix 2

the english at the battle of maldon

names given in capitals are of men mentioned as actually present at the battle; other names are those which occur in the text of the poem. Ealdorman Byrhtnōth has been excluded from this list, which is intended to help identify the 'minor' participants. The figure in brackets after each name refers to the line(s) of the poem in which the name occurs.

ÆLFHERE (80) One of the English defenders of the ford between the Viking camp and the mainland.

ÆLFNOTH (183) One of the companions who stood next to Byrhtnōth at his death, and subsequently lay dead alongside him.

Ælfric (209) The father of Ælfwine, and possibly the same man as Ælfric Cild who took over the ealdormanship of Mercia, and was sent into exile the following year.

ÆLFWINE (211, 231) The son of Ælfric and grandson of Ealhelm; quite probably the sister-son of ealdorman Ælfheah of Hampshire, from whom he received a bequest of land. This high-born warrior refers (in the speech attributed to him by the poet) only to his grandfather Ealhelm, possibly because his father and uncle were political opponents of Byrhtnōth over the issue of monastic reform. He claims at line 224 to be related to Byrhtnōth, perhaps by marriage.

ÆSCFERTH (267) The son of Ecglāf, and a Northumbrian hostage (*gysel*) in Byrhtnōth's entourage.

Æthelgār (320) The father of the loyal Gōdric.

Æthelred (52, 151, 203) Ethelred the Unready, the contemporary king of England.

ÆTHERIC (280) The brother of Sibyrht and a keen fighter. A man of the same name is believed to have plotted to assist Sven Forkbeard when he lodged in Essex as leader of a Danish army in 994. There is nothing in the fragment of the poem to suggest that Ætheric died in the fight at Maldon.

Byrhtelm (92) The father of ealdorman Byrhtnōth. There is no record of him as an ealdorman in his own right.

BYRHTWOLD (309) The 'old companion' of Byrhtnōth's hearth-troop. Æthelflæd, Byrhtnōth's sister-in-law, left a grant of land to a man of this name (spelt Brihtwold) at some time before 991.

Ceola (76) The father of Wulfstān.

DUNNERE (255) A *ceorl* or yeoman who made a short speech of encouragement to the remaining defenders after Byrhtnōth's death.

EADRIC (11) An English warrior who had made a vow before Byrhtnōth; possibly a member of the hearth-troop.

EADWEARD (117) An English warrior, possibly the same man as EADWEARD SE LANGA (the Tall) who charged and broke through the Viking shieldwall where he was slain (line 273).

EADWOLD (304) The brother of Ōswold, both of whom uttered speeches of encouragement.

Ealhelm (218) Ealdorman of Mercia from 940 to 951; grandfather of Ælfwine.

Ecglāf (267) The father of Æscferth.

Gadd (287) The kinsman of Offa; this curious name is recorded in early forms of the place-names Gasthorpe (Norfolk) and Gaddesby (Leicestershire). It may be a Viking name, derived from the Norse word *gaddr* meaning 'a sting'.

GÓDRIC (187, 235, 237) The son of Odda who, with his brothers, fled the battlefield first and caused the English force to be routed.

GÓDRIC (321) The son of Æthelgār, with whose death our fragment ends.

GODWĪG (192) The son of Odda; he fled with Gōdric.

GODWINE (192) The son of Odda. The name is actually spelt Godrine in the transcript, which may represent this name, or possibly Godrinc; the characters approximate much more closely in Saxon script.

LEOFSUNU (244) A noble warrior from Sturmer in northern Essex.

MACCUS (80) One of the Englishmen set to guard the ford. This name is actually an Irish form of the Viking name Magnus, and occurs in the place-name Maxey (Northamptonshire).

Odda (186, 238) The father of the three deserters.

OFFA (5, 198, 230, 286, 288) An English nobleman and encourager of the remnant after Byrhtnōth's death. From the context of the poem he was evidently a close friend and adviser of the ealdorman; he may have been a major Essex landowner. This name became popular in England following the dramatic success of the Mercian king who bore it; he in turn was named after an earlier king who led the small Baltic tribe on their expansion into continental Europe.

ŌSWOLD (304) The brother of Eadwold; an encourager of the warriors.

SIBYRHT (282) The brother of Ætheric; Queen Æthelflæd granted land to a kinsman of hers of the same name.

Thūrstān (298) The father of Wīstān. This name is derived from, or influenced by, the Norse name Thōrsteinn.

Wīgelm (300) A kinsman of Wīstān.

WĪSTĀN (297) The son of Thūrstān; a bold warrior who slew three Danes before the foe overcame and slew him.

WULFMÆR (113) The sister-son of ealdorman Byrhtnōth; he was one of the first to fall in the battle.

WULFMÆR *SE GEONGA* (155, 183) (the Young) The son of Wulfstān. An attendant of Byrhtnōth's who is perhaps to be identified with 'Offa's kinsman' at line 5.

WULFSTĀN (75, 79, 115) The father of Wulfmær the Young and the son of Ceola. The mainstay of the English defence of the ford. A will exists pertaining to land in the Maldon area, made out by one Leofwine son of Wulfstān, and dateable to the late tenth century.

Glossary

Words in italics are Old English words used in the text; the others are ordinary English words with an unfamiliar meaning.

æðeling	An 'atheling', prince or nobleman.
beot	A warrior's boast or vow before his comrades.
burh	A 'borough', stronghold or fortified residence.
būrdēn	An officer in a nobleman's household.
byrnie	A protective coat of mail or armour.
ealdorman	A provincial governor, a nobleman.
eorl	A warrior hero; later, the same as ealdorman.
folc	A province of the nation, or the men of that province.
fyrd	An army of levied troops.
hearth-troop	A bodyguard of trusted warriors; also hearth-band.
heriot	A tax levied for the upkeep of the army.
hide	A plot of land sufficient to feed one family.
hundred	An administrative division of the shire, based on a royal manor.
jarl	A Norse chieftain or earl.
lindenwood	A poetic name for a shield.
ord	The point of a weapon, or the forefront of the fyrd.
ring-giver	A poetic name for a lord who distributes gifts of treasure.
shire	A division of a kingdom, often governed by an ealdorman.
thane	A royal official of noble blood; a knight.
wergild	The legal recompense for the slaying of a freeman.
Witan	A council of wise men, the king's advisers.

BIBLIOGRAPHY

Almgren, Bertil, *The Viking*, A. B. Nordbok, Gothenburg 1975

Arbman, Holger, *The Vikings*, Thames and Hudson, London 1961

Ashe, Geoffrey (ed.), *The Quest for Arthur's Britain*, Pall Mall Press, London 1968

Bain, George, *Celtic Art – The Methods of Construction*, Constable, London 1951

Barney, Stephen, *Word Hoard*, Yale University Press, London 1977

Bates, Brian, *The Way of Wyrd*, Century Publishing Co., London 1983

Bengtsson, Frans G., *The Long Ships* (translated by Michael Meyer), William Collins and Sons, Glasgow 1954

Birkebæk, Frank and Barren, Charles, *The Sea Wolves: The Viking Era*, A. B. Nordbok, Gothenburg 1975

Branston, Brian, *The Lost Gods of England*, Thames and Hudson, London 1957
    Gods and Heroes from Viking Mythology, Eurobook Ltd, London 1978
    Gods of the North, Thames and Hudson, London 1955

Brent, Peter, *The Viking Saga*, Weidenfeld and Nicolson, London 1975
    Britain in the Dark Ages, HMSO, London 1974

Brondsted, Johannes, *The Vikings*, Penguin Books, Harmondsworth 1965

Brooke, Christopher, *The Saxon and Norman Kings*, B. T. Batsford, London 1963

Cameron, Kenneth, *English Place Names*, B. T. Batsford, London 1961

Campbell, James, *Essays in Anglo-Saxon History*, Hambledon Press, London 1986

Cunnington, C. W. and P., *Handbook of English Mediaeval Costume*, Faber & Faber, London 1952

Ekwall, Eilert, *Concise Oxford Dictionary of English Place-Names*, Oxford University Press, Oxford 1936

Elliott, R. W. V., *Runes: An Introduction*, Manchester University Press, Manchester 1959

Ellis Davidson, H. R., *Pagan Scandinavia*, Thames and Hudson, London 1967
    Gods and Myths of Northern Europe, Penguin Books, London 1964

Embleton, G. A. and Banting, D. R., *Saxon England*, Almark Publishing, New Malden 1975

Finberg, H. P. R. (ed.), *The Agrarian History of England and Wales*, Volume I,
  Cambridge University Press, Cambridge 1972

Foote, Peter and Wilson, David, *The Viking Achievement*, Sidgwick and Jackson, London 1970

Garmonsway, G. N., *The Anglo-Saxon Chronicle*, J. M. Dent & Sons, London 1953
      An Early Norse Reader, Cambridge University Press, Cambridge 1928
      An Introduction to Old Norse, Oxford University Press, Oxford 1957

Gordon, Ida (ed.), *The Seafarer*, Manchester University Press, Manchester 1979

Graham Campbell, James, *The Viking World*, Frances Lincoln Publishers, London 1980

Graham Campbell, James, and Kidd, Dafydd, *The Vikings*, Trustees of the British Museum, London 1980

Hamer, Richard, *A Choice of Anglo-Saxon Verse*, Faber & Faber, London 1970

Hasloch-Kirkby, Michael, *The Vikings*, Phaidon Press, Oxford 1977

Helms, Randell, *Tolkien's World*, Thames and Hudson, London 1974

Humble, Richard, *The Saxon Kings*, Weidenfeld and Nicolson, London 1980

Hunter-Blair, P., *Roman Britain and Early England*, Thomas Nelson, London 1963

Jones, Glynn, *A History of the Vikings*, Oxford University Press, Oxford 1968

Kerr, N. and M., *A Guide to Anglo-Saxon Sites*, Granada, London 1982

Keynes, S. and Lapidge, M., *Alfred the Great*, Penguin Books, Harmondsworth 1983

Koch, H. W., *Mediaeval Warfare*, Bison Books, London 1978

Kocher, Paul, *Master of Middle Earth*, Thames and Hudson, London 1973

Laing, Lloyd and Jennifer, *Anglo-Saxon England*, Routledge & Kegan Paul, London 1979
      Celtic Britain, Routledge & Kegan Paul, London 1979

Laing, Samuel, *Heimskringla*, J. M. Dent & Sons, London 1930

Leslie, R. F. (ed.), *The Wanderer*, University of Exeter, Exeter 1985

Magnusson, Magnus, *Hammer of the North*, Orbis Publishing, London 1976
      Viking Expansion Westwards, The Bodley Head, London 1973

Magoun, Francis P., *The Oral-Formulaic Character of Anglo-Saxon Narrative Poetry, Speculum* **XXVIII** 1953

Mitchell, Bruce and Robinson, Fred C., *A Guide to Old English*, Basil Blackwell, Oxford 1982

Morrison, Ian, *The North Sea Earls*, Gentry Books, London 1973

Newark, Tim, *The Barbarians*, Blandford Press, Poole 1985

Nicolle, David, *Arthur and the Anglo-Saxon Wars*, Osprey Publishing, London 1984

Oakeshott, Ewart, *Dark Age Warrior*, Lutterworth Press, London 1974

Onions, C. T. (ed.) *The Oxford Dictionary of English Etymology*, Oxford University Press, Oxford 1966

Page, R. I., *Life in Anglo-Saxon England*, B. T. Batsford, London 1970
      Runes, Trustees of the British Museum, London 1987

Palsson, H. and Edwards, P., *Egil's Saga*, Penguin Books, Harmondsworth 1976

Potter, Simeon, *Our Language*, Penguin Books, Harmondsworth 1950

Quennell, M. and C. H. B., *Everyday Life in Anglo-Saxon, Viking and Norman Times*, B. T. Batsford, London 1926

Schucking, Levin, 'The Ideal of Kingship in Beowulf', trans. in *An Anthology of Beowulf Criticism*, University of Notre Dame Press, Notre Dame, Indiana 1929

Scragg, D. G., *The Battle of Maldon*, Manchester University Press, Manchester 1981

Sorrell, Alan, *Reconstructing the Past*, Batsford Academic, London 1981

Sweet, Henry, *Anglo-Saxon Primer*, Clarendon Press, Oxford 1900

Tolkien, J. R. R., 'Beowulf: The Monsters and The Critics', Proceedings of the British Academy 1936

Watkins, Alfred, *The Old Straight Track*, Methuen & Co., London 1925

Whitelock, Dorothy, *The Beginnings of English Society*, Penguin Books, Harmondsworth 1952
(ed.), *Sweet's Anglo-Saxon Reader*, Oxford University Press, Oxford 1967

Whitlock, Ralph, *Warrior Kings of Saxon England*, Moonraker Press, Bradford-on-Avon 1977
In Search of Lost Gods, Phaidon Press, Oxford 1979

Williamson, Craig, *A Feast of Creatures*, Scolar Press, London 1983

Wilson, David M., *The Anglo-Saxons*, Thames and Hudson, London 1960
(ed.) *The Northern World*, Thames and Hudson, London 1980
The Vikings and Their Origins, Thames and Hudson, London 1970

Wise, Terence, *Saxon, Viking and Norman*, Osprey Publishing, London 1979

Wood, Margaret, *The English Mediaeval House*, J. M. Dent & Sons, London 1965

Wood, Michael, *Domesday*, BBC Publications, London 1986
In Search of the Dark Ages, BBC Publications, London 1981

acknowledgements

Illustrations published courtesy of the following:
Ashmolean Museum, Oxford, p 140, 141; B. T. Batsford Ltd, p 12 bottom, 13, 20, 29 centre, 74, 75, 103, 111, 115, 122, 157, 167, 169, 170; Bodleian Library, Oxford, p 70, 106, 114, 166; British Library, London, p 19, 26, 27 top, 73, 76, 80, 92, 93, 96, 100, 103, 116, 118, 121, 125, 133, 138, 155, 174; British Museum, London, p 10, 14, 18, 23, 24, 28, 29 top, 41, 43, 53, 59, 61, 69, 71, 81, 82, 83, 88, 90, 99, 102, 104, 109, 110, 112, 113, 122, 144, 145, 147, 156, 158, 161, 163 bottom, 165, 172, 173, 174; Corpus Christi College, Cambridge, p 37; Hulton Picture Library, p 11, 89, 131, 154; Pitkin Archives, p 30, 34 (Museum of London), 76, 127, 128 (Durham Cathedral), 134, 145, 151 (Merseyside Co. Museum); Trinity College, Cambridge, p 22; Victoria & Albert Museum, p 129; Weidenfeld Archives, p 14, 69, 70, 71, 102, 114, 156, 161, 174; Wiltshire Archaeological Society, Devizes Museum, p 164.

index

Note: numbers in italics indicate pages on which illustrations fall.